GREAT STORIES
FOR GAINING DECISIONS

Louis Torres

Printed by:
Remnant Publications

Great Stories for Gaining Decisions
This edition published 2013

Cover design: Tabatha Nethken Mattzela

Published by:
TorresLC Ministries
P.O. Box 688
Gaston, Oregon 97119

Printed in the United States of America

ISBN 978-0-9703553-7-9

Throughout this publication all emphasis is supplied by the author unless otherwise noted, and all biblical references are from the King James Version unless otherwise indicated.

Contents

FOREWORD

This work is a follow-up to the first book I wrote entitled, *Gaining Decisions for Christ: A How-to Manual*. The inspiration for it came from a former student of mine, Pastor Mark Howard, who was visiting and, upon my request, was holding a series of evangelistic meetings for Mission College of Evangelism. During his stay, he suggested that we spend time together and requested that I help him especially in the area of public appeals. One thing for which he had a great need was stories and illustrations to incorporate with or in his appeals.

One day he said, "I think you ought to write a follow-up book to *Gaining Decisions* and call it *Great Stories for Gaining Decisions*. The result is that after seeing his need. I remembered that I was a young preacher myself struggling with the same. I was convinced, after prayer and thought, that others could benefit from this book.

My earnest prayer is that many souls will be encouraged to take their stand for Christ as they hear the stories and illustrations from this book. In gratitude for the support and encouragement from my dear wife Carol, I wish to dedicate this work to her.

Chapter 1

ESSENTIAL APPEALS

Someone once told me, "If you give a man a fish, you have fed him for a day. If you teach him how to fish, you have fed him for a lifetime."

This adage is just as true in the science of soul winning. Many pastors invite evangelists to help them and their lay people "bring their interests across the line." Hence, the evangelists are giving the pastors a "fish," rather than "teaching them how to fish." It then goes without saying that the weakest link in the work of ministry is the art of persuasion. Leading others to Christ in public meetings or in private is not their strong suit. The result is that many a soul goes on indecisively because the minister or gospel worker has not discovered, or learned the essence of decision-making. Many a sermon flies aimlessly through the air without finding any landing or making an impact on their hearers. This occurs because the speaker does not know how to make an appeal, is afraid to, has misconceptions about it, or does not see the need to do so.

One of my young ministerial interns told me "soul winning was not his calling." This was his comeback to my inquiry in my first interview with him. I asked him how many souls he had won since he entered the ministry. His resistance made the answer obvious. In order to train him, I gently coerced him to hold his first evangelistic meeting. Doing it only because his supervisor required it, the intern reluctantly obeyed. I did not visit the site until two days prior to the end of the series. While in the audience, I heard a wonderfully orchestrated, well developed, and forcibly delivered sermon. I could sense and see that the visitors were stirred by the message. However, he concluded the presentation without an appeal.

After the meeting, when everyone was dismissed, I said, "That was a wonderful message, why didn't you make an appeal?" "What for?" He retorted. "There is no one here to respond. Besides, what if I made an appeal and no one responded? I would have stood there looking silly." "Oh no," I answered, "had you made an appeal, I sensed that at least four people would have responded." "Sure!" He sarcastically responded.

Thinking of a way to get him over his fear and resistance, I said, "I am coming back tomorrow for your last presentation, and I want you to make an appeal." "Me?" He questioned with his voice cracking. "Yes, you," I said. "I will write it out for you, and if it does not work, you can put the blame on me."

The next night I was there, fully expecting an appeal—and he knew it. When he was finishing his presentation, I felt he came near to making the appeal. But, he moved away from it. I could tell he became extremely nervous. I began to pray. Coming back the second time, he approached the appeal and then moved away from it again. It was like a flight student coming down for his first landing and the fear of it made him take the plane back into the air. Once again, he came around to the appeal for the third time. "Help him land it," I prayed. Finally, out of sheer mandate, he read the appeal. To his great surprise, four people responded. He was moved to tears. These souls were the first baptismal candidates in his ministry. He was never the same. Excited by the success, when he moved into his own district, he continued to hold meetings and make appeals.

So many preachers are like my former intern. They preach great sermons but make no appeals. Oftentimes, it is not because of lack of desire, rather it is the fear that no one will respond, or they feel self-reproach—who am I to appeal to people? Still others feel they are stepping on "holy ground." In other words, this is an area relegated only to the Holy Spirit—man is to keep off this terrain. Whatever the sincere conviction or misguided notion, they serve as obstacles to successful harvesting through preaching. Perhaps it could be that those hesitant appealers have never been taught this art form or just do not know what constitutes a good appeal. They may lack material (e.g., stories, illustrations, etc.) to develop an effective closing or have not had a resource to reference.

Sadly, so many good, well-delivered sermons fail in making an impact because of a weak appeal or none at all. But we are counseled, "at close of every meeting, decisions should be called for."[1] "For the

---

1. E. G. White, *Testimonies for the Church*, Vol., 6, 65

secret of our success and power as a people advocating advanced truth will be found in making direct, personal appeals to those who are interested, having unwavering reliance upon the Most High."[2] In every discipline and vocation there are "tricks of the trade" for success. In this last statement the secret to successful preaching is revealed—that of making "direct, personal appeals." So, if a person wants to be a successful preacher, it is crucial that the "secret" be discovered and exercised.

"Why should appeals be made?" You may ask. "Aren't people mature enough to know what to do with the message they have heard? Besides, isn't that the role of the Holy Spirit?" The truth of the matter is that people must be led to make decisions. It is not by second nature that a person comprehends his or her initiative in this matter. First, there is an enemy of the soul who is waiting to catch away the precious seed (the Word of God) before it can have its effect on the hearers. Jesus said:

> A sower went out to sow his seed: and as he sowed, some fell by the way side; and it was trodden down, and the fowls of the air devoured it. Now the parable is this: The seed is the word of God. Those by the way side are they that hear; then cometh the devil, and taketh away the word out of their hearts, lest they should believe and be saved. (Luke 8:5, 11-12)

The battle for the mastery becomes intense when a person attempts to leave the ranks of the enemy. The devil is unwilling that any who have served under the banner of darkness make the transition to serve the Prince of Life. It is at this time that "all the mental and physical energies be drawn upon [on the part of the worker] to make the very strongest stand, to array evidences in the clearest light, and set them before the people in the most pointed manner, and urge them home by the strongest appeals."[3]

Second, when it comes to spiritual matters, the Bible says that people are like sheep. (See Isaiah 53:6; Luke 15:4-7.) Therefore they must be led, enticed, compelled, or encouraged to make decisions. The reality is that "there are souls in every congregation who are hesitating, almost persuaded to be wholly for God. The

2. E. G. White, *Review and Herald*, September 30, 1892
3. Ibid.

decision is being made for time and for eternity; but it is too often the case that the minister has not the spirit and power of the message of truth in his own heart, hence no direct appeals are made to those souls that are trembling in the balance. The result is that impressions are not deepened upon the hearts of the convicted ones; and they leave the meeting feeling less inclined to accept the service of Christ than when they came. They decide to wait for a more favorable opportunity; but it never comes."[4]

On the other hand, others, though convicted of sin and feel the need of the Lord, procrastinate and make no move toward the Savior. Circumstances of life are comfortable. Hence, they feel no urgency to make their salvation sure. If there is no pointed application of Christ's message to the heart, they will not sense their danger. So if words are not spoken at the appropriate moment and decisions are not called for, the convicted individuals pass on oblivious to their golden opportunity. The conviction wanes, and they do not take the forward-step to identify themselves with Christ. Generally speaking, there is danger that these persons will gradually become apathetic and never take a stand for the Lord.

Third, while it is true that the Holy Spirit is the one to make impressions on the heart, God uses human instrumentalities. Christ appealed to John and Andrew to follow him. With this invitation, the foundation of the Christian church was set. Andrew found his brother Peter and called him to the Savior. Philip was then called, and he in turn went in search of Nathaniel. It was Peter who, on the day of Pentecost, crystallized for those dwelling in Jerusalem what should be the appropriate response to the promptings of the Holy Spirit. Paul was instrumental by using spoken and written admonitions in appealing to the Agrippas, the jailors, the Greeks, and the Jews to yield their lives to Christ. These examples should underscore the importance of the human agent's role in putting forth personal effort to make direct appeals to our relatives, friends, and neighbors.

When men and women of spiritual understanding conduct Bible studies, they need to tell the Bible student how to yield to the conviction and power of the Holy Spirit. When this is done, it will aid to establish them more fully in Bible truth. As they

---

4. Ibid.

surrender to that spiritual influence, the power of God will be made manifest. We must remember that:

> It is not the human agent that is to inspire with life. The Lord God of Israel will do that part, quickening the lifeless spiritual nature into activity. The breath of the Lord of hosts must enter into the lifeless bodies. In the judgment, when all secrets are laid bare, it will be known that the voice of God spoke through the human agent, and aroused the torpid conscience, and stirred the lifeless faculties, and moved sinners to repentance and contrition, and forsaking of sins. It will then be clearly seen that through the human agent faith in Jesus Christ was imparted to the soul, and spiritual life from heaven was breathed upon one who was dead in trespasses and sins, and he was quickened with spiritual life.[5]

It is only the divine power of God that will reach and melt the sinner's heart and take him, a penitent, to Christ. Clearly, the Scriptures indicate that the disciples themselves could not have gained such access to the hearts and accomplished the grand results that "turned the world upside down." Men and women felt the influence of a superior power and involuntarily yielded to it.

Therefore, in order to realize this phenomenon, the preachers of God's truth should "ever represent the life and teachings of Christ; then will they have power over the hearts of men."[6] The result will be that the revelation of Christ in the character will have a transforming power upon all who listen. Let Christ be made evident in the presentations, and He will reveal the creative energy of His words—a gentle, persuasive, yet mighty influence—to recreate in other souls the beauty of a changed, transformed life. Let the worker contemplate Christ crucified, Christ resurrected, Christ rising into the heavens, and Christ returning again. This will soften, hearten, and fill the mind. Thus, the presentation of these truths to the people made in love and deep earnestness will make Jesus palpable to them and not to the speaker.

---

5. E. G. White, *SDA Bible Commentary*, Vol. 4, 1165 (emphasis supplied).
6. E. G. White, *Review and Herald*, August 8, 1878, 11.

For this reason the preacher must be alive and imbued with the Holy Spirit. There must be earnestness in his delivery. His preaching must give evidence that he himself is convicted about the message he is preaching. Remember this: "Little conviction, little reaction; great conviction, great reaction!" As he speaks, let there be a practical and close application of the truth to the hearts of the listeners. It will be extremely difficult to estimate the loss resulting from preaching without the unction of the Holy Spirit.

Wherever I have preached, I have seen that in every congregation souls waver—almost at the brink of deciding to be committed to God. As the prophet Joel declared, they are "in the valley of decision" (Joel 3:14). A person who is indecisive, by default, is deciding. Hence, decisions are being made, but too often the minister conveys the message without the Spirit's power. No direct appeals are made to those in the balance. As a consequence, the convicted ones may have secretly desired to be urged, but they leave inwardly disappointed that there was no calling out from them an outward response to the inner longings.

Because there is a God-given message to bear to the world, it needs to be borne in the rich fullness of the Spirit's power. Let ministers deliver the message coupled with heartfelt conviction, and then at the appropriate moment make direct appeals to the unconverted.

Fourth, all preachers want to experience a measure of success. In any discipline there are "secrets" or "tricks of the trade." There are videos galore about tips to make you successful in this or that, which is because those who have had success have either studied or inadvertently stumbled unto the secret of succeeding in their respective area of expertise. What about in regard to preaching? Notice the statement again. "For the secret of our success . . . is in making direct personal appeals."

If, therefore, there is a secret to effective preaching, it is found in making appeals. This is the example that the Great Teacher gave. The best way to reach souls is by direct, personal appeals. The young pastor who encouraged me to write this said, "I noticed if I preach a lousy sermon but have a good appeal, it saves the sermon. But if I preach a powerful sermon but have a lousy appeal, the message seems to go over like a lead balloon … it just does not speak to the hearts of the listeners."

MAKING THE MESSAGES EXPERIENTIAL
AND SPIRITUAL IN NATURE

I have heard homilies in which the content or subject matter is purely intellectual in nature. The assumption is if it makes intellectual sense, it should lead the listeners to automatically get the point and independently of any outside insistence or external influence make their own decision. Thus, a decision should be the natural outcome. It is true that the subject matter should be cohesive, logical, well-organized, and fluid. This is true because:

Some minds [of preachers] are more like an old curiosity shop than anything else. Many odd bits and ends of truth have been picked up and stored away there; but they know not how to present them in a clear, connected manner. It is the relation that these ideas have to one another that gives them value. Every idea and statement should be as closely united as the links in a chain. When a minister throws out a mass of matter before the people for them to pick up and arrange in order, his labors are lost; for there are few who will do it.[7]

This statement makes it absolutely essential to have the sermon well-organized and connected.

However, when it comes to making a practical application to the heart, reaching the intellect is not sufficient to produce the looked-for outcome. When making an appeal, the speaker must turn from the intellectual to the emotional. Hopefully, by this time the intellect has been engaged. It is the heart that must be reached. Therefore, as stated before, there must be a practical application to the heart —"making earnest appeals that will reach the heart."[8]

As the dew and the still showers fall upon the withering plants, so let words fall gently when seeking to win men from error. God's plan is first to reach the heart. We are to speak the truth in love, trusting in Him to give it power for the reforming of the life. The Holy Spirit will apply to the soul the word that is spoken in love.[9]

---

7. E. G. White, *Review and Herald*, April 6, 1886, 9.
8. E.G. White, *Evangelism*, 280.
9. E.G. White, *The Ministry of Healing*, 157.

We should "speak with the force and intensity necessary in order to reach the heart."[10] This intensity is the natural outworking of a close relationship with Christ. For "when the hearts of the workers are brought into sympathy with Christ, when he abides in them by living faith, they will not talk one-half as long, nor manifest one-half the smartness, that some do now; but what they say in love and simplicity will reach the heart, and they will be brought in close sympathy with teachers, scholars, and church members."[11]

In making a public call that reaches the heart, there should be pathos in the tone of voice and an obvious yearning for the soul. To aid in the appealing process, it is important to have heart-touching illustrations and stories. Practical stories and illustrations have a way of helping God's truth make its way into the heart. They enable the mind's eye to see with the heart the importance of the message. Jesus Himself used illustrations and stories that riveted in the minds of His hearers the sublime truths He sought to impart to them. In fact, the entire Bible is filled with stories and illustrations of human experiences that give practical meaning to God's message of love.

But the question is, "Where do I get appealing stories?" It is hoped that this book will help in meeting that void. Rather than getting another "fish," it is my desire that this will aid in making fishermen. Obviously, the best stories are your own life experiences that you have lived. Pray that God can help you remember those experiences that will nail down in some soul, through your appeal, the wonderful truths of God's good news of salvation.

But if you lack in this area, then as you sit and listen to sermons, pay close attention especially to appeals that successful preachers make. Give attention to their stories and analogies. Write them down and make a list of them for future reference. Then when you are ready to give a sermon, first state a purpose for it. In other words, why are you preaching this sermon? What do you hope to accomplish with it? Are you hoping that the message will engender in the hearer a desire for heaven, forgiveness, victory over sin, etc.? Then as you develop the sermon, stay close to the stated purpose. Finally, when you reach the appeal, flesh it out.

10. E.G. White, *Counsels on Diet and Foods*, 138.
11. E.G. White, *Counsels on Sabbath School Work*, 167.

Give thought to the particular material needed for the invitation. Then when the moment comes for the appeal, give it with reliance upon the Most High.

Some audiences and groups of people may not be used to either hearing or responding to appeals. Thus, they may be reticent to embark upon this would-be quagmire. I understand this perfectly well. At times I have been invited to speak to congregations and audiences where this has been the case. While in Germany for example, I was doing a training seminar on gaining decisions. In the evening I would give a practical demonstration of the principles taught in a nightly community presentation. Prior to my presentation, I informed my translator that I was going to make an appeal. "Oh no," he said. "Germans are private people and do not show their emotions openly. They are not used to the American style of appeals." I then told him, since I had been teaching his students about public calls, and since I sensed that I needed to make one, just to do as I did and said.

As the appeal was made, my translator could not believe what was happening. German men and women were standing up and responding to the appeal. My translator was moved to tears. Afterwards he said, "I need to change my whole thinking on this issue."

This mindset, concerning public calls and the level of discomfort both on the part of indigenous workers and their perceptions of their people and audiences, I have seen repeated over and over again. This precaution has been voiced to me while working among the Norwegians, Austrians, Australians, Hungarians, Polish, and other technologically advanced societies or countries. The truth of the matter is that all humans have emotions. All have hearts. Generally speaking, the problem lies not with the audience but rather in the lack of experience, resistance, reticence, or misunderstanding about this topic. Wrong perceptions lead people to wrong conclusions.

I was invited to teach a group of home-schooled young people in the state of California. During my presentation I noticed two ladies who appeared to be uncomfortable about something. After I finished with the children, the women approached me and said, "Who do you think you are?" Not sure of their assumptions, I asked, "What do you mean?" "You are trying to do the work of the Holy Spirit, and we are upset that you are teaching these kids to do the same," one smarted. "How am I doing the work of the Holy Spirit?" I questioned. "You are teaching these kids to make appeals. That is not for us to do. Our part is just to live our lives and let the Spirit bring the conviction when He wants," the other one interrupted.

"Ladies", I said, "I am sorry that you feel offended about what I have done. But if these children are not taught how to bring their friends to accept their Savior, then who will?" "That is not our work," and with that statement, they left.

Unfortunately, many well-meaning Christians, in not understanding this sacred responsibility, stand in the way of precisely the One they think they are defending. A few months passed when my phone rang. After identifying herself as one of those ladies, she said, "Pastor, I am calling you to ask your forgiveness. Just this past Sabbath my minister made an altar call. It was the first time that any of our pastors made an altar call. I was so moved by it that weeping, I went forward in response. Now I understand. Please forgive me." I was grateful to the Lord for enlightening those ladies concerning the correct posture that all should take concerning this matter. As Moses stated, "I would that all of God's people were prophets" (Numbers 11:29, author's paraphrase).

Chapter 2

PUBLIC CALLS

Let us address public calls. Making public calls or appeals is as critical as pulling in the line once the fish is hooked or gathering the fruit when it is ripe. The following statements underscore the importance of this element of preaching. "At the close of every meeting, decisions should be called for."[12]

The concern and love of God for the lost in the hearts of ministers will lead them to make earnest appeals. Some people need to be entreated, others warned, and still others reproved. If this work is neglected, "souls will continue in sin, confirmed in a wrong course by those who have spoken to them only smooth things."[13] "In every discourse, fervent appeals should be made to the people to forsake their sins and turn to Christ."[14] This matter of urging is not unbiblical. Joshua exhorted:

> Now therefore fear the Lord, and serve him in sincerity and in truth; and put away the gods which your fathers served on the other side of the flood, and in Egypt; and serve ye the Lord. And if it seem evil unto you to serve the Lord, choose ye this day whom you will serve; whether the gods which your fathers served that were on the other side of the flood, or the gods of the Amorites, in whose land ye dwell: but as for me and my house, we will serve the Lord. (Joshua 24:14, 15)

Elijah demanded, "How long halt ye between two opinions? If the Lord be God, follow him: but if Baal, then follow him" (1 Kings 18:21). Jesus likewise encouraged his disciples to "compel them to come in" (Luke 14:23). Thus, "the people should be urged to decide just now to be on the Lord's side."[15]

---

12. E. G. White, *Testimonies for the Church,* Vol. 6, 65.
13. E. G. White, *Gospel Workers,* 448-9.
14. E. G. White, *Evangelism,* 280.
15. E. G. White, Letter 29, 1890..

There is a caution, however, that needs to be addressed: Do not treat an appeal or call as some addendum to your real message. The whole message must be structured as an appeal to the heart. Then and only then can a call for decision be truly effective. Do all that you can to treat every subject as an appeal to understand truth as it is in Jesus—as it relates to practical godliness. With your own heart filled with the convicting power of the Holy Spirit, strive to guide your listeners to a desire to follow your blessed Savior in whatever the truth may be, however doctrinal or prophetic, the subject matter. As you do this, an appeal or call will follow naturally.

EXTREMES TO SHUN

1. Shunning to declare the whole counsel of God (Acts 20:27). Sometimes we think that if people are told the whole truth it will serve to discourage the candidate. It is true that you don't want to flood a person to the level of "information saturation." Neither do you want to preempt yourself—that is, giving information before the candidate is ready to receive it. However, you do not want to mislead an individual by short-changing them. In more than a few cases, persons have been led to think that they are only being baptized in Christ, only to discover on their day of baptism that they are joining an organized church. This approach leads these people to feel they have been tricked.

2. "Weaving into the labors an element which moves the feelings and leaves the heart unchanged."[16] Feelings will be moved when the work is properly done in harmony with divine principles. But too often, there is the danger that we can manipulate the feelings while leaving the life without the power-changing influence of the Holy Ghost. "A sensational religion is to be dreaded, for it is hard work, when once it has been woven into the experience, to ever make the individuals feel that they must go deeper than mere emotional exercise; that they must practice true godliness."[17]

---

16. Ibid.
17. E.G. White, *Evangelism*, 281.

3. "Hammering at the people in an un-Christlike manner or talking in a way that they think you are provoked."[18] When calling for a decision, the use of spiritual intimidation or of verbal force will never accomplish what the Holy Spirit is able do. We need to manifest the compassion, tenderness, and the loving spirit of Christ!

CREATING AN ATMOSPHERE OF CONVICTION

As I have already stated, "Watch, watch!" Remember, "Every fresh display of the conviction of the grace of God upon the souls of unbelievers is divine."[19] If it is a "display," then it should be observable—something opened to the careful, watchful eye of the worker.

As a young pastor my focus was mostly centered on the precision and accuracy of my content and delivery. But as my experience deepened and grew, I discovered that more important than correctness was a need to concentrate on watching for the moving of the Holy Spirit on the hearts of the hearers. So, as your preaching is executed, watch for the response of the hearers. It is said of Christ: "He spoke directly to every mind and appealed to every heart. He watched the faces of His hearers, marked the lighting up of the countenance, the quick, responsive glance, which told that truth had reached the soul."[20] "Jesus watched with deep earnestness the changing countenances of His hearers . . . As the arrows of truth pierced to the soul, breaking through the barriers of selfishness, and working contrition, and finally gratitude, the Savior was made glad."[21]

As a speaker is delivering a message, "he will not dismiss a congregation without presenting before them Jesus Christ, the sinner's only refuge, making earnest appeals that will reach the hearts."[22] I have known some speakers who are afraid to follow this counsel. One told me, "What if I make an appeal, and no one responds? I'm afraid I will stand there looking silly." These fears keep many from becoming effective in their public speaking.

18. Ibid.
19. Ibid, page 284
20. E. G. White, *Education*, 231.
21. E. G. White, *Evangelism*, 95.
22. Ibid., 280.

This apprehension is born, not of a supreme concern for the people, but of an overriding concern for looking good. And while it is true that the message suffers if the speaker looks bad, generally speaking, it is not this trepidation that keeps preachers from appealing. This unwarranted concern needs to be laid aside. However, the reality is this: if insipid and feeble Christless entreaties are made, then what can be expected but the result of self-fulfilling prophecy—no congregational response! But if we learn how to communicate earnest appeals, those fears will become merely unrealized anticipations.

But let's suppose that the feared anticipation occurs. Suppose that no one responds, then rest in this: you have done your part. It either means that everyone has already made a commitment, or they are not able to respond. In that event, there are always those who are struggling within themselves. I then simply give an opportunity for those who possibly fit into this category to lift their hands for prayer. I have found that people may not be able to make the full commitment, but they do appreciate knowing that though they were unable to respond to God, He does not cast them off. Give hope to the struggling.

MAKING HEARTFELT APPEALS

In order to make heart-moving appeals, one must "cultivate earnestness and positiveness in addressing the people."[23] There may be those who, after reading this statement, remain convinced that this is not part of their personality. Maybe that is where the root of the problem lies. Some will take a "spiritual inventory test" to determine their gifts or talents. Once they take the test, they rely on the results to dictate their static abilities. But let's consider these thoughts: "Do not wait until some human examination pronounces you competent to work, but go out unto the highways and hedges, and begin to work for God."[24]

"God can and will use those who have not had a thorough education in the schools of men. A doubt of His power to do this, is manifest unbelief; it is doubting the omnipotent power of the One with whom nothing is impossible. Oh, for less of this uncalled-for,

23. E. G. White, *Evangelism,* 296.
24. E. G. White, *Testimonies,* Vol. 7, 281.

distrustful caution! It leaves so many forces of the church unused; it closes up the way, so that the Holy Spirit cannot use men; it keeps in idleness those who are willing and anxious to labor in Christ's lines; it discourages from entering the work many who would become efficient laborers together with God, if they were given a fair chance."[25]

Listen, we must look to Him "that is able to do exceeding abundantly above all that we ask or think, according to the power that worketh in us" (Ephesians 3:20). So when our will cooperates with God's, then our will becomes omnipotent. Therefore, whatever He commands can be accomplished in His power. When He bids you to do something, He will enable you to do it.

If God has commanded, "Go ye and preach," then don't depend on a test to determine your spiritual abilities; rather, depend on a "thus saith the Lord." If you put your trust in His commands, then you will be able to preach and make appeals. The primary reason truth-professing Christians have so little power is that they do not put into practice the abilities the Lord has given them. The reasons vary. "Not my gift." "Don't have time." "Someone else can do it better." "That's why I pay my tithe." "It is the pastor's job." "I am too shy." "Don't know enough." Or "People may reject me."

These self-centered reasons make them partners with the man who hid his talent in a napkin. But talents do not increase without exercise: just as strength does not come by inactivity. The example of Christ's lowly fishermen exercising their talents eloquently underscores this point. As they sought to win souls to Christ, the abilities increased. Their increase in eloquence, refinement, and fervor gives evidence to the truth of Christ's parable concerning the other two who had either five or two talents. By using them, they not only increased, they were doubled. God did not add—He multiplied their talents. As we are willing in childlike faith to obey His commands—thrusting out into the deep—the Lord will aid us.

This is the intent for our spiritual gifts. We are to use what we have. God will then give the increase. The woman at the well, as well as the demoniac, did not have the opportunity to attend the rabbinical schools of training. Neither did they have the prerogatives of Christ's personal coaching to the disciples.

---

25. E. G. White, *Christian Service,* 25.

Nevertheless, they immediately put into action what they received, and God blessed their efforts a hundredfold. "As we use our powers, we shall increase our ability to use them, and thus be enabled to do the highest kind of service. We shall be able to put our talents to a wise use; but if we do not use those qualifications of mind and body that God has given, however precious they may be, they will be valueless."[26]

To be successful in any field, one must apply the rules that have been proven to lead to success. If the speaker is not personally moved by the message presented, it will be hard to move others toward a positive appeal response. The subject matter may be excellent and poignant. In fact, it could be just what the people need, but there must be mingled with the message positiveness with persuasive entreaties. A good way to develop this is to practice preaching the message in front of a mirror. Observe the gestures, body language, and tone of voice, or have someone listen to the potential speaker and indicate the areas where improvement is needed. Have the person make the adjustments, and deliver the message again ensuring that the recommended changes are implemented. By this method, the speaker can then modify his or her delivery and improve his or her effective communication for the Gospel. Then, "let your preaching be short and right to the point, and then at the proper time call for a decision. Do not present the truth in a formal manner, but let the heart be vitalized by the Spirit of God, and let your words be spoken with such certainty that those who hear may know that the truth is a reality to you."[27]

Though making public appeals may seem frightening to a speaker who is attempting it for the first time, it is really not that difficult. If the Lord has placed you in the position to deliver a message, then the appeal should not be made as though you are the one inviting but rather as though you are God's mouthpiece. He is the one calling, not you. With this confidence, you have the freedom to appeal directly to the hearts of your hearers.

While making your appeal, here are a few points to remember. I believe these following points are necessary to an appeal's power. Some may consider them perfunctory, but they are the elements

26. E. G. White, *The Youth's Instructor,* February 6, 1896.
27. Ibid.

that will make or break the appeal. Let us consider these three essential elements to making a successful public appeal. Bear in mind that they must become an integral part of your thought process as you launch each appeal.

1. **What:** What am I asking these people to do? You have presented the message, so what do you want them to do with it? If the subject was on heaven, will you invite them to want to be there?

2. **How:** How am I telling them to indicate their response? Are they to raise their hand, stand, walk forward to the altar, or fill out a decision card? You must make the response action clear. Otherwise, the people will be left frustrated, unsure how you expect them to respond.

3. **When:** At what point during the appeal am I requesting them to show their response? Example: "Oh friend, isn't it time for you to give your heart fully to Jesus? If that is your desire, would you raise your hand now just where you are?"

Here are two "sample calls." The first is a general call. The second is a specific call ending with a general call in the event the speaker feels it is appropriate. God will bless as you work to make your messages as appealing as possible under the guidance of the Holy Spirit!

CALLS

SAMPLE GENERAL CALLS
(to be used after the "heaven" presentation)

"What a marvelous place heaven is! I want so much to be there."

"Wouldn't you like to raise your hand with me to say, 'Yes, I too want to be there.' Is that your desire? (Raise your own hand.) Yes, just raise your hand right now." (Go directly into prayer with your hand raised.)

"Father, you see our hands raised. Please help us to keep our priorities straight. And help each one of us to be ready to live with You so we may realize this desire of our hearts. We look forward to this experience. Thank you for making all this possible through Jesus Christ our Lord. Amen."

SAMPLE SPECIFIC CALL:
[after a major message such as the mark of the beast]

"To some of you, this message has come as a real shock. You may need time to study it thoroughly, and pray to God for strength to follow His revealed Word. But for others here tonight, this comes as a wonderful revelation, the missing piece of the puzzle, the light that clearly reveals the pathway of God. You hear God's voice speaking to you saying, 'My son, my daughter. Will you stand on My side? Will you stand up for truth? Will you commit your life to being an example of pure religion, undefiled by human inventions and traditions?'"

"Friend, if you hear God's voice calling you, will you just stand to your feet and be counted on His side right now?"

1. (If there is an immediate response, respond with):

- "God bless you."
- "Are there others? Yes, God bless you."
- "Are there still others who are ready to take your stand with Jesus?"
- "We'll wait and pray." (Pause in attitude of prayer)
- "Are there others? Thank God." [Now go into prayer or move to your general appeal.]

2. (If no quick response):

"I know that this is a very serious decision. A lot is at stake. The question each one of us must answer is: 'Is this what Jesus wants? Is this His way?' And if it is, friend, He is faithful. He will help you; He will guide you. He will strengthen you. But you must make the decision."

"Is there one who is ready to say, 'Yes Lord, here I am. You can count on me.'"

"If you are that one, will you stand just where you are?"

(If there is a response, you should go back to #1. If there is still no response, go on to the general appeal.)

MOVE TO GENERAL APPEAL:

"There are two other groups I want to include in this appeal."

"Because of the serious nature of this message, perhaps some do not have, just now, the strength to make this commitment, but who want to ask God for special help. This is the first group."

"The second group, I am sure, includes many of you. Others here tonight have previously committed their lives to live fully in harmony with God's revealed will, but tonight your hearts have again been strangely warmed, and you would like to say, 'Lord, you can count me in—I still pledge to stand for You and for Your truth.'"

"If you are in either of these two groups, you need strength to stand. Or would you like to recommit your life to God and His truth? Would you join me in standing for Jesus?" (If some responded before, then say, "Would you join these who are standing now?")

(Prayer)

"Father, here we stand, an army of Your children. Prepare us for combat, but even more, Father, prepare us for victory!

"You know, there are those standing here tonight who do not yet have the strength to move forward in your truth. Oh God, draw close to them. Guide their thinking, encourage their fainting hearts, and we will give You the praise and glory.

"And those who for the first time have stood in response to such a challenge, please keep them faithful and give them the strength of purpose that they need to move ahead with Christ from victory to victory.

"When You come, Father, and may it be soon, may we all— every person here tonight—be found faithful to You and ready to meet You in peace is my prayer in Jesus' name. Amen."

Sample Appeal Phrases:

These are some thought provokers!

1. Will you be ready?
2. This is God's plan. Will you let Him include you?
3. What a beautiful message of hope. Do you have this hope?

Make a list of your own appeal phrases as you listen to others speak, and spend personal time with God's Word.

Chapter 3

STORIES FOR EVANGELISTIC SERMON APPEALS

The forthcoming chapters provide stories, illustrations, and appeals for a typical series of evangelistic meeting presentations. This is not to say that these stories and illustrations have only a limited use in a series of meetings. They can also be adopted for use in other settings. However, the primary purpose is to provide those who are doing evangelistic preaching a suggested appeal for each subject.

At least one story is provided for each subject coupled with an appeal, but in most cases more than one story and appeal accompanies each subject. These stories and appeals are also well suited for the worship service, or the prayer meeting. These appeals have also been used in youth rallies, week of prayer meetings, and revival meetings. All levels of people have responded to these appeals with a good measure of the Lord's blessing, which includes different ethnic and language groups.

When the occasion calls for it, or the situation is conducive for it, these illustrations and analogies can be employed with some measure of good response by either experienced or inexperienced speakers. Obviously, I should caution that it is the Holy Spirit that brings the heart to conviction. We simply are His mouthpieces.

Once I was requested to participate in a "block preaching" campaign at the Projects in the lower section of the Bronx in New York City. The "Projects" are generally a group or clump of apartment buildings erected by the city government. The buildings can reach twenty-five stories or higher. Doing a street campaign is difficult in the sense that one does not know who is listening. Preaching is done by faith believing that someone will be tuning in, and that the Holy Spirit will take the sermon and plant it inside some attentive heart.

At the conclusion of my message, I would cast an appeal in the open air. Though it appeared like I was casting to the wind, before long, people began to come out the front doors of their respective buildings. Yes, they were listening from inside their own abode and catching the message through their windows. The Holy Spirit took my words and found lodging in those hearts that He knew were wistfully looking toward heaven. I was then reminded of that passage in the Scriptures that says, "In the morning sow thy seed, and in the evening withhold not thine hand: for thou knowest not whether shall prosper, either this or that, or whether they both shall be alike good" (Ecclesiastes 11:6).

During two weeks in August 2006, from the 17th to September 2nd, in Mindoro Island of the Philippines, I mentored twenty-two teams of both pastors and lay people. Some were from Austria, others from Switzerland and Germany, and a few from the United States. My role was to coach them in the morning concerning the message, how to deliver it, what illustrations to use, and how to deliver the appeal. Then each team would go to their respective site and preach to the attending crowds. Many of the illustrations they used are those that you will find in this book. At the conclusion of the effort on September 2, we had the privilege of baptizing 1,175 souls.

Though most of the group was inexperienced, the Lord blessed their efforts as they preached utilizing the sermon illustrations and appeals. Each speaker gained the awareness of the importance that preaching the word with illustrated appeals plays in the outcome of soul winning.

The following will be the illustrations and appeals divided into different evangelistic topics normally presented in an evangelistic series of meetings.

Chapter 4

THE CHOICE BETWEEN GOOD AND EVIL

FOLLOWING THE SHEPHERD

A boy was herding his father's sheep. Not far away across a little valley, a neighbor boy was herding his sheep for his father. The boys were good friends and often called to each other across the valley. One day a severe storm arose suddenly, and the boys took refuge under a ledge with their sheep. But when the storm was over, and it was time to go home, the boys had a problem; they could not separate the sheep. They knew some of the sheep, but they were not sure about the others. Finally in desperation, and fearful that they would be scolded, they started for home—one going down one path and the other down another. And what happened? The sheep separated themselves perfectly, each sheep following his own shepherd.

APPEAL:

Here is the question. Who is going to be the shepherd of your life? It is up to you! Remember this: The devil will never come to your door and say, "Good morning, lady. I am the devil, and I've come today to tempt you." No, he'll never come to your store and say, "Good afternoon, sir. I am the devil, and I've come to tempt you to cheat this fellow in this deal." No! He is full of wisdom. Perfect in beauty. Who will it be? Will it be the love of power, or the power of love? We are at the cross. Who is going to reign in your heart? Choose your shepherd! The Savior offers you: humiliation, trouble, poverty, sorrow, tears, love in your heart, and a glorious eternity of love and peace.

Satan offers you: wisdom, popularity, fame, money, a good time. He offers you all these things with hopelessness, darkness, and ashes in the end. Satan hates you. Jesus loves you. Will you give your heart to my Christ? He is the only hope for your soul and my mine. Would you stand in testimony to your surrender to Him? Will you say, "I will follow Him?"

CAN GOD BE JUDGE?

Billions of the lost were scattered on a great plain before God's throne. Some of them talked heatedly—not with cringing shame, but with belligerence. "How can God judge us?" Said one. "What does He know about suffering?" Snapped a brunette. She jerked back a sleeve to reveal a tattooed number from a Nazi concentration camp. "We endured terror, beatings, torture, and death!"

In another group a black man lowered his collar. "What about this?" He demanded, showing an ugly rope burn. "Lynched for no crime but being black! We have been suffocated in slave ships, been snatched away from loved ones, and toiled till death gave release."

Far out across the surface of the land were hundreds of such groups. Each had a complaint against God for the evil and suffering He permitted in this world. How lucky was God to live in heaven where there was no weeping, no fear, no hunger; no hatred! Indeed, what did God know about what man had been forced to endure in this world?

So each group sent out a leader, chosen because he had suffered the most. There was a Jew, a black, an untouchable from India, an illegitimate, a person from Hiroshima, and one from a Siberian slave camp. There were others who had also suffered inhumanely from different ages. So they gathered and consulted with each other. At last they were ready to present their case.

It was rather simple: before God could qualify to be their judge, He must endure what they endured. Their decision was that fairness demanded that God be sentenced to live on earth as a man! But since He was God, they set certain standards to be sure He could not use His divine powers to help Himself. Let Him be born a Jew. Let the legitimacy of His birth be in question so that none can know who His father really is. Let Him stand for a cause so just, but so radical, that it brings down on Him the hate, condemnation, and efforts of every major traditional and established religious authority to eliminate Him. Let Him try to describe what no man has ever seen, tasted, heard, or smelled. Let Him try to communicate God to man. Let Him be betrayed by His dearest friends. Let Him be indicted on false charges, tried before a prejudiced jury, and convicted by a cowardly judge. Let Him see what it is to be terribly alone and completely abandoned by every living thing. Let him be tortured, and let Him die not an ordinary death, or a silent death, but as a common criminal!

As each leader announced his or her portion of the sentence, loud murmurs of approval went up from the great throngs of the people. But when the last had finished pronouncing sentence, there was a long silence. No one uttered another word. No one moved. For suddenly, all knew. God had already served His sentence.

APPEAL:

Yes, God understands the pain. His dear Son endured it all for you. He knows firsthand your trial, your temptations, and your pain. The Scriptures say, "For in that he himself hath suffered being tempted, he is able to succour them that are tempted" (Hebrews 2:18). "For we have not an high priest which cannot be touched with the feeling of our infirmities; but was in all points tempted like as we are, yet without sin. Let us therefore come boldly unto the throne of grace, that we may obtain mercy, and find grace to help in time of need" (Hebrews 4:15, 16). Yes, He understands your heartache, your trials, and your woes. And because he knows, he invites you to place your every care on Him. Will you come to Him? Will you trust Him? You can trust Him because He loves you. Will you come?

TAKE MY SON AUCTION

A wealthy man and his son loved to collect rare works of art. They had everything in their collection, from Picasso to Raphael. They would often sit together and admire the great works of art. When the Vietnam conflict erupted, the son went to war. He was very courageous and died in battle while rescuing another soldier. The father was notified and grieved deeply for his only son.

About a month later, just before Christmas, there was a knock at the door. A young man stood at the door with a large package in his hands. He said, "Sir, you don't know me, but I am the soldier for whom your son gave his life. He saved many lives that day, and he was carrying me to safety when a bullet struck him in the heart, and he died instantly. He often talked about you, and your love for art."

The young man held out this package. "I know this isn't much. I'm not really a great artist, but I think your son would have wanted you to have this." The father opened the package. It was a portrait of his son, painted by the young man. He stared in awe at the way the soldier had captured the personality of his son in the painting. The father was so drawn to the eyes that his own eyes welled up with tears. He thanked the young man and offered to pay him for the picture. "Oh, no sir, I could never repay what your son did for me. It's a gift." The father hung the portrait over his mantle. Every time visitors came to his home, he took them to see the portrait of his son before he showed them any of the other great works he had collected.

The man died a few months later. There was to be a great auction of his paintings. Many influential people gathered, excited over seeing the great paintings and having an opportunity to purchase one for their collection.

On the platform sat the painting of the son. The auctioneer pounded his gavel. "We will start the bidding with this picture of the son. Who will bid for this picture?" There was silence. Then a voice in the back of the room shouted, "We want to see the famous paintings. Skip this one." But the auctioneer persisted. "Will somebody bid for this painting? Who will start the bidding? $100? $200?" Another voice said angrily, "We didn't come to see this painting. We came to see the Van Goghs, the Rembrandts. Get on with the real bids!" But still the auctioneer continued, "The son! The son! Who'll take the son?"

Finally, a voice came from the very back of the room. It was the longtime gardener of the man and his son. "I'll give $10 for the painting." Being a poor man, it was all he could afford. "We have $10. Who will bid $20?" "Give it to him for $10. Let's see the masters." "$10 is the bid. Won't someone bid $20?" The crowd was becoming angry. They didn't want the picture of the son. They wanted the more worthy investments for their collections. The auctioneer pounded the gavel. "Going once, twice, SOLD for $10!"

A man sitting on the second row shouted, "Now let's get on with the collection!" The auctioneer laid down his gavel. "I'm sorry, the auction is over." "What about the paintings?" "I am sorry. When I was called to conduct this auction, I was told of a secret stipulation in the will. I was not allowed to reveal that stipulation until this time. Only the painting of the son would be auctioned. Whoever bought that painting would inherit the entire estate, including the paintings. The man who took the son gets everything!"

Two-thousand years ago, God gave His son to die on the cross. Much like the auctioneer, His message today is, "The son, the son, who'll take the son?" Because, you see, whoever takes the Son gets everything. It is written, "He that hath the son hath life" (1 John 5:12). "He that spared not his own Son, but delivered him up for us all, how shall he not with him also freely give us all things?" (Romans 8:32).

APPEAL:

You might have suffered in this world. Your lot might be hard. But God gave his Son. Through that gift, He too suffered the cruelty, the indifference, the mockery of a trial, and finally death. Yes, my friend God understands your heartache. He alone can soothe the aching heart. He can bring comfort in pain, and finally victory out of your greatest disappointments. Trust Him! He who has promised is faithful. You must put your trust in Him. He loves you. Satan hates you. Who here will respond to His loving entreaty and come to Him? Will you give him all your heartaches, your pain, your delusions? Will you accept His promise of a better world to come? Will you raise your hand?

MOTHER PROTECTING HER CHILDREN

Word was spreading about the unfortunate lot of many poor families who had been slain. A band of criminals declared they were doing them a favor by taking them out of their misery.

A single mother being greatly concerned for the welfare of her six children determined to protect her siblings at whatever cost to herself. Each night she put her children to sleep in the little hut she had erected. Then with a machete in hand, she would stay up being vigilant during her night guarding.

Finally, news came that the police had surrounded the wicked convicts in a sugarcane field. Fire was set to the cane field. Unwilling to surrender the gang came out shooting, but their attempts of escape proved unsuccessful. With what relief did the mother receive the news! At last her children were safe, and she could find rest.

APPEAL:

There are many things in this world that are unfair, wrong, and cruel. But the day is coming when God will make everything right. Just like that mother, you too can rest when the Lord comes to set all affairs aright. The One who has brought so much suffering and pain, that has caused so much agony and death, will finally be brought to his end.

Yes, friend, just like that dear mother who was relieved when justice was met, so you too can trust that God will bring justice out of this chaos. Does your heart yearn for that day? Do you long for the day when anxiety will be a thing of the past? When trouble and misery will forever be gone? Do you long for the Lord to come? Who here will stand and say, "Even so come, Lord Jesus"? Please come and bring an end to this misery and pain. Please come and usher in that promised era of eternal bliss! Come and wash away all tears from our eyes. Bring the time when there will be no more pain, crying, sickness, or death. Will you stand? Yes, Amen!

CAN YOU EVER COME BACK TO GOD?

An American pastor was visiting in Romania. As he walked to his usual place of prayer upon a hill, he came across a shepherd tending to his sheep. Noticing that the pastor was not from his country, the shepherd approached and engaged him in a conversation. After the initial introduction, the shepherd asked a sobering question. "If you leave God, can you ever return to Him?" The shepherd asked.

Surprised at the question coming from a shepherd, the pastor began to share the wonderful story of the Great Shepherd, and the reality that God has an open door for any who desire to come to Him. Enwrapped in the conversation, the shepherd forgot all about his sheep. Then realizing they were all scattered, he jumped into action. Using his rod, he struck the ground on the far right, and then running to the opposite side, he struck the ground again. As he did so, the sheep turned and reunited.

APPEAL:

If you lose your way, can you come back? Perhaps you have lost your way. Maybe you never knew that you were lost. But as you have listened to the message and realize that God made a plan to save you—He gave His Son—as your heart is moved, as God is inviting you, will you respond to His invitation? Will you take what God is offering? Will you give yourself to Him now?

Chapter 5

CHOOSING CHRIST'S KINGDOM

DANIEL

MARCH OF THE NATIONS

From this marvelous revelation in Daniel, chapter 2, of the march of the nations, God has revealed who ultimately is in control. Man may wield his might. It may appear that he will have the final say. But it is God who sits enthroned in the heavens. It is He who has declared, "They shall not cleave together," and man has not been able to step over that boundary. Jesus declared, "Whosoever shall fall on that stone shall be broken; but on whomsoever it shall fall, it will grind him to powder," (Luke 20:18).

APPEAL:

Oh, friend, this world is in trouble. For centuries man has made efforts to make a better life. But man is powerless to change the current of things. The leaves of all the past world orders have fallen to the ground. What we need is for Jesus to come. What the old world needs—the sin-sick human needs—is for Christ's kingdom to come. We ought to pray that prayer, "Thy kingdom come!" Without the prophecies of Christ to describe the end of the world and the setting up of God's eternal kingdom, man would have little or no hope for the future.

But now we can see that God sits enthroned. Thank God that man will not have the final say. The Stone is coming! Christ is about to set up his eternal kingdom. Oh friend, do you want to fall on that Stone and be broken? Will you put your trust in Him? Or will you wait until it is forever too late to accept Him? Will you decide just now to prepare for His coming kingdom? Will you raise your hand toward heaven and say, Yes Lord, let Thy kingdom come and make me a part of it! Will you lift your hand toward heaven now? Amen!

ROMANIAN PILOT

A well-dressed pilot approached the speaker after the night's presentation. It was obvious that the visitor was troubled. "I believe what you say," he said to the preacher, "and I would like to become a Christian. But I am afraid if I do, I will loose the woman that I love. I know that it is wrong the way we live, but I don't know what to do."

"How much does salvation mean to you?" asked the preacher. "It means a lot," he replied. "What is a lot?" Responded the speaker. After a long pause, the man said, "Everything." "Alright," said the preacher, "if you want, I would be willing to go and speak with her about your choice." "Would you?" Replied the delighted man. "Yes, I will be able to do that tomorrow afternoon about one o'clock," the pastor assured him.

The next day, due to unforeseen circumstances, the evangelist was unable to keep his appointment. Feeling somewhat embarrassed that he had not met his appointment, and concerned that it probably did not go well with the man, the pastor prayed. That evening, he was surprised to see the man in a completely different frame of mind than the previous night. He was walking into the meeting hall and straight toward the speaker with a woman's arm wrapped around his.

"I am very sorry that I was not able to meet my appointment," the speaker began. "It is quite all right," responded the pilot. "I knew when five minutes to one o'clock came and went, and you had not arrived, that something was wrong. I became quite nervous. When the hour came and went, and you were nowhere in sight, I began to perspire. But when ten minutes past the hour came, and you did not show up, I realized that I was on my own. I was fearful of the outcome, and I knew then that there was no other alternative. So, with a heavy heart, I sat her down.

"With tears running down my cheeks I told her how great my love was for her. Then I shared my concern. 'I can't continue to live this way any longer. I have decided to become a Christian and be baptized.' To my surprise, she broke down and started crying. 'For a long time,' she began, 'I felt uncomfortable living the way we were. My desire was to become a Christian as well. But I thought that if I told you, you would leave me.' I was amazed at her response. I couldn't believe my ears. We joyfully embraced and decided to commit our lives to God. We have come to tell you that we decided to bring our lives in harmony with God and be baptized." They were married and baptized.

APPEAL:

Three months later as this reputable helicopter pilot was routinely training a new pilot, something went wrong. The rookie pushed the wrong lever, shut off the fuel, and the helicopter went down plunging both to their deaths. Little did he know that his decision was the most important one he ever made. What about you? Have you made your decision to follow the Lord at whatever the cost? Yes, life is insecure, but with Christ, you can secure your salvation right now. Will you come to Christ? Will you surrender yourself to Him just now?

GIVE YOU THE KINGDOM

Ninety-four-year-old Salomon Mendoza was taking a Bible study. He had served in the Baptist church for 70 years, but had never learned the things of prophecy he was now learning. At the Bible study, the leader purposed to take a big grease board to draw out the image of Daniel 2. Salomon was really excited that the Bible worker had brought it.

At the conclusion of the study, Salomon was asked three questions: Where in the image are we living today? What is the very next thing that takes place in the dream after the description of the feet? And finally the third question was asked, but before asking the last question, he was directed to the Gospel of Luke to answer this question. "Seek ye first the *kingdom of God*; and all these things shall be added unto you. Fear not, little flock; for it is your Father's *good pleasure* to give you the *kingdom*" (Luke 12:31, 32; emphasis supplied).

He was then asked, "Brother Salomon, what is the Father's good pleasure?" There was silence in the home for a moment. He thoughtfully looked at the verse again, looked at the drawing of the image on the grease board, and then he slowly turned his eyes from the grease board to the Bible instructor. The instructor noticed his eyes began to twinkle and shine. With a shaky voice he answered, "To give us His kingdom." In the midst of his answer, tears were running down his wrinkled face. He continued to share how beautiful the study was in the book of Daniel, and that from that day forward he was going to seek first the kingdom of God, and not allow the problems in his family, the war situation in this country, and all the worries of this world to discourage him because he was a son of the King.

They both knelt together and prayed. His prayer was one of the most beautiful and sincere prayers ever heard. In his prayer, he mentioned his 70 years of walking with the Lord, and how he thought he knew the Bible, but that he realized there was much more he needed to learn and experience.

It's amazing to see how one of the most basic prophecy studies can have such a powerful affect on a man's heart.

APPEAL:

Yes, it is a simple prophecy, but oh, such an important one. Referring to this prophecy, Jesus declared, "Whoso falls on this rock shall be broken, but on whomsoever it falls upon, it will grind him to powder." Oh, friend, it is Jesus' desire to give you the kingdom if you will have it! Do you desire to have the kingdom? Remember, He invites us to pray, "Thy kingdom come." Is that the prayer of your heart? Yes, even the last prayer of the Bible is, "Even so, come Lord Jesus."

We are living on the very edge of earth's history. Soon all the earthly kingdoms will pass. But God's kingdom will stand forever. Do you want to be a part of that kingdom? If that is your desire, will you lift up your hand?

Chapter 6

CHOOSING CHRIST AS THE SAVIOR
PROPHECIES OF CHRIST

CHOOSING

It's not necessary to have an opinion about Alexander the Great, Karl Marx, John F. Kennedy, or Queen Elizabeth I. They have passed on from the scene of life. They have had little if any impact on your life. But when it comes to Jesus Christ, we are brought face to face with the reality—we have to choose sides. This choice Jesus placed before all who heard Him, including His disciples. He asked, "What think ye of Christ?" "Who do you say that I am?" So today, you have come to the same crossroads. As we have talked about Him, there is the sense that one cannot remain indecisive—indifferent.

APPEAL:

Will you choose Him now? Will you make Him your Savior? What do you think of Christ? The answer to that question will decide your destiny. Why not make Him your Savior now? Who here will say, "Yes!" Will you lift your hand / stand to your feet / come to the altar? (The level of readiness of the audience should determine which response the speaker selects.)

EVA FROM POLAND

Eva was a very enthusiastic Jehovah Witness. When she received a flyer announcing an American evangelist holding a series of prophecy seminars, she decided to attend. As she listened to the first few presentations, she decided that the visiting speaker needed some help with Bible doctrines. After the meeting ended one night, she approached the speaker and suggested that he needed some things to consider that would correct his teachings. The speaker welcomed the opportunity to learn what he could, but he stipulated that everything had to come from the Bible.

Night after night they would meet along with another Jehovah Witness in a room at the church. Eva would carry her resource materials, which she kept just under the table where we were sitting. When a point arose that she could not immediately answer, she would glance at her reference material and scan for an answer. Night by night she fought to convince the speaker of her "truths," but she finally realized that her positions were not as well supported as she thought.

One night the subject was on the Holy Spirit. After the meeting, Eva thought she now could help the American see his error. As the study began, it was not long before Eva could see that the speaker's position was well supported by the Bible. Her idea that the Holy Spirit was merely an essence like electricity was not supported at all from the Bible. Eva became nervous. "Can you see, Eva, that the Holy Spirit is a divine being?" asked the speaker. Eva could not deny it. What about Jesus, then? Who is he?

As the speaker went from text to text, Eva could again see the truth about Jesus. Feeling driven against the wall, Eva began to cry. "Can you see that Christ is a divine Savior?" Eva then brought out the material she had underneath the table. Crushing the papers in her hands she said, "They have ruined my life." "Eva," said the pastor, "will you accept Christ as Thomas did when he said, 'My Lord, and my God.'" "Gladly," she responded. "Shall we kneel?" suggested the pastor. Then kneeling together, Eva accepted Christ as her Lord and Savior.

APPEAL:

Many a sincere person has been confused on this point. Yes, you believe Jesus was born as a man about 2,000 years ago. Yes, you accept the fact that as a man, he bled and died for your sins. But they had never seen him as that One who was preexistent, the One who has life-unborrowed, the Mighty God, the Everlasting Father, the Prince of peace. But now as you have heard the Word of God, you realize you are not dealing with just a mere man. In proportion to your understanding concerning the true character of

Christ, will be your appreciation of Him. Will you like Eva accept Him as not only your Savior, but also your God? Will you stand to your feet, and by so doing, declare that you accept Him as your Savior, Lord, and God? Will you stand just now? Let us pray.

WHO DO YOU SAY THAT I AM?

Bob was a logger in the mountains of the northwestern United States. As he was logging one day, his boss, who was not religious at all, drove up to him and said, "Bob, I read this text someplace in the Bible where Jesus is talking to one of his disciples, Peter. Jesus says He's going to build His church on the rock. What does that mean? Is He going to build a church on what Peter said, or on Peter himself? I want to know." Bob replied, "I don't know, but I'll find my Bible and tell you tomorrow."

So Bob drove down the mountainside and began to reflect on how his life was changing a bit. He later remarked that strange things had been going on in his life and noticed that his heart had changed, feeling more tender and kind. When he got to his house in the village below the mountain where he was cutting the trees, he found in an old trunk the Bible that his mother had given him 20 years before. He hadn't touched it since she had given it to him. He dusted it off and read in the Scriptures the text in the book of Mark where Jesus made the statement to Peter.

The next morning when the boss came by again, Bob said, "I think it is very obvious, as you read the Scriptures, Jesus is going to build His church on the confession of Peter that Jesus was the Christ, the Son of God." That satisfied Bob's boss, so Bob put on his earmuffs, started his big chainsaw, and began cutting the big trees. As he was cutting the trees, he heard a voice. The voice repeated the words of Jesus to Peter, "Who do you say that I am?" Bob looked around—no one was there.

Again, Bob returned to cutting the trees and heard the voice the second time. He looked around, and again, there was no one. He heard the voice all day, and he said later that he thought he would loose his mind that day. The voice kept saying, "Who do you say that I am? Who do you say that I am?" That night he could not sleep. He kept thinking about the voice.

The next day he went back to the mountains and began to cut trees again. Though he wore his big ear muffs, and the chainsaw was roaring as it cut through the trees, he heard the voice again ask, "Who do you say that I am?" He quickly looked around, and once more, no one was there. He turned off the saw, and in the little clearing there in the woods he fell on his knees and said, "You are the Christ, the Son of the living God." There on his knees, Bob surrendered his life to Jesus.[28]

APPEAL:

Oh, friend, who do you say that He is? Will you make Him your Savior now? Did someone just tell you about him? Perhaps like Bob, you have long forgotten your Lord. Perhaps you have turned away from Him, and just now, you would like to return. Whoever you are, why not accept Him now? Will you come to Him? Just rise, and like the prodigal say, "I will arise and go to my Father and say, 'I am not worthy to be your son.'" Remember, He has promised to receive you. Come just as you are.

THE ALLIGATOR AND THE BOY

Some years ago, on a hot summer day in south Florida, a little boy decided to go for a swim in the old swimming hole behind his house. In a hurry to dive into the cool water, he ran out the back door, leaving behind shoes, socks, and shirt as he went. He flew into the water, not realizing that as he swam toward the middle of the lake, an alligator was swimming toward the shore.

His mother was in the house. When she was looked out the window to her horror she saw the two as they got closer and closer to each other. In utter fear, she ran toward the water, yelling to her son as loudly as she could. Hearing her voice, the little boy became alarmed and made a U-turn to swim to his mother. It was too late. Just as he reached her, the alligator reached him.

From the dock, the mother grabbed her little boy by the arms just as the alligator snatched his legs. That began an incredible tug-of-war between the two. The alligator was much stronger than the mother, but the mother was much too passionate to let go. A farmer happened to drive by, heard her screams, raced from his truck, took aim, and shot the alligator.

28. Duane McKey, *Sermon Illustrations*, 5.

Remarkably, after weeks and weeks in the hospital, the little boy survived. His legs were extremely scarred by the vicious attack of the animal, and on his arms were deep scratches where his mother's fingernails dug into his flesh in her effort to hang on to the son she loved.

The newspaper reporter who interviewed the boy after the trauma asked if he would show him his scars. The boy lifted his pant legs. And then, with obvious pride, he said to the reporter, "But look at my arms. I have great scars on my arms, too. I have them because my Mom wouldn't let go."

APPEAL:

You and I can identify with that little boy. We have scars, too, not from an alligator, or anything quite so dramatic, but the scars of a painful past. Some of those scars are unsightly and have caused us deep regret.

But some wounds, my friend, are because God has refused to let go. In the midst of your struggle, He's been there holding on to you. The Scripture teaches that God loves you. If you have Christ in your life, you have become a child of God. He wants to protect you and provide for you in every way. But sometimes we foolishly wade into dangerous situations. The swimming hole of life is filled with perils—and we forget that the enemy is waiting to attack. That's when the tug-of-war begins. If you have the scars of His love on your arms, be very, very grateful. He did not, and will not, let you go.

Have you let go of God? Do you have scars of regret? Have you tried to get away from God but have realized that He will not let you go? You long to return, but you don't know how? All you have to do is to make the decision to return to Him. He says, "With an everlasting love have I drawn you. You are mine." Will you be His? Is that your desire? Will you respond to Him now? Will you raise you hand?

EARL WILLIAMS—BARREN SOUL

One morning as the preacher got up to present his sermon, he noticed a long, red-haired and red-bearded man slip in and sit down. The visitor looked enraptured by the message presented that morning. But as soon as the preacher ended his message, the man slipped away and vanished just as he had appeared. At the conclusion of the service, the pastor asked, "Did you see that long, red-haired man?" "What red-haired man?" Questioned the deacon. "He was sitting right there," responded the pastor. But no one had seen him.

The next weekend the same thing occurred. As soon as the preacher got up to deliver the sermon, in slid the red-haired man. This time the deacons saw him. The pastor noticed again that the man had an intense interest in the spoken Word. He seemed glued to every word. Once more, no sooner had the sermon ended than the man disappeared.

This time the pastor sensed in the young man someone desperately hungry for the Word. "Please bring him back again," prayed the pastor. The next weekend the pastor began his homily. The man appeared and took his seat. Unbeknownst to the visitor, the pastor had prepared a special message in the event that the man would return. So at the right moment, the pastor slipped in the specially prepared sermon. At the conclusion of the sermon, the pastor made a special appeal. Gripped with conviction, the man rose to his feet and made his way to the front weeping.

After the church service, the pastor invited the troubled man to meet with him in private. "Tell me about yourself. Where are you from, and what do you do?" With tears still running down his face he confessed, "I grew up as a Christian. I was married as a young man and had two children with my wife. But I became restless. I got interested in a rock group, and before I knew it, I became bored and disenchanted with the church. I abandoned my wife and children for another woman and abandoned everything I knew that was decent."

"Then I got into drugs and drinking. At first it was exciting. Then I began to get bored with life. From one woman to another, from club to club, I wandered. I began to feel a miserable void; nothing seemed to satisfy me anymore. Then in one of my empty, lonely moments, I thought of my vagrant soul. I wished there was something that could satisfy it. Then I thought of church. If only I could hear something that could water my soul, I mused. I came with the hope that I could hear something to fill my soul, but I had no plans to come back. Oh, I have been so barren—so empty."

APPEAL:

Oh, friend, have you been trying to fill your soul from dry cisterns? God has made a special place that He only can satisfy. Jesus says, "Whosoever drinketh of this water shall thirst again, but whosoever drinketh of the water that I shall give him shall never thirst; but the water that I shall give him shall be in him a well of water springing up into everlasting life" (John 4:13, 14). "For my people have committed two evils; they have forsaken me the fountain of living waters, and hewed them out cisterns, broken cisterns, that can hold no water" (Jeremiah 2:13). The Lord invites you! Listen, "And the Spirit and the bride say, Come. And let him that heareth say, Come. And let him that is athirst come. And whosoever will, let him take the water of life freely" (Revelation 22:17).

Are you longing for something to satisfy the deep yearnings and hunger of the soul? Then lift up your hand toward heaven and say, "Lord, fill me." As the song is being sung (for example, *Fill My Cup Lord*), will you let Him come into your heart? Will you come as the words are being sung?

THE TESTIMONY OF THOSE WHO LIVED IN CHRIST'S DAY

Put John the Baptist on the witness stand, and let's ask him, John, what do you say about this man Jesus?
Behold the Lamb of God.

Simon, the aged prophet, waiting for the salvation of God, what do you say?
I have seen the salvation with mine own eyes, O Lord.

The wise men from the east, what are your testimonies?
We have seen His star in the east and are come to worship Him.

John the Beloved, you who lived with Him, you who sat, you who ate with Him, you who watched Him, you who heard Him, you who spent three years with this man, what do you say about Jesus?
In the beginning was the Word and the Word was God.

Nathaniel speaks loud and clear.
Thou art the Son of God: thou art the King of Israel.

The woman of Samaria, as you spoke with Him, what was your response? Who do you say He is?

Is not this the Christ?

The disciples on that stormy sea, as the waves were beating that small boat, you were struck with horror. Men, what is your testimony—what do you say?

What manner of man is this, that even the winds and the sea obey him?

Nicodemus, scholar, leader of Israel, let us hear what you have to say.

We know that thou art a teacher come from God.

The Samaritans after hearing Him themselves, what do you have to say?

We have heard Him ourselves, and know that this is indeed the Christ, the Savior of the world.

The officers of the temple who arrested Him, what do you say?

Never man spake like this man.

Pilate, you've seen many criminals. You know men. Great philosopher, what is your testimony?

I find no fault in Him.

Judas, the betrayer, after you have sold Jesus, what is your testimony concerning this man?

I have betrayed innocent blood.

Finally, let's go to the shadow of the cross. There, as we approach it, we find a thief hanging. You remember, he was on the left side. And as the shadows of the day are coming, the sun is casting its glare on Calvary. We hear the thief cry out:

Lord, remember me when thou comest into thy kingdom.

Thomas, what do you have to say about your Savior after you put your fingers in His wounds?

My Lord and my God.

I want to share with you nine proofs of Christ's divinity:

Number 1:   Jesus had the power to read human hearts.

Number 2:   He had the power to foretell the future.

Number 3:   He had creative power. He fed thousands
from just a few pieces of bread.

Number 4:   He could give life—resurrected many.

Number 5:   The power of absolution—He could forgive sins.

Number 6:   He could receive worship.

Number 7:   He had life inherent, unborrowed.

Number 8:   He could transform hearts. As many as received
Him, to them gave He power to become the sons
of God.

Number 9:   He never made a mistake. He never had to take
anything back. He had the power of infallibility.

APPEAL:

I have to add to these testimonies my own testimony. My Savior has changed my life. *Note to the reader: The following is the author's personal testimony. Please share your own testimony.*

Forty years ago, I was a lost man—following a reckless riotous life. Plunging deeper into the abyss, I went about strumming upon a bass guitar, running wild in clubs, and trying to find happiness in activities or things. But when the Master touched my life, He changed me. And I can testify that He is not just a man. He is my Savior, the living God; the One who is altogether lovely.

Oh, friend, what do you say? What do you think of Christ? Who is He to you? Troubled soul, what is Jesus to you? Will you accept Him as your Lord and Savior? Will you say yes to Him now?

THERE IS NO SUBSTITUTE

A new pastor had arrived in his new church district. As he was unpacking, there was a knock on his door. A well-dressed lady, one of his new members asked to have a word with him. She explained that her husband was a well-known skeptic, but did not have long to live. He had done much against Christianity and had displayed no interest in God at all. Would he please go and visit with her husband immediately? "Well," he said, "I'll go as soon as possible." "He may not receive you. He can be very unkind, but please don't delay; his sister and I will be waiting." The next day the pastor made his way to the house. It was a large and beautiful home. Nervously, he knocked at the door. The lady of the house opened the door and was thrilled to see the pastor. He is upstairs. We will be praying for you while you visit with him."

The pastor made his way up the winding staircase. His heart was beating quickly. As he reached the landing, he came to the door. He knocked and waited. A very tall striking looking gentleman came to the door. The pastor explained that he was new in the area, was told of his condition, and asked to visit him.

Then he told him of his specific errand. "I have come to ask you to accept Christ as your Savior." The old, distinguished man asked him to enter. "You see all these books? They are all written by skeptics and infidels. In fact, I have written a few of them. But sir, they offer no substitute. Here and now, I give you my hand and accept your invitation." They then knelt, and a new soul was born into the kingdom.

APPEAL:

Oh, friend, the world can offer you all sorts of ideas and theories, but they leave your heart empty. They offer you no assurance, no peace. They try to take away Christ, but they offer you no substitute. There is only one Savior! Will you accept Him? Troubled heart—anxious soul—why not make Him your Savior now? Will you raise your hand indicating your election? Will you do that just now?

REMEMBER, I LOVE YOU!

In the recent rescue efforts resulting from the earthquake in China in May 2008, a woman was found. When the rescue team discovered her, she was already dead. She had been killed by the house that collapsed on her. Through the debris and destruction, the position in which she died could be seen. She was kneeling, with her whole body in a forward position, using her hands to support her body. Her position was somewhat similar to how people prayed in the olden days, except that the shape of her body was somewhat changed, and it looked a little scary.

A rescue worker squeezed his hand through all the debris just to confirm that she was dead. He shouted a few times, using his baton to knock a few times on the bricks, but there was no response inside. When the crowd walked to the next building, the team leader suddenly ran back again, shouting, "Come quickly!" He went to her dead body, and he used all his might to feel under the woman's body. He seemed to have felt something . . . then he shouted, "There's someone; there's a child, still alive." After some struggle, the team and volunteers helped to clear all the debris and took out her child from under her body. He was wrapped in a red blanket that had a yellow floral pattern, and he was about three or four months old. Because of his mother's protection, he was completely unscathed.

When they removed him, he was still sleeping peacefully. His sleeping face warmed everyone's heart. The accompanying doctor performed some checks on him and found a hand phone inside the blanket. He read the screen, and it read, "My dearest child, if you are able to survive, you must remember that I love you." The doctor, who in his life had experienced many births and deaths through his career, cried. The phone was passed around. Everyone who saw it couldn't help but shed tears.[29]

APPEAL:

Oh, friend, more than 2,000 years ago, your Creator and Redeemer bent his body over to take your blow. "He was wounded for our transgressions, he was bruised for our iniquities:

---

29 www.flickr.com/photos/26599733@N04/2496870006/in/photostream/

the chastisement of our peace was upon him; and with his stripes we are healed" (Isaiah 53:5). Yes, friend, He died, but he left this message: "My son, remember I love you". Those outstretched hands were for you. He took your beating, your punishment to protect you. Will you accept Him as your Savior? Will you give your heart to Him now?

Why not give your heart to Him just now? He loves you and died so you can live. Will you lift up your hand just now? Will you accept his love?

Chapter 7

HOW TO GET
RID OF YOUR GUILT!
THE SANTUARY
AND CHRIST'S MEDIATION

MARTIN LUTHER

Martin Luther was a great man, but he was a great sinner too; he admitted to the last. One day he was very discouraged. One thing the devil does to you and me is to egg us on. He tempts us until finally we step over the line. When a human being steps over the line, plunges into some fault, some sin, does he get encouragement from the devil? No, no! Discouragement. See what you did! He taunts. What hope is there for you? There is no use trying. You are lost. I committed one sin, and God cast me out of heaven. Do you think He will save you with all those sins—you, a church member; you, a Christian; you, who did so well? There's no hope for you. Then he tries to plunge you into the slough of despair.

Martin Luther felt that way one day. It just seemed as if there was no use trying. Finally, he had a dream. He dreamed that the devil came into his room in Wartburg Castle. Everything was dark; everybody was against him. It may have been more than a dream, but it seemed like a dream. The devil came in person, and he had a long piece of paper, a parchment, that reached down to the floor. He held it up, and on that piece of paper was a record of all Martin Luther's sins. He held it up and asked, "Did you commit all these sins, Brother Martin?" Luther hung his hand. "Yes," he said, "I committed them all." "Then what hope is there for you?" Taunted the devil.

Luther was profoundly discouraged, but he noticed all the time the devil was keeping his hand over something down in the bottom of the list. Finally he said, "What is that under your hand? Take your hand away; let me see it all." He made the devil take his hand away, and what do you suppose was written there? In red ink it said, "The blood of Jesus Christ His Son cleanseth us from all sin." The devil will keep his hand over that verse when you're discouraged, but, my friend, look at it and believe it. Then you will be on the other side of the great ledger, and the red mark will cover all.

APPEAL:

A day of reckoning is coming for everyone. God will judge all men by "that Man whom He hath ordained." Tonight I offer you the opportunity of meeting Christ in the judgment as your judge, or of going in through that great courthouse with him as your advocate. Oh, friends, it is a wonderful thing, when you go to court, to walk in with a lawyer who has never lost a case, isn't it? My brother, and sister, here tonight, don't you want to be represented in the heavenly tribunal by that Man? He is the only One who has the right to plead before that court. God has appointed Him to represent you. Let me give you another text. It is Romans 2:12, 16: "For as many as have sinned without law shall also perish without law: and as many as have sinned in the law shall be judged by the law ... In the day when God shall judge the secrets of men by Jesus Christ according to my gospel."[30]

You see, we are going to be judged by Christ according to the Gospel, the law as lived in Christ. That is the promise here in the Word of God. Judged by the law according to the Gospel! Thank God for that. According to the gospel! If the Bible simply said, "You are going to be judged by God's law: there would be no hope for any of us." But it says, "according to my Gospel." I thank the Lord for that completed sentence: according to my Gospel. We must face the court of God's righteous judgment, the Bible tells us. But it also brings the blessed promise that if we give our hearts to God, Jesus' death will be accounted for us, and we shall stand there before the judgment pardoned and cleansed because somebody else took our place.

Do you want to give your heart to Jesus? Or do you want to be judged by the law alone? You will be, if you do not give your heart

30. *The King James Version*, (Cambridge: Cambridge), 1769

to Him. You will be judged by that holy law without the perfect life of Christ unless you have given your heart to God and ask Him to take Jesus' righteousness in the place of your unrighteousness. Unless we do that, we cannot stand in the judgment; we shall be ashamed in the judgment.

Who here, when your name comes before the review of the universe, when your name is called, wants to lift up your hand and say, "Oh, Lord, have mercy on me! O God, there is a Mediator! There is One who is going to help me!" Will you plead, "Dear Savior, answer for me when He calls my name"?

IT HURT THAT MUCH

In the city of Baltimore, Maryland, a gospel worker was seeking for a person named on the Bible study enrollment card he was holding. Arriving at the address, he knocked and waited. After a little while, a young woman named Cynthia opened the door and demanded the reason for his presence. Her appearance looked haggard, and her eyes glassy giving indication that she was under the influence of narcotics.

He showed the card and asked if the individual named on the card was residing there. "Naw," she responded and began to shut the door. "Well," said the gospel worker, "this is a special study on the Bible, and it is free. Would you be interested in taking it?" Handing it to her, she took it and began looking at the lesson. "Let me come in and show you how it works," he said, so she invited him in. When he entered, he was surprised at the condition of the apartment. Her little boy was in an unkempt condition. Her dwelling looked like a tornado had gone through it. There were dirty dishes piled up in the sink, clothing strewn over the living room, and a very stuffy atmosphere typical of drug abusers.

He showed her the lesson, explained how to study it, and asked if the following week would be a good time to return to see how she did. She gave an immediate consent. He prayed with her and left. The next week he returned. He discovered that she had not done the lesson, nor did she know where she placed it. Having another on hand, he opened it and began studying with her. Though still in the same mental condition, Cynthia listened intently. At the conclusion of the study she was asked if there were any questions? "No," she responded. After a short prayer, the gospel worker left with the assurance that he would return the next week.

This went on for several times. On one particular appointment, the gospel worker returned with the fifth study. When she opened the door, he noticed something different about her. Her hair was combed, and her eyes had a clear sparkle. There was a change in her dwelling also. The dishes were clean and in the cupboards, and the house was clean. The smell of the apartment was fresh and her child was nicely dressed and clean.

When they sat down and the study was about to begin, she began to explain why the change. "I woke up yesterday and realized how disorderly my house was. So, I started by trying to pick things up. I noticed that on my living room end table, there was a porcelain bust of Christ. It looked very dusty so I decided to dust it off. As I was wiping the grime and dust, I got pricked by one of the thorns decorating his head. I pulled my finger back from the sharp pain that seem to race all the way through my body. The blood began to trickle out. As I held my finger cringing from the pain, the thought struck me. 'If this hurt me that much, then what about the pain that he must have suffered with those thorns on his brow?' Then I realized that He suffered greatly for me. I knelt down and decided to commit my life to Him, and that changed my life."

APPEAL:

That painful encounter convicted her enough to change her life. He can change your life also if you will let Him. Look at Him hanging on that cruel cross of Calvary. Hear that agonizing cry— "Father, forgive them for they know not what they do!" Watch Him as drops of blood fall from that innocent brow. He suffered it all for you! But have you felt the pain? Have you opened your heart to Him? There is no other way to get rid of your guilt. Will you accept Him today? If you give Him your guilt—your sins, he will replace them with peace of heart and a quiet conscience. Oh, sinner, will you take refuge in Him now? Will you accept Him now? Will you stand?

PRISONER IN DEATH ROW

The state of Pennsylvania had a governor named Pollock. During his administration, a young man, the only son of a widow in the mountains of central Pennsylvania, committed a crime—killed his dearest friend in a drunken brawl. He was condemned to death, sent to Harrisburg, and put into the old Eastern Penitentiary to die. Different people pleaded for him. The citizens got together and sent a plea, "His mother is a widow; he is her only support; he did it when he was drunk." They sent a delegation to see Governor Pollock, and they said, "Can't you let this young man off, or at least commute his sentence to life imprisonment?" His mother is a widow, and he is her only son. Her heart will be broken, and she will die, governor, if you don't do it." He said, "Gentlemen, I'm sorry. I have sworn to uphold the law, and the law must take its course."

Then the ministers of the time, with a Jewish rabbi and the Catholic priest, got together, and went down to see Governor Pollock. He heard their pleas, but said, "Gentlemen, the law must take its course. I can't pardon him."

Then last of all, his mother went. The governor didn't want to see her, but it was his duty; so she went, weak and trembling, her cheeks sunken, her lips ashen, her hair disheveled, her clothing unkempt. She staggered and dragged her way into the governor's presence, and, oh, how she pled for her boy! She said, "Oh, governor, don't kill my boy; he's all I've got. Don't kill my boy, governor. Oh, governor, let me die in his place. Don't kill my boy." And she fell fainting to the floor. The governor picked her up tenderly and laid the poor emaciated form on the sofa there. Tears ran down his face as he walked out of the room and said to his secretary, "John, if I can't pardon him, I can at least tell him how to die."

So Governor Pollock took his Bible and went down to that old Eastern prison. He went down to that death cell. The young man did not know who he was. The governor opened his Bible and read the great promises of God's Word to that poor condemned boy. He read John 3:16 and 1 John 1:9. He read the story of the cross and of the thief on the cross. That day there was a soul born again.

Then the governor shook hands with the young man, wished him well for the terrible ordeal the next day, and went away. After he was gone, the boy turned to the guard and said, "Guard, who was that man who came in here and read the Bible and prayed with me?" "Why," came the reply, "don't you know?" "That was Governor Pollock."

The young man threw his hands to his head. "Governor Pollock!" He cried. "If I had known that was Governor Pollock I would have thrown my arms around him. I would have buried my fingers in his flesh and said, 'governor, I won't let you go until you pardon me.'" The next day he stood on the scaffold, his feet and hands tied, black cap and shroud on. His last words were, "Oh, the governor here, and I …" He dropped down into eternity.

APPEAL:

Oh, friends, there is One greater than the governor here—the Lord Jesus Christ—and He waits to be gracious. Will you give your heart to Him now? In this great audience, wherever you are, will you not stand and say, "God help me; I need help. Please pray for me, because I wish to be with Him; I want Him to be my advocate in the judgment, my Savior. I wish my name to come up with Him. I want Him to present my case, and stand before the judge and take my place—Jesus." Who here would like to stand and say, "Pray for me!"[31]

CONDEMNED PRISONER

Years ago in the state of Ohio, a young man was found guilty of a terrible crime and was sentenced to death. Appeals to change his sentence to life imprisonment failed. Finally, his parents came and begged the governor at least go and see the boy. He agreed and went without announcement. The young man saw him approaching his cell and said to himself, "Here comes some preacher to bother me—I won't see him."

As the governor stepped up to the bars, he said, "Good morning, James." But the young fellow just turned his back and would not answer. "Your friends have been talking to me about you, and I have come to see you," said the governor. "I don't care to talk today." "If you knew the importance of my message, I'm sure you would give me an audience." "I don't care to talk. You'll

31. H.M.S. Richards, *Revival Sermons*, 248-256.

do me a favor and go away." "Very sorry; good-day, sir."

Soon afterward, the guard came by and asked, "Well Jim, how did you and the governor come out?" "The governor! You don't mean to tell me that little man who looked like a preacher was Governor Nash!" "Yes, he came to see if he could do anything for you."

His opportunity was gone, and a few days later, they put the black cap over his face, he cried out, "Oh God, what a fool I was! He wanted to help me, and I wouldn't let him."[32]

APPEAL:

My friend, you and I are under condemnation in the prison cell of sin. Come to God! Christ wants to help you now. May He not say of you, as of some others, "Ye will not come to me, that ye might have life." John 5:40. Come, friend, come to Christ now, and through faith receive life—everlasting life—for "He that believes in the Son has everlasting life, and he that believes not the Son, shall not see life, but the wrath of God abides on him" (John 3:36). When the Savior comes in glory, it will be too late to find salvation. So do it now! Be ready, be waiting, and be praying. Will you accept Him now? He wants to help you now. What will keep you from receiving His offer?

I HAVE HAD NO PEACE

An elderly woman approached the evangelist after his presentation and requested to speak with him alone. After the audience was dismissed, she and the pastor sat down in an adjacent room. As she began to talk, she could not contain her tears.

"Let me tell you my story," she confided. "When I was a young wife, to my great delight I discovered I was pregnant. I just couldn't wait until my husband came home to tell him the great news. When he arrived, I served him his meal and then told him the great news. To my shock, he said, 'Get rid of it. I don't want any children.' I was struck with grief. I thought that maybe he had just had a bad day.

"The next day, after he returned from work, I again approached the subject. He then blew up, and told me that it was either it—or

32. H.M.S. Richards, *25 Sermons*, 55-56.

him—and, he was serious. Pastor, I did not know what to do. I just could not bear the thought of loosing him. So in my distress, I had an abortion. Since then, I have never had peace. I killed my child. I have prayed and prayed, but my conscience still tortures me. What can I do?"

Opening the Bible, the pastor turned to 1 John 1:9. There he read these words, "If we confess our sins, He is faithful and just to forgive us our sins, and cleanse us from all unrighteousness." "But how can that be true?" she queried, "How can God with just a few words wipe out such a cruel crime?" "No, it is not just a few words. This promise is backed by the supreme sacrifice He provided in giving his own Son," the pastor responded. "It is true because He promised it. It is up to you to believe it or not. Do you want to accept His offer, or do you want to continue torturing your soul?"

Realizing the reality of God's sure promise, the elderly woman knelt down, and with a grateful heart, claimed the forgiveness offered and went home in peace.

APPEAL:

Perhaps, like that elderly lady, you have been carrying a burden on your heart. At times it seems like the sin has just blocked your entrance to heaven. You might even feel, "What's the use of praying, I am too great a sinner, and God will not hear." But friend, it is not about how you feel, it is about what he has promised. The condition is laid out before you, "If." Will you take God at his Word? Will you have peace in your heart? Do you long for, and want, His forgiveness?

Then why not do what that elderly woman did? Just kneel where you are, and confess it all to Him. He has not only promised to forgive but to cleanse as well. You must take Him at his Word. He has promised. Will you accept His invitation just now? Will you kneel, confess, and claim His wonderful promise?

Chapter 8

BAPTISM
HOW TO BURY YOUR PAST

WASTED SO MANY YEARS

An elderly gentleman attended an evangelistic meeting. As he was on his way out of the hall at the conclusion of one of the presentations, he approached the speaker and said, "Can you visit me at my home?" "Yes," responded the evangelist. "Here is my address and directions to my home." At this, he turned and departed.

The next day the speaker made his way to the address. He was taken back. The old man appeared very poor, and here he was before a mansion. He was wondering if he was at the right place when he heard, "This way, preacher." The old man motioned in his direction. Up a small winding staircase they went until they reached a little room. "Please sit down," the old man said. "Let me tell you why I asked you to come. When I was young, I was an unbeliever. The only thing I believed in was the all-mighty dollar. Then I fell in love with a beautiful young woman. I determined I was going to marry her. And I did. The only problem was that she was a Christian. That didn't bother me for I knew that in just a short time I could pull her away from that.

"I told her that I was going to make her the happiest girl in the world. I vowed that by the age of thirty-five I would be a millionaire. I was going to buy her a house in Europe, the States, and we would travel and see the world. But to my disgust, all she said was, 'What would make me the happiest is for you and me to spend eternity together.' I became upset with her. 'Nonsense!' I said. 'You are too beautiful and smart to buy that fairy tale,' she cried."

"Then what happened?" The visitor asked. "I determined that I was going to break her faith. Instead, I broke her heart. I am afraid I sent her to an early grave. When she died, I lost interest in everything. This house, I had built for her, and when she passed away, I could not bear to live here without her. So I left it. I went abroad.

Like a madman I began to live a reckless life. First, I lost one eye and then got crippled in my leg in the process. I lost everything, but nothing mattered. For, what I loved the most, I lost. I never thought I would see her again." Then taking a locket from around his neck he said, "Look at her. Isn't she beautiful? I have been a fool! I came back here to finish out my hopeless, empty life. The people who bought this house were kind enough to let me rent this little room.

"I thought I would never see her again until I attended your meetings. Now, I look forward to seeing her, and how glad she will be! Pastor, can I be baptized?" "You may if you believe with all your heart," said the pastor. "Oh, I do," he responded. Right there and then, the old man and the pastor knelt and prayed.

On the day of his baptism, there stood a group of onlookers as the pastor waded into the lake. Then, the old man began to limp toward the water. Wishing to help the candidate, some men stepped forward to assist him. "No, gentlemen. Thank you for the help. I have been walking on these legs for the last sixty years for the devil, now I want to use them for the Lord." Then he proceeded to where the pastor was. After offering a benediction, the pastor baptized the man. Coming up out of the water, the old man with tears of joy running down his face exclaimed, "I will see her again, I will see her again."

On the shore there was a well-dressed family. The thirteen-year-old girl turned to her father and said, "Father, I have wanted to be baptized for a long while. You have kept telling me to wait for you. Dad, I can't wait any longer." And with that, she also walked into the water to be baptized. The father with tears streaming down his face likewise took off his jacket and followed his daughter to be baptized. And there that day were three souls born into the kingdom of God.

APPEAL:

Oh, friend, have you been born into the kingdom of God? Perhaps like this old man, you have been wandering aimlessly, with dashed hopes and a troubled conscience. Jesus can wash that all away. Jesus says, "Though your sins be as scarlet, they shall be as white as snow. Though they be like crimson, they shall be like wool" (Isaiah 1:18). "Repent and be baptized for the remission of your sins," is the call, "and ye shall receive the gift of the Holy Ghost" (Acts 2:38). Do you desire to begin a new life? Why not accept the Lord's invitation? Will you do it just now? Will you stand? (Raise your hand or fill out a decision card. Use the one that is appropriate.)

CAN GOD FORGIVE ME?

In a tent meeting one night, a man and a woman walked in and sat in the back row. The evangelist could see by his shadowy outline that he was a big man. It was dark in the tent for the speaker was using slides with his presentation. At the conclusion of the sermon, the couple abruptly got up and left. By the time the speaker reached the exit to greet the people, they were gone. No one knew who they were.

The next night as the evangelist got up to speak, the same couple returned and this time sat closer to the middle of the tent. Again, as the message of the night ended, the couple quickly got up and left. Still no one knew who they were, or why they were leaving so soon from the meeting place. The next night they came earlier and sat even closer to the front. He was a hulk of a man. The woman also was obviously into body building. This particular evening the preacher made an appeal. He invited anyone who would to rise and come to the altar. Among others was this couple.

With tears streaming down his face, the gentleman stepped up and let it be known that he needed time with the preacher alone. After all were dismissed, the man threw a question at the evangelist, "Can God forgive me?" "Of course!" Responded the preacher. "How do you know? You don't even know who I am, and what I have done," stated the troubled man. "You are right. I do not know who you are or what you have done, but I know who God is and what He can do!" Then the preacher opened his Bible and read, "If we confess our sins, He is faithful and just to forgive us our sins, and cleanse us from all unrighteousness" (1 John 1:9).

"How can that be true?" Inquired the man. "With man things

are impossible, but with God, all things are possible," was the reply. Then the pastor continued and asked, "What do you think you have done that you think God can't forgive you?" "I have killed 3,500 people." "Three thousand five hundred lives? How did you kill that many people?" Asked the amazed listener.

"My father was a hired killer," began the visitor. "From my childhood up, I developed the thirst for blood. But I did not want to be like my father—always hiding. At an early age, I began to body-build so that I could beat up on people. But it was not enough. I was unsatisfied, so decided to join the military at age seventeen. I became a helicopter pilot and volunteered for Vietnam. Finally I was excited for the opportunity to kill legally. Convinced that I could kill more than all the other pilots I suggested taking bets. I volunteered for every search and destroy mission. It was this way that I destroyed 3,500 lives.

"What is strange about it is that I never felt guilt or remorse about this until I came here to this tent meeting. You know why I came? We were driving by and I told my wife, 'Let's go into that tent and see what is going on.' I always enjoyed going to places and starting something so that I could have the pleasure of taking somebody's face and twisting it. But things here were not what I expected. Now I am in turmoil over my past. Will God really forgive me?"

The pastor again turned to the promise in 1 John 1:9, and read it. The he said, "If you determine to turn your life over to God, and with a contrite heart ask for forgiveness, He will forgive you and give you a new heart. Is this what you want?" asked the pastor. "Yes," responded the man. Then together they sank to their knees, and he poured out his heartfelt plea to the Lord. Yes, that hour there was a new soul born into the kingdom.

APPEAL:

Have you committed a sin that you have felt God could never forgive? Have you had pleasure in sin for a season and feel the burden of that terrible deed? Do you long for cleansing? Remember, if we confess our sins, He will not only forgive you, but also cleanse you. Is that your desire? Will you come to the Lord just as you are? Will you rise to your feet and come just as you are? Will you come "without one plea, but that His blood was shed for you?" Will you come?

JUST A LITTLE DIRT

A young evangelist was visiting a lady who was attending his seminar. He was trying to encourage her to accept the truth of biblical baptism. The woman insisted she had already been baptized by sprinkling and that was good enough for her. Despite the facts presented to her that Jesus was immersed, the Ethiopian was immersed, and the word baptism itself means, "to put under, or submerge," she would not yield.

As he conversed with her, he was silently praying, "Lord, what can I say?" Then the thought struck him. Her little puppy had, just prior to his arrival, been crossing the road and was killed. "What are you going to do with your dead dog?" He questioned. "I am going to bury it," she said. "Well, I suppose you are going to just take a few grains of sand, throw them on the animal, and that will bury it?" Asked the evangelist. "Of course not!" She said. "I will need to dig a hole, place the animal in it, and then cover it with dirt." As soon as she said that, the meaning of baptism by immersion struck her. She now understood that a few drops of sprinkled water was not biblical baptism. Then and there she made her decision to be baptized.

APPEAL:

Perhaps you too have been christened and have felt that sufficient for you. But now you realize that with God this is not sufficient. You need to be buried. The Scriptures remind us:

> Know ye not, that so many of us as were baptized into Jesus Christ were baptized into his death? Therefore we are buried with him by baptism into death: that like as Christ was raised up from the dead by the glory of the Father, even so we also should walk in newness of life. For if we have been planted together in the likeness of his death, we shall be also in the likeness of his resurrection: Knowing this, that our old man is crucified with him, that

the body of sin might be destroyed, that henceforth we should not serve sin. (Romans 6:3-6)

Jesus is your example. He was buried for you that you might have life. But you must follow His counsel. "Why tarriest thou? Arise and be baptized, calling on the name of the Lord." Will you respond to His voice now? Who here will lift up your hand and say Lord, "Wash me completely." Will you do it now?

PATTY

She was a young wife with a strong faith. She kept herself very active in her church. Her husband, however, was an unbeliever. Patty tried her best to get him to believe but to no avail. One day, there was a knock on her door. The man inquired as to whether the young man who had sent in a card requesting Bible studies was at home? Looking at the card, she recognized the handwriting. "This is my husband's handwriting," she said. "But it must be a mistake. Someone must be playing a joke." "Is it his handwriting? Inquired the man. "Yes," she said, "but I am sure he did not send it. He is an unbeliever." The man suggested that he would leave the first lesson for her husband, and would return to see if he was serious about the studies.

Upon his return, Patty informed him that her husband had no interest. Then the man asked, "Will you take them?" She consented and started the weekly study. When she began to put into practice the light that she was receiving, it aroused opposition. Three ministers showed up to see her on different occasions. Strangely, no one had ever visited her before. They gave her literature to dissuade her, but when she compared it with what she had read herself in the Scriptures, she could see their error.

Patty loved the studies, and all that she was learning about her Lord. Finally the day came when she arrived at the church to be baptized. Her mother also showed up unannounced. Right in the midst of the service, the mother stood up and railed on her and the Bible worker. She did everything to embarrass Patty. But though frail in stature, Patty was strong in spirit and determined to follow her Lord whatever the cost. Contrary to all opposition, Patty went ahead and was baptized.

APPEAL:

Perhaps you are going through the same things that Patty did. No one paid much attention to you until you decided to study the Scriptures and walk in the wonderful light God has been unfolding to you. The opposition of loved ones is always painful. Jesus was also opposed by his family. He well understands the struggle.

But if you will determine to make him first in your life, He will strengthen you just as he did Patty. That young woman was an eloquent testimony of the courage God can give even to the most frail. Are you tried? Determine to follow Him, come what may. Jesus will strengthen you. He says in Isaiah 41:10, "Fear thou not; for I am with thee: be not dismayed; for I am thy God: I will strengthen thee; yea, I will help thee; yea, I will uphold thee with the right hand of my righteousness." Will you rise to stand on Christ's side? Will you do it now?

THE BRENT WALKER STORY

In 1970, during the Vietnam crisis, a group of soldiers were caught under enemy fire. One of the soldiers radioed for help, and a helicopter was sent in for rescue. A helicopter pilot noticed the soldiers and lowered its rope ladder. As one of the soldiers was climbing up, the medic above watched the ascending soldier drop his rifle and then his radio. He also began to fall backwards; fortunately, his foot got caught in one of the rungs of the rope ladder. The medic who saw this happening scampered down the ladder and pinned the soldier's leg against the ladder. There they were like a flying trapeze, dangling from this ladder. The bullets flew everywhere, so the pilot of the helicopter decided to rise as quickly as possible.

As it did so, the pilot had to be careful not to go so high as to lose the men, but high enough to get away from the enemy fire. The helicopter then headed toward safety. You can imagine the scene with this helicopter flying with two soldiers dangling: one unconscious and one hanging on for dear life, not only for his own, but also for the life of the unconscious one.

Finally, they lowered the man and took him off to the hospital. The soldier that risked his life to save his comrade climbed back into the helicopter, and off they went to find others that they could deliver. In the meantime, Brent Walker, the unconscious soldier, finally began to regain consciousness. All he could remember was climbing up the ladder. He didn't know how he got to the hospital. In response to his inquiry, they told him of the scene of the helicopter with the two dangling soldiers. He was one of them—unconscious—while the other was holding onto him and to the rope ladder for all he was worth. He then realized that soldier had risked his own life to save him.

This story came to the attention of one of the television programs some years later, and they investigated to see if this story was actually true. They decided to try to get all the players together. We are talking about thirty years later. During those thirty years, Brent Walker thought to himself, if only I could meet my rescuer, if I only could thank him personally for what he did.

Brent Walker was married with children and had grandchildren. He had lived a very successful life stating, "I would have never been able to accomplish what I have accomplished if it had not been for . . . him. I would have never had my wonderful wife, my children, or grandchildren if it had not been for . . . him. Oftentimes," Brent said to himself, "I wish I could meet him. If I could just meet him, I could thank him personally for what he did."

Thirty years later they were sharing the story on television. Unbeknownst to Brent, all the players in the episode were brought together. Brent walked on stage. The host of the show asked him to repeat the story and its details as well as he could remember. "Is it true? Did it really happen?" Asked the Host. "All I can tell you is I remember being caught under enemy fire and radioed for help. I remember the helicopter coming down, I remember climbing the ladder, and the rest is history. They told me what happened," Brent responded. Then he was asked, "Have you ever desired to meet that fellow?" "Yes, a thousand times. I would love to meet him and give him my personal thanks."

The television host turned around and said, "Ladies and gentlemen, welcome to the stage Sergeant Gibbons." From behind the curtain walked out this Specialist 5 ranked sergeant who had risked his life to save Brent Walker. "Now please remember that they have not met for thirty years," the host continued.

When Brent Walker saw the man, he jumped up from his seat, ran to his rescuer, hugged him, and sobbed for joy that after thirty years he had finally met the man. As far as he was concerned, he owed everything to him. As they were clutched in their embrace, the whole audience erupted with applauding, weeping, and rejoicing. Then the host said, "We have a special recognition for Sergeant Gibbons." From behind the curtain came two high-ranking officers with a letter of accommodation from the United States president and a special medal of recognition. After thirty years they finally awarded him for his bravery.

APPEAL:

How grateful are you? This man, for thirty years, yearned to thank his rescuer. How much do you yearn to meet your rescuer? Are you grateful for the sacrifice He has made for you? Have you made Him your Lord and Savior? Jesus Christ came down to this dark earth to rescue you. He declares, "Behold, I have graven you in the palms of My hands; with loving-kindness, I have drawn you. You are Mine."

That thought causes me to ask myself, "How grateful am I?" What about you? Have you given yourself to the One who has loved you even to His death? Do you desire to give yourself to Him? Is it your desire to commit your life to Him in baptism? Will you lift up your hand and say, "Thank you, Jesus? Thank you for dying for me. I give myself to you. Here I am! I want to seal my complete commitment to You in baptism." Will you lift your hand to heaven now?

JESSICA—YOUNG GERMAN GIRL

Fifteen-year-old Jessica was attending a weekend series of lectures in Germany. She had gone to hear the American speaker, Louis Torres. Her presence there was merely out of curiosity. However, the more she heard, the more she became convicted. She determined not to yield herself to Christ. It was not that she did not believe in Him, it was just simply that she wanted to enjoy life before becoming too serious about religion.

On Sunday morning, the last presentation was to be given. Though advised concerning the impracticality of making a public call due to the people's resistance to such public display, the speaker nonetheless made an appeal. As Jessica listened, she began to have a great struggle in her soul. Later she admitted that it seemed as if her heart's throbbing would push it out of her chest. But she had purposed that she would not, at this young age, make such a serious commitment. She resisted until she could no longer resist. The promptings of God's Holy Spirit she could not deny.

As Pastor Torres made a fervent appeal for baptism, Jessica could no longer hold back. With tears streaming down her beautiful, fair complexion, Jessica finally decided to stand, and by doing so, made a public declaration that she would not only get baptized, but surrender her life completely to the Lord. After the meeting, with tears still freely flowing after an hour, she told the pastor about her struggle, and the gratitude she had for his appeal.

APPEAL:

Perhaps, like Jessica, you too are struggling with the temptation to resist. There are plans that you have, which, if you were to make the decision, would have to be discarded. There are pleasures that you feel you would miss. But your heart throbs— just like Jessica's. You know what you should do. You know what God is offering you. And He says, "And now why tarriest thou? Arise, and be baptized, and wash away thy sins, calling on the name of the Lord" (Acts 22:16).

Oh, friend, don't put off your decision to a more convenient season. A man named Felix in the Bible said, "Come back in a more convenient season." The problem was that it never came.

Will you yield your heart to Christ today? Do you desire to have your sins washed away? Do you want to start with a completely clean record? Is it your desire to give yourself to Christ? If that is your desire, will you raise your hand just now?

THE ALCOHOLIC

One night during an appeal, the local drunkard responded. He had been listening, though at times, he would show up drunk to the meetings. After the appeal the old man requested help from the preacher. He now believed with all his heart, and wanted to begin a new life through baptism. But he had a problem. He and his woman were living together, and he knew he could not begin a new life without righting that matter. However, he felt if the preacher would speak with the woman, there would be a better chance of taking care of the problem. His request was granted, and an appointment was made.

Climbing up the steep hillside, the pastor made his way and arrived at the little shack where they lived. When the pastor met the woman, he then understood why the man requested his help. She was terse and unwilling to cooperate. The pastor made his plead in behalf of the man's desire to begin a new life. But in order to be baptized, he needed to get married. In spite of the fact that they had been living together for fifteen years and had ten children together, she refused to marry him.

With a downcast countenance, the old man gave evidence that he was terribly disappointed. But the pastor was determined not to give up. On another day the preacher made his way to the shack alone. He wanted to talk with the woman to discover why she was so reticent to marry the man. He discovered that the woman did love her man. But when she was a young woman, she was in love. She wanted to marry her lover, but her father refused.

It was then that she vowed to God that if she could not marry the one of her choice, she would never marry anyone. The pastor insisted that the vow she made to God was made in ignorance of His counsel, to which she agreed. She then admitted that a great change had come over her man since he had been attending the meetings. He had stopped drinking, cursing, and had become a better mate.

"What then will keep you from getting married?" She then presented her dilemma. She had no birth certificate and no money to pay for the license. Then she surprised the pastor by telling him that if she could get married, she too wanted to begin a new life with God and with her husband. What joy came to the old man to know that the great obstacle standing in his way to begin a new life was removed! They were married, and they both began a new life together in Christ.

APPEAL:

What is in your way of giving yourself to Christ? With Him, nothing is impossible! Do you, like the old man, long to be cleansed—to start a new life—but there are obstacles? Is there something in your life that you know needs to be removed in order to begin a new life in Christ? Why not come to Him? With man things are impossible, but with God, all things are possible. He will work out the problem if you will give yourself to Him. Will you come?

OLD COUPLE REBAPTIZED

They were living together for thirty years. The man was now incapacitated and bedridden. As they studied the Word of God, they confessed that though they had been baptized by immersion, they had never really studied the Bible. The more they studied the more their hearts burned to recommit their lives to Christ. But when they went over the Ten Commandments, they showed an uneasy look. Yes, though they had lived together for thirty years, they had never legally married. The aged woman began to cry. "They baptized us, but they never told us that we were living in sin nor studied with us.

"Now we know in verity that your teachings are from God. We want to get baptized, but we first must make our lives right. We want to get married before the Lord."

A few days later, the groom was dressed lying on the bed. The elderly woman was attired with a beautiful dress. And in their bedroom, the wedding took place. When the day of the baptism arrived, strong men picked up the aged man and placed him in a wheel chair. Then at the baptismal site, they hoisted up the wheel chair and candidate into the baptismal pool.

The old man and his wife beamed as they enter the watery grave of baptism. How thankful they were to be cleansed from all sins! Now, they were not baptized in their sins, but without their sins. When the old man was taken out of the baptistery, something wonderful happened. Whereas, before he could not sit up, after the baptism, he was able to sit and attend the rest of the meetings.

APPEAL:

Perhaps you are like the old couple. Deep inside you love God and want to serve Him. But as you have been hearing the messages, you sense that your first baptism just does not meet the longing of your heart. Perhaps you were baptized as a baby, and now you realize that in reality; you were never really baptized as the Bible commands. Now you want to do it right and for the right reasons. Will you arise and come to the Lord? Like the disciples of John the Baptist, though you have been baptized, it is now your desire to recommit your life to Christ in rebaptism? If that is your desire, will you lift up your hand?

BISHOP FRATELLI OF NEW YORK CITY

Bishop Fratelli, a Catholic living in the borough of Queens, New York, had a neighbor. Every time she had an opportunity, she offered him some Christian literature. Though he took it, he always threw it away. Then one day, he had to present a message and discovered that the title on the literature was just what he needed. He took it, and it turned out to be just what he needed.

When he saw her, he expressed his appreciation for the material. This started a more cordial relationship. One day, she was going to a special prayer seminar and invited him to attend. Though a little reluctant, he accepted and went with her. It turned out to be just what he needed. He had never heard people pray like he heard praying that night. Since it was a week-long seminar, he attended every night.

By the conclusion of the week, he had come to the realization that though a bishop, and a man of sixty-nine years of age, he had never really known the Lord. Prayer was tedious to him. Now prayer was a joy. He learned that he could communicate directly with heaven. This newly found experience resulted in his decision to read more into the Bible. It was then that he realized his need of starting anew and being baptized.

He decided to set a date and invite all his friends to celebrate his birthday. When the occasion arrived, priest, bishops, and others attended. Though surprised that the chosen site was a Protestant site, the friends waited anxiously to discover what was going on.

The program began with a brief introduction, then after a special musical item, Bishop Fratelli spoke. He said, "Thank you all for coming to celebrate my birthday with me. However, I am not celebrating my physical birthday today, but my spiritual rebirth. I have decided to be baptized."

"You may ask, 'Why are you being baptized when you have already been baptized?' I was baptized as a baby. My parents decided that for me. I had no part in the decision. They meant well for they did what they thought was best for me at that time. However, I have discovered that baptism is a divinely ordained ceremony. It is to be done as a direct result from a personal conversion to Jesus Christ. But in order to be converted, there must be repentance—a sorrow and a turning away from sin of which I had no part when I was sprinkled.

Today, I am being baptized as a testimony of my personal love for Christ—a public confession of my faith in Him as Lord and Savior and a washing of my past sins.

APPEAL:

Friend, if Bishop Fratelli, a man of sixty-nine years of age could sense his need of being rebaptized and of turning away from tradition to follow a "Thus saith the Lord," then what about you? Do you sense your need of being washed? Will you just now respond to the calling of the Lord and arise and be baptized?

THE LEPER

As Jesus spoke throughout the synagogues and cast out devils, a man with leprosy ran up to him. In his loathsome condition, he threw himself to the ground. Leprosy was a much feared and dreaded disease. It did not matter who contracted it. The consequences were cruel. Not only did the person have to be separated from family, friends, and society, but with it came the reproach of being singled out by God as a great and hopeless sinner. Thus leprosy was a symbol of sin.

Apparently this man must have been observing the movements of the Savior. When he saw the opportunity, he ran to Jesus. He was so desperate in his aim that he did not make the usual cry of "unclean." So determined was he that he dare not miss the opportunity. The Scriptures say, "And it came to pass, when He was in a certain city, behold a man full of leprosy, who seeing Jesus fell on his face, and besought him, saying, Lord, if thou wilt, thou canst make me clean" (Luke 5:12). Notice that the man sensed his need of cleansing and saw Jesus as the only One who could do what he so much needed.

In response to his pitiful plea and his demonstration of unwavering faith, "Jesus, moved with compassion, put forth His hand, and touched him, and saith unto him, I will; be thou clean" (Mark 1:41).

In another episode, Jesus was with His disciples. It was the night of the Passover. Jesus approached Peter with a basin and began to wash his feet. Peter's response was that of consternation. "After that He poureth water into a basin, and began to wash the disciples' feet, and to wipe them with the towel wherewith He was girded. Then cometh He to Simon Peter: and Peter saith unto him, Lord, dost thou wash my feet?" (John 13:5, 6). Though Jesus cautioned that he would understand later, Peter refused the washing and said, "Thou shalt never wash my feet." Then Jesus' sobering words aroused his fear and struck his heart, "If I wash thee not, thou hast no part with me" (John 13:8).

APPEAL:

Oh, friend, there is nothing more terrible than the thought that we will have no part with Jesus. Like the leper, we not only need to recognize our true sinful condition, we must also acknowledge that Jesus is the only One who can cleanse us. Friend, if you have not been washed, remember Jesus said, "Except a man be born of water and of the Spirit, he cannot enter into the kingdom of God" (John 3:5). Do you want to enter? Then arise and wash away your sins calling on the name of the Lord, and you shall be saved. Will you lift up your hand to heaven now?

GERMAN WOMAN WRESTLER

In Herbolzheim, Germany, a young woman had heard of a week-long series of meetings near her home. She decided to attend. As the biblical messages were being delivered and an appeal for baptism was made, she responded. At the conclusion of the meeting, the speaker met with those who had responded. Having some personal questions, she waited until she had an opportunity for a private talk.

"I want to be baptized, but I have a problem," she began. "I have been a champion wrestler. Though I have been successful in my career, I always felt that something was missing. I did not realize that it was God until I attended this meeting. But that is not my major problem," she continued as she brushed away her tears. "I live with a man, and I realize now that before I can seal my life with Christ, I must abandon my sinful life. I need some time to get things in order."

The next day she returned to the meeting. This time she brought some friends with her. When the speaker noticed her, he took note that she looked different. There was an obvious joy and peace on her countenance that was not present when she began attending the meetings. After the presentation, she met with the pastor.

"You look different as if a great load has been lifted from you," the pastor said. "Yes," she replied. "I sat down with the man I was living with and told him of my decision to be baptized and give my life to the Lord. Then I told him that he needed to go back to his wife. Then I called his wife and told her she needed to take her husband back. There is nothing like having peace of mind and knowing that Christ is willing to wash our sins and give us a new start. Now, I am ready to be baptized."

APPEAL:

Maybe you are like that woman wrestler. You sense the Lord speaking to your heart and feel the need to give yourself to Him. Like her, you know there are things you need to set in order. As the Spirit speaks to your heart, you want to make that commitment, but wonder how to do it. Remember this, Jesus said, "For without me, ye can do nothing" (John 15:5). Do you want to ask the Savior to help you? You want to be cleansed and start a new life with Christ: will you give Him your heart now? Will you respond to Him now? If that is your desire, will you lift your hand to Him now?

NEWSPAPER REPORTER

"I want to tell you that I was at some of your presentations fifteen years ago," said an attending newspaper reporter to the visiting preacher. "I would love to have an interview with you tomorrow for my newspaper." After it was agreed to have the interview, she left.

The next morning the pastor made his way to the newspaper building where he would meet his appointment. Happy that he had arrived, she began to open her heart. "As I told you last night," she began, "I attended your meetings fifteen years ago. I felt then that I should commit myself to Christ. And I fully intended to do it, but I had other things I wanted to do first. One thing led to another. I got involved with the theater life, singing, and the dog-eat-dog of show business life. I was unhappy. And though in the back of my mind the impression made at your meeting lingered, I could not break away from what I was doing. I have wasted and lost fifteen years of my life trying to find meaning in life, but to no avail."

Then she told the pastor that her hopes revived when she heard that he was back in town. Determined to be there, she changed her schedule. "Last night as I listened, the deep movings of God that I had felt fifteen years ago revived. Back then I remember the desire I had as I watched others being baptized to experience the same myself. But I didn't follow through. After fifteen years, I have determined by God's grace to catch up on lost time. I am going to be baptized, and begin a new life."

APPEAL:

Have you, like that reporter, felt the promptings of God's spirit, but like that reporter, things have gotten in your way? Time has past, and as you contemplate, you realize that you have wasted precious time. As you listen, your conviction has revived that you need to catch up on lost time. You see that nothing you have tried has brought the peace that your soul needs. And just now, as God's voice is speaking to you, like that reporter, you are determined this time not to let the moment escape you.

Just now you want to say, "Lord, I have squandered precious time. I have been drinking from dry cisterns, and my soul is empty.

I desire to turn my life over to you just now." Like that reporter you want to say, "I make my decision right now to commit my life to you in baptism." If that is your heart's desire, will you stand?

FIGHTER AND A DRINKER

At a visit from a pastor, he sat and listened. The pastor tried to encourage his friend to accept Christ and be baptized. Then asking permission to speak, the Gypsy man addressed the group then present. He shared with those listening that he had been a fighter and a drinker—a rough man. Unbeknownst to him, his son began to have an interest in spiritual things and was baptized.

By his son's witness, the man's wife also desired a new beginning and was baptized. This made him glad because now as a Christian, she would no longer be nagging him to quit his wild living, he reasoned. He knew there was something different in his family, but pride and stubbornness kept him from their influence. Then she invited him to the church by saying, "Just come once. If you do not like it, you do not need to return." Feeling this was a way to get her off his back, he consented. But his plan was to argue with the members, and, therefore, insure himself he would never be welcomed again.

When he entered the church, he found the people loving, kind, and pleasant. They took him in like family. He later confessed that this completely troubled him. It was not how he had planned it: what he gambled for. While at the church he began to feel a tug on his heart. Deep within he desired a change of heart, victory over his violent temper, and the enslaving habit.

The love and acceptance he found at the church caused him to open his heart. Through the spoken word, he found power to overcome, and a loss of desire for alcohol. He also noticed a change in his temper. This awakened a desire in him to completely forsake his old ways and experience the washing away of his old life in baptism. Then he said to his friend, looking him straight in the eye. "I was then baptized and am a new man. You need to do the same!" With a downcast glance the friend responded, "You are right! Right here and now I make my decision to be baptized."

APPEAL:

Some in this audience can identify with that Gypsy. You may be caught in an abandoned lifestyle, but deep inside you long for a different way. Perhaps like the Gypsy, your pride and stubbornness has prevented you from seeing your true condition and need. But as you have listened to the message, there has awakened in you a longing to be set free. You desire a fresh start, a new beginning. Why not start now?

As the spirit of God has awakened in you those desires, that awakening comes with the assurance of power to overcome, and to set you free. But it is up to you. Do you want a fresh start? Does your heart long for deliverance? Will you lift your hand toward heaven and say, "Lord, deliver me. Help me to change." If that is your heart's desire, I invite you to respond just now.

DON'T LET PRIDE KEEP YOU FROM GETTING BAPTIZED

A man, his wife, and adult son, and daughter were attending a series of meetings. From the appearance the entire family were baptized Christians. However, the pastor discovered the contrary when the son and daughter approached him and asked if their father could receive a visit. He had been married for fifty years to his god-fearing wife and only permitted his children to attend Christian schools for their education. While all his family members were baptized committed Christians, he was not.

From night to night he attended the meetings and seemed to enjoy them. His expression gave evidence that his heart yielded to the biblical teachings presented. But he would never make a move when appeals were made. Curious as to why he was so compatible with the Gospel and yet not accept it, the preacher made a home visit. Upon the visit, the daughter was asked to translate because the man was not fluent in English. He had no problems understanding the presentations for they were being translated.

When the pastor asked the first question, the daughter translated. However, the daughter did not appreciate the apparently arrogant response. So rather than translate, she began to chide her father. Sensing that this would not work, the pastor asked the son to translate.

At the next visit, the family gathered around the table. The pastor presented the first question. This time the mother chided him for the way he responded. The pastor then asked the mother to get drinks for them all to remove her from the discussion. Realizing the situation, she acquiesced. This time the pastor was able to freely ask questions without interference.

"Have you ever had a desire to commit yourself to Christ in baptism?" Asked the pastor. "Honestly, yes." He responded. "Would you like to do it?" Was the second question. "Yes, but because I am too timid, I would like to do it just with my family present." He said. "Alright," said the pastor, "we can do it this weekend." "Fine," was the response.

"Pastor," said the daughter privately, "my dad is not going to be baptized. He just likes you and does not know how to say no." "No," said the pastor, I believe him to be sincere in his decision." "But you don't know my father," she said.

At the next meeting, the father said, "I have changed my mind. I want to be baptized in front of the entire church." Drawing the pastor aside, the daughter said, "See, I told you. My father being baptized in front of all the church, impossible! I know my dad— he is too timid. He just doesn't know how to say no to you so as to not offend you."

"You will see," said the pastor. At the next meeting the man made another request. "I would like to say something to the congregation before I am baptized and have my daughter translate for me. Is that possible?" "Of course," said the pastor. Once more in private the daughter remonstrated with the pastor insisting that her father changing all the time indicated unequivocally that he would not do it.

When the night of the baptism arrived, the father was present. He went and changed into his baptismal robe. As he descended the steps of the baptistery, the daughter took her place at the podium to translate. As the father began to speak, his daughter was overcome with crying and could not translate. The brother then stepped up and translated.

"For fifty years," he began, "I witnessed the love and care of a godly wife. I saw her raise my children to become a wonderful son and daughter. But because I was a Communist, and too proud to surrender, I have held back all these years from giving my heart to God, but He has been merciful. Today, I stand in testimony to the powerful influence of a godly family. Friend, don't make the same mistake that I have made. Don't allow pride to keep you from giving your heart to God."

APPEAL:

Have you allowed pride to keep you from giving yourself to God? Have you resisted knowing deep inside that this is the right thing to do, but you cannot bring yourself to surrender your heart to God? Is it too humiliating? Friend, take the advice of one who suffered a tortured conscience all those years, because he would not humble himself. Give yourself to God now. Don't allow the enemy to keep you back from peace of mind, cleansing of heart, and a pardoned life. Just think how much people lose out on simply because they are unwilling to yield, unwilling to admit, yes, they are right.

Will you allow the Lord to have His way into your heart? Will you say, Lord, I have held back all this time, I will not keep you waiting any longer. Will you arise and come to the Lord? Will you come just now?

Chapter 9

CHOOSING TO LIVE FOREVER
THE MILLENNIUM

MAN SHUT UP IN MAUSOLEUM

The man was wrapped up in his grief and sorrow. His fiancé had died. Little by little those present at the gravesite slipped away as they sensed the need to give him time alone. As tears rolled down his cheeks, he reflected on their experiences and his great loss. Finally, he brought himself into composure and began to make his way to the door. In his reflections, he had lost track of time. The only light in the mausoleum was candlelight. In the dim light, he had not noticed that the door was shut. As he approached the door and pushed to open it, he discovered it was locked. His thoughts ran quickly. Oh, no! I am locked inside, buried alive. He began to knock but no response.

Perspiration began to ooze its way out of his brow. The horrible thought terrified him. "I have been left inside here," he thought, "and no one may realize it until it is too late." His grieving turned to anxiety and dread. Buried alive! No, no! Then he awoke.

APPEAL:

The time will come when those outside the Holy City will realize that they are locked into the terrible fate of being lost forever. There will be no reversing of the doom, no room for repentance, and no one to plead their case. Unlike the man who dreamed with dread that he was buried alive, the awful realization will dawn on the lost of their irreversible plight—lost forever. Oh, friend, why not seal your decision tonight to be with your Lord inside the city? Why not say, Oh, Lord, I want to have the desire to follow you, to be on your side, to dwell with you forever? Can you say, "I desire salvation?" Is that the longing of your heart? Will you respond to your Savior's invitation? He has made every provision, but you must accept it.

YOUNG FIANCÉ BEGGING
HER LOVER NOT TO GET BAPTIZED

At a baptismal service the candidates were getting ready for the special occasion. Many had made their decisions to give their hearts to the Lord and seal their decisions in that sacred rite. As the speaker was walking to check on the preparations, he happened into a situation. There before him was a young man already dressed in his baptismal robe and a young lady clutching unto it and weeping. Being moved by the scene, the pastor decided to see if he could render some comfort.

Seeing the speaker approaching, the young woman turned to him and said, "Please tell him not to do it." "Do what?" Asked the speaker. "Tell him not to get baptized now. If he does, my parents will not allow me to marry him. Oh please, tell him not to go through with it. After we are married, then he can do it."

The pastor looked at the weeping, heart-torn young man and asked, "How do you feel about it?" "I love her, but I need to follow the Lord."

APPEAL:

Oh, friend, what in this world is worth losing your soul over? Are there things in your life that tug at your heart, telling you that the sacrifice is too great? Jesus said, "What shall it profit a man, if he shall gain the whole world and lose his own soul? Or what shall a man give in exchange for his soul?" (Mark 8:36, 37). How is it with you tonight? Is there anything worth missing out on when compared with all that the Savior offers you? Those outside the city will realize all too late that nothing gained on this earth is worth losing all that God offers.

Friend, will you ask God to help you with that struggle? Perhaps it is that certain person, or that opportunity, or that habit that you know will keep you out of the city and cost you your eternal salvation? Will you lift your hand to heaven and like that young man choose to be with God? Oh, friend, don't let anything keep you out of that city.

PARDON THROUGH CHRIST

When the Civil War broke out, there was a man in one of the far southern states that enlisted in the southern army. He was selected by the general and sent to spy on the northern army. As you know, armies have no mercy on spies if they are caught. This man was caught, tried by court-martial, and ordered to be shot. While he was in the guardroom waiting the day of execution, he would call Abraham Lincoln by every name that entered his mind.

One day while he was in prison, a northern officer came into his cell. The prisoner, full of rage, thought his time had come to be shot. The officer, when he opened the door, handed him a free pardon, signed by Abraham Lincoln. He told him he was at liberty; he could go to his wife and children. The man who had before been full of hatred asked, "Abraham Lincoln pardoned me? I have never said a good word about him." The officer responded, "If you got what you deserved, you would be shot. But some one interceded for you in Washington and obtained your pardon. You are now at liberty."[33]

APPEAL:

Yes, if you or I got what we deserved, we should suffer the consequences of our sins—lost forever. The Bible says, "For the wages of sin is death" (Romans 6:23). But thank God, someone interceded for you! Yes, with His own life, Jesus paid for your sins and mine that we might receive pardon. We might have been a Christian living in the world and serving as a double agent.

Our lot should be sure. Because of our transgressions, we should be outside the city destined to eternal destruction, but today, who can find the word pardon by your name? Today, if you will accept it, you can go free in Christ. Will you accept the pardon? Will you choose to be with the righteous enjoying eternal bliss? If you will, will you respond to this appeal? Will you raise your hand (stand, or invite them to the altar) just now?

---

33. *Christian Endeavor World*

THOSE LOST

The Scriptures say, "But the fearful and unbelieving, and the abominable, and murderers, and whoremongers, and sorcerers, and idolaters, and all liars, shall have their part in the lake that burneth with fire and brimstone: which is the second death" (Revelation 21:8). Again, it says, "And whosoever was not found written in the book of life was cast in the lake of fire" (Revelation 20:15). Now this could be a very sad ending, but friends, God does not want to destroy sinners. He finds no joy in destroying sinners. He says, "I find no pleasure in the death of the wicked but that he turn from his wicked way. For why will you die? I give you life! Why will you accept death?"

But those who accept life, it says, "Nevertheless we, according to his promise, look for a new heavens and a new earth, wherein dwelleth righteousness" (2 Peter 3:13). "And I saw a new heaven and a new earth: for the first heaven and the first earth were passed away" (Revelation 21:1). What a wonderful promise! What a wonderful day that will be, when with God our Savior, we'll be able to be with Him for all eternity!

A new earth made new. Life springs up again. Flowers will never fade. Imagine, no death. No one will say I'm sick, and you won't have to count birthdays either. What a wonderful thing! What do you say? The lame will be straightened up again, the blind will see far better than an eagle. We'll be able to enjoy all the pleasant things that God initially wanted us to enjoy, and this time no one will be able to take them away from us.

Oh, what a hope! What a hope the Bible gives us! What a hope the Lord gives us! What a wonderful hope! And with everything that God offers us, it's hard to understand why people would choose death, why people would choose sin. But they do.

I had a young man talking to me. He pierced himself with many sorrows. How sad, when God offers life, health, and strength, when God offers salvation, when God offers a clean conscience, when God offers you eternal life. What can you pay for eternal life? Can you buy it? People in the past have done everything to find eternal life. They tried to find fountain of youth to no avail. Scientists are trying to figure out the secret of life. Oh, if he or she could only discover it! But thank God life is in Jesus' hands!

I would hate to think, my friends, that humankind could continue forever in the way it's going. If it can be as evil in fifty years as Hitler was, what would it be if it lived a thousand years? What would it be if it lived a million years and never died? Can you imagine the atrocities? Thank God that He cut the life of humanity short, and that He is preparing a place of eternity only for those who want to live in harmony with the principles of love, peace, and joy forevermore. I want to be in that new earth. What about you? As you think about that, listen to the words of this song entitled, "I Dreamed I Searched Heaven For You."

APPEAL:

I would like to close tonight with just a very simple appeal. Some of you here tonight have been coming night after night. Last night, there were those of you who made a decision. So we rejoice because God says that heaven rejoices over one sinner who repents, more than ninety-nine just men who need no repentance. What a wonderful thing to know that heaven is interested in us. Heaven poured out its heart as it suffered on Calvary in giving its Son, for you and for me—all to ensure that you will not miss heaven.

Tonight, I wonder as you've heard the appeal song, as you've been thinking about it in your own heart, I wonder as you've heard the Spirit of God speaking to you, if it is not time for you to say, "Lord, I want to choose the right side. I want to be on the right side. I want to be on the inside looking out and not on the outside looking in." I wonder if there's someone here tonight who can identify with what I'm saying.

God's Spirit is speaking to you, and you'd like to say, "Tonight, I want to make that full and complete commitment to my Lord. I want to come and give myself to Him. I want to take my stand. I want to be baptized. I want to have all of my sins washed away. I do not want anything to stand in the way of my having the assurance that I can be with God in His kingdom." If that's the way you feel, if there's someone here tonight who would like to respond by standing, please just quietly rise to your feet where you are.

RESPONDING TO AN APPEAL

A young man was in a meeting when an appeal began to be made. Strangely, there came over him a sudden chill. He began to shiver and his teeth began to chatter. It was warm in the hall, so this was unexplainable. He realized that there was a struggle raging within himself. He felt strongly that the invitation was for him, but he could not move. His brother, sitting next to him, noticed what was happening and wondered at the strange occurrence. As the appeal continued, the cold effect seemed to have a grip on the young man.

As he shivered, he wondered at the strange phenomenon. Then it occurred to him what was happening. Satan was trying to keep him attached to that chair so he would not respond to God. He then mustered up a prayer in his mind to God, "Give me strength. I know You're speaking to me. I need to respond." And so he closed his eyes and said to himself, "No matter what it takes I'm going to stand up and if I fall, I fall. At least God, You'll know that I'm making an attempt to stand for You." When he stood up, the chill left him, and the nervousness unleashed its grip on him. He felt a peace and warmness return to him. Then he went to the altar in response to the appeal. Oh, what victory the Lord gave that young man!

APPEAL:

What will be your response? Is there someone here who would like to stand and say, "I want to prepare for baptism. I want to stand! I want to be among that group." Amen. God bless you and you too.

Let us pray. "Our Father, we thank You so much for those who have stood. We thank You, Lord, for those who stood last night, and the reason they're not responding is because they already have made their commitment. We thank You for these who have joined them. Now, Lord, as they make their preparation, as they have placed their hands by faith in Your hand, as they look forward to the time when Jesus shall come and be among those who are first caught up, or first resurrected, may Thou seal them tonight, we pray. May You put in their hearts that hope, and may they look forward to that day when Jesus shall come and rescue them. Lord, all of us who have already made our decisions, we recommit ourselves to You again tonight. We don't want anything to keep us back. So Lord, accept us again. Thank You for hearing us in Jesus' precious name. Amen."

THE HILO TIDAL WAVE, MAY 23, 1960

In Hilo, Hawaii, sirens began to shriek in the night. A tidal wave was headed toward Hawaii at 450 mph. Hilo residents had three hours and fifteen minutes to evacuate.

But Hilo had been through many tidal-wave alerts. Usually nothing happened. Some moved to higher ground. Some didn't bother. An eyewitness reported that some people actually went to the beach to get a first hand look at the large waves.

Suddenly the sirens stopped. All was quiet. It was like a death hush. Then came a rumbling like the roll of a distant drum. It was almost inaudible at first, then it grew louder. Then with a fierce rumbling and force impossible to describe, it was there, a wall of water thirty feet high and moving with the speed of a jet. The screams of anguish were drowned in the deafening roar. Then it was quiet again, that awful silence again.

In the morning, seventy-eight bodies were discovered among the ruins, seventy-eight people who didn't need to die. They knew! They heard the sirens. They understood the risk. They just didn't bother to do anything about it.

APPEAL:

God has so mercifully unfolded the fate of the unrighteous and that of the devil. The righteous will enjoy the bliss of eternal youth—a place where there will never be pain, sorrow, tears, or death. Heaven's warnings have been heralded. What will be your lot? Will you choose to be inside the Holy City or outside? Will you determine by the Lord's grace to make your move toward the kingdom? God wants you inside. But will you allow Him to help you? Will you raise your hand just now toward heaven?

FRANK TRACY

He woke up sweating. It was early in the morning, about 5:00. But what he had just experienced through the night was too urgent to wait until later. So he called the pastor and begged him to immediately make his way to his home. When the pastor arrived, there was a very solemn and distressed man waiting. "Come on in pastor." Once in, the pastor enquired about the reason for the urgent visit.

"During World War II," he began, "we were ordered to take a Japanese stronghold on a hill. The problem was that the hillside was made of gravel. When the first wave tried, they were cut down. Finally, we were the last to go. I made it halfway up the hill, but there was nowhere to go. I was an open target. Next to me was my first sergeant. All of a sudden there came a grenade. It missed me, but wounded the sergeant. I picked up my wounded sergeant ·and held him in my arms. Then once more, another grenade was thrown. This time it hit the sergeant in the head and killed him. There I stood with him in my arms and nowhere to hide. I knew it was it for me. I expected a shot to ring out.

"Instead from nowhere, a soldier came, grabbed me and rushed me out of harm's way. I did not know where he came from, and I never ever saw him again. Why was I spared?" This brought him to talk about the immediate episode that prompted the urgent visit. "I don't know what it was, but it was so real that I woke up sweating."

Then he shared that he found himself in a single-file line with people in front of him and behind him. He was not able to identify anyone. Way in the front, he could see that people arrived at a gate. There they met someone. There seemed to be a brief interview. They went through the gate, and then gradually disappeared into an abyss. He wanted to get out of the line, but there was nowhere to go. It seemed as if all were locked into the line. As he was approaching the gate, he was gripped with an unknown dread. Then all of a sudden, a bright light shown above his head. As he looked up, there was a retinue of people, joyful and holy, flying upward through the air. Among the crowd of happy people were his Christian girlfriend and her son. They were oblivious to him.

It was then that he realized he was eternally lost. When he approached the gate, the attendant looked inside a book. Then the gate was opened, and he was compelled to enter. No matter what effort he made, he could neither turn to the left nor the right. Down the plank he descended into the darkness below. He was so terrified that he awakened drenched in sweat.

APPEAL:

It is that unknown dread that will torment the lost. They could have been saved, but for whatever reason, they are lost. There will be no reversal of the sentence. The time to plead for mercy has expired. The lost then keenly realize how dreadful is their lost condition. Oh, how they long for that voice of entreaty and compassion! If only they had taken advantage of all that heaven had proffered them. But now it is forever too late.

Ah, friend, why not choose now to be in God's kingdom? Why not determine by God's grace to be inside looking out, rather than outside looking in? God has made every provision for your salvation. Will you accept it now? Will you put your all on the altar?

Chapter 10

DECIDING TO BE IN HEAVEN
OUR ETERNAL EXISTENCE!

(If possible, have someone sing the song,)
"I Dreamed I Searched Heaven For You."
Words by Kitty Wells

I dreamed I had gone to that city

That city where never comes night

And I saw the bright angels in glory

I saw their fair mansions of light.

I gazed for long, long years of rapture

On the face of my Savior so true

And I sang with the seraphim holy

Then I dreamed I searched heaven for you.

Chorus

I dreamed, I searched heaven for you

Searched vainly through heaven for you

Oh, won't you prepare to meet me up there?

Lest we should search heaven for you.

I looked on both sides of the river

That flows through the city of God

I searched through bright mansions celestial

And streets of gold pavement I trod.

The faces of saints by the millions

I scanned in my yearning to see

That face I had cherished so fondly

The face that had grown dear to me.

Chorus

I dreamed, I searched heaven for you

Searched vainly through heaven for you

Oh, won't you prepare to meet me up there?

Lest we should search heaven for you.

There is another more contemporary appeal song by the title
"I Want To Go To Heaven" by Rick Metcalf.

I want to go to heaven and pick a never fading flower;

From the mountain overlooking the temple of my God.

I want to go to heaven where all this light and glory.

How I long to be with Jesus! How I long to be with God.

Chorus

Sometimes I think I can stay here no longer.

I feel very lonely here for I have seen a better land.

Oh that I had wings like a dove,

Then would I fly away and be at rest.

I want to go to heaven; I want to hear the voice of Jesus,

"You have washed your robe in My blood,

Stood stiffly for My truth."

And I want to get to heaven and cast my crown at Jesus' feet.

I want to praise His name forever! He has done so much for me!

Chorus

Sometimes I think I can stay here no longer.

I feel very lonely here for I have seen a better land.

Oh, that I had wings like a dove,

Then would I fly away and be at rest.

APPEAL:

Jesus' prayer in dark Gethsemane was, "Father, I want them to be with me where I am." He even promised, "I go to prepare a place for you. And if I go and prepare a place for you, I will come again, and receive you unto myself; that where I am, there ye may be also" (John 14:2-3). Jesus has made every provision. God has given you every incentive—streets of gold, glorious mansions, and a life that equals with the life of God are offered to you. Why all this? God's only reason is that He wants you to be with Him forever!

Oh, friend, God longs to be with you. The Scriptures clearly declare, "Behold the tabernacle of God is with men, and He will dwell with them" (Revelation 21:3). The question is, do you long to be with your Savior? Just think friends, life everlasting, joy unending, and friendships that will never end. God has done His part; now He invites you. Will you accept the invitation? If that is your desire, will you raise your hand to heaven just now? Will you say yes to God?

I wonder whether there are those here (today or tonight) who would like to say. "I wish you would pray for me. I want to be there, and I accept my Savior's call. I accept it. Will you pray for me?" I wonder whether all who say that would be willing to stand. Those who would like to be remembered in prayer, wherever you are, stand just now. God bless you! Anybody else? Yes—and you, and you! Let us pray.

LITTLE TYKE:

A mother lioness in the Seattle Zoo killed her newborn cubs—all but one. The little cub was rescued and given to a friend of the zoo to raise. He was a butcher and thought, "It will be simple to feed this lion because I can feed it with scraps from my butcher shop." But amazing as it sounds, the lion, which he named Little Tyke, would not touch meat. From the first to the last of its life, Little Tyke was a vegetarian! She was so peaceful and gentle.

Her owner trained her and would often display her in public gatherings. On stage, before a live audience, a couch would be placed on the platform. From the wings a live lamb would be carried and placed on the couch. Then without bars, chains, or a leash, there came a large, full grown lion. She would take one look at the audience and everyone gasped to realize that there were no restraints. The lion could have run right down into the audience and what a stir of panic that would have caused. She would sniff the air, catch sight of the lamb, and run straight to the helpless lamb on the couch and jump right up with it. When she lay down beside the lamb with her paws cuddling it, the audience breathed a sigh of relief.

APPEAL:

Oh, friend, God is preparing a real place for real people. Think of it! The time will come when all that destroys will be changed. God will make a new heaven and a new earth. God has revealed all the wonderful incentives that tell us, He wants you and me there with Him. The question is, do you want to be there? Jesus said, "I go and prepare a place for you." Don't you long for that day? Don't you want to be with your Savior who at such great personal expense has made it possible for you to be there? Will you say to the Lord, "Yes, Lord! I desire to be with You." Will you lift your hand to heaven now?

THE RICH YOUNG RULER

In Matthew 19, a rich young ruler approached Jesus and asked, "Good Master, what must I do to have eternal life?" Jesus said, "Keep the commandments." The young man responded, "All these have I kept from my youth." Then Jesus said to him, "Go sell all that you have and give it to the poor; and come and follow me."

When the young man heard this, he went away sorrowfully because he had great wealth. Also in Matthew 19, a publican approached Jesus. His name was Zacchaeus. He was so anxious to see Jesus that he climbed up a tree to see Him. When Jesus came to the spot where Zacchaeus was in the tree, He said, "Zacchaeus, you come down, for I am going to your house today." At the house, the publican said, "Lord, all my goods I give to the poor, and if I have taken from another by fraud, I have returned back fourfold." Then Jesus said, "This day has salvation come to this house."

APPEAL:

Ah, friend, the first rich man was looking for eternal life without Jesus. He turned away sorrowfully when presented with the cost. "All should consider what it means to desire heaven, and yet to turn away because of the conditions laid down. Think what it means to say "No" to Christ. The ruler said, 'No, I cannot give You all.'"[34] The second man, the publican, desired Jesus so much

---

34. E. G. White, *The Desire of Ages*, 523.

that he cared not about the cost. He gained eternal life. How much does eternal life and heaven mean to you? Do you long to be with the Savior? He longs to be with you. He promised, "I go to prepare a place for you. And if I go and prepare a place for you, I will come again, and receive you unto myself; that where I am, there you may be also" (John 14:2, 3).

Do you long to be with Jesus? Like Zacchaeus, are you so desirous that you are willing to have Him and eternity at any cost? If that is your desire, will you respond now? Will you lift your hand toward heaven and say yes to Jesus?

THE YOUNG RUNAWAY

She chaffed at the reproof and longed someday to get away from the "don'ts." She was but fourteen years old, but she was incorrigible. One day she planned her escape. When everyone was asleep, she took the rope she hid in her closet, flung it out the window, climbed down to the front yard, and made her way in the darkness to her long-desired freedom.

Now that she was free, she headed to the big city of Chicago. There she felt she could get lost in the crowd and never be found. As she reached downtown, she began admiring the big stores. While she was admiring a ladies clothing store, a fancy large car drove up and parked at the sidewalk. A well-dressed man sat at the driver's seat. Looking at the young girl, he said, "Nice clothing, aren't they?" Surprised at his questioning, she glanced to see who was talking to her. Looking like a well-meaning man, she responded, "Aha." He got out of the car and approached her. Sticking out his hand to shake hers, he said, "My name is John, what's yours?" "Mary," she said. "Well, are you just window shopping, and are you from around here?" The stranger asked. Not being sure why he was questioning, she just said, "Just window shopping."

Then changing the subject, he asked, "I am going to get a bite to eat, are you hungry?" "Well, kind of," she answered. "Well, I am going right next door, and it's on me," he said. He seemed to be such a kind person. She began to feel at ease and felt that her parents' admonition about strangers in the big city was overstretched. During the meal, the stranger plied her with several questions. She felt that he was interested in her and seemed to want to befriend her. After they finished, he asked, "Are you going home?" "Well," she said, "not exactly." "Are you tired?" he asked. "Well, kind of." "Well, if you want, you can go to my home and rest. I have a guest room that you can use." Reluctantly, she went.

As she got into the fancy car, she could not believe how she struck luck. When they reached the house, she was taken back by how big it was. Once inside, he showed her the guest room and said, "It's yours to use. If you need to take a shower, the towels are clean. Make yourself at home." "Can this be true?" She wondered. After the shower she laid down in a bed that she could only dream about. When she woke up after a nap, he invited her to eat, and then asked, "What do you think if we go out and buy you some of the clothing you were admiring earlier in the shop." "Really?" She asked. "Sure," he said.

When they returned, she brought in the beautiful clothing just bought. "Why don't you hang them up, get some rest, and tomorrow we can talk some more." When she awoke, there was breakfast on the table. The man met her and after breakfast he asked, "How are you going to pay for all the clothing I bought you?" Surprised and fearful, she questioned, "Pay for them?" "Sure," he said, "you didn't expect to get them for free, did you?" "Well, I don't have any money. How can I pay for them?" So Mary was introduced into prostitution.

At first she did not like it. But then she got used to it, and finally, she began to enjoy it. She had everything: nice cars, nice clothing, and a beautiful house. Then one day her boss noticed a rash on her. As he checked it out, things immediately changed. He could no longer use her. It didn't take long for Mary to find herself in the streets. Now she had nothing. Sick and alone, she became a street dweller. In order to protect herself from becoming a victim, she got herself a knife. At night she would cover herself with the cardboards to protect herself from the chill of the night.

While in her desperate condition, she began to think about home and her parents. She longed for home and the companionship of her loved ones, but felt she could never return. What would her parents think of her if they discovered what kind of life she had been living? What shame and reproach would be theirs! She tried to dismiss her yearnings, but to no avail. Then she thought, "I will call them collect and ask them if they want me back home." So she got up her courage and called. Fearing rejection, she braced herself for the worst. She was overwhelmed with joy to hear her father and mother beg her to return and promise to send her the money for the bus fare. As she boarded the bus and took her journey, she began to go over her turn of events.

She remembered the modest, yet, pleasant home. The night escape from her supposed bondage she regretted. Then the fall into abject slavery of both body and soul were painful memories. She wondered whether anyone other than her parents would even want to see her after all that she did. As the bus rounded the corner and began to approach the station, there was a crowd of people waiting. Not only her parents but also all her cousins, aunts, uncles, and friends greeted her. As she disembarked, her father broke through the crowd, ran up to her, and embraced her in a clutch of relieved joy—swinging her as he held her.

APPEAL:

Jesus said, "There is joy in heaven over one sinner that repents" (Luke 15:7). Perhaps you feel you have been too great a sinner to come to Him? Some of us may feel that we are very far away from home. Oh, my friend, if Jesus came all the way from the outer reaches of the universe to save you, then there is no distance too far for Him to encompass in order to receive you.

Remember He declares, "Him that cometh to me I will in no wise cast out" (John 6:37). Do you, like Mary, long to return? Why not "Come to yourself" like the prodigal and say, "I will arise and go to my father and will say unto him, Father . . . I am no more worthy to be called thy son" (Luke 15:18, 19). Oh, friend, just like that father running out of the crowd to embrace his lost daughter, so God will receive you if you will come to Him. Will you arise just now and come? The Lord is waiting. Will you come?

Chapter 11

YIELDING TO
THE HOLY SPIRIT

YOUNG MAN AND DWIGHT MOODY

One night during one of his lectures, Dwight L. Moody made an appeal. People began to respond. While people were moving forward to the altar during the appeal, Mr. Moody noticed a well-dressed young man being stirred, but he did not respond to the call. The appeal finished, and the young man did not accept the invitation. At the exit, the evangelist bid people a good night. When the young man came to the door, Mr. Moody said, "Young man, I noticed that you were convicted, but you did not commit yourself to the Lord. Why not do it now?" "Oh, not now," the young man nervously replied. "But I promise that I will do it. I give you my word." "All right," responded Mr. Moody. And with this, the young man hurried away.

Several weeks later as Dwight Moody was walking down the streets of Chicago, he met the young man again. After the initial greeting, Mr. Moody reminded the man about his promise. Have you given your heart to the Lord? "Well, not yet. Business has picked up, and I have not had a chance," he said. "Well, why not give your heart to the Lord now? You can do it right here," Mr. Moody encouraged.

"Oh no," begged the young man, "we are right in the middle of the street and everyone will be watching. Please, Mr. Moody, not now. But I promise you I will do it. Don't worry, I will do it. But please not here." "All right young man, you promise you will?" "Yes, I give you my word." Then he left.

Several months later Dwight Moody was awakened late in the night. "Mr. Moody you must come quickly. There is a young man desperately ill, and the parents have requested that you come without delay. They feel the young man does not have much time. The preacher got dressed and went with the messenger. They made their way through Chicago and boarded a waiting boat. When they arrived on the island, they rushed Mr. Moody to the bedside of the sick young man. It was the same person who Mr. Moody had encouraged to give his heart to the Lord.

Sensing the urgency of the situation Mr. Moody immediately began to appeal to the young man. "Young man, it is Mr. Moody. Have you given your heart to the Lord?" But there was no response. Moody attempted to gain the man's attention, but there was still no response. Then Mr. Moody noticed the patient's lips moving. Bending over and placing his ear close to his lips, Mr. Moody hoped for a gleam of hope.

To his sorrow, he heard the young man utter words he was quoting from the book of Jeremiah. Here are the words, "The harvest is past, the summer is ended, and I am not saved" (Jeremiah 8:20).

APPEAL:

Why let your spiritual summer end? Don't put your salvation on hold. The Lord says, "Behold now is the day of salvation. Harden not your hearts." While God's Spirit is speaking to your heart, why not say, "Lord Jesus, I will not put you off any longer. Here I am. Take me, and come into my heart." Will you do it just now? Why delay? When Jesus called his disciples, the record states, "And straightway (at once) they left their nets and followed him" (Mark 1:18).

Jesus said, "Follow me. But he said, Lord, suffer me first to go and bury my father. Jesus said unto him, Let the dead bury their dead: but go thou and preach the kingdom of God. And another also said, Lord, I will follow thee; but let me first go bid them farewell, which are at home at my house. And Jesus said unto him, No man, having put his hand to the plough, and looking back, is fit for the kingdom of God" (Luke 9:59-62). Will you come? Will you stand for the Lord? Just raise your hand where you are, signifying your pledge to heaven of your commitment.

I AM LOST, AND I DON'T CARE!

A young man was taken ill one night. His mother called a doctor. The doctor, upon examining the young man, saw that he could not live more than twenty-four to thirty-six hours at the most. He called the mother into another room and told her that the boy would not live. The mother was overcome with grief, especially because she knew the boy was unsaved. Finally, after a time, she regained her composure. She telephoned her pastor to come and talk to her boy about his soul.

Then endeavoring to hold back her tears, she went into the sickroom and said to her boy, "Son, the doctor says that you cannot live more than thirty-six hours. I have telephoned my pastor to come over and talk with you."

The boy looked his mother in the eye, and said, "I don't want to see your preacher. I will not let him talk to me. I am lost, and I don't care. Two years ago I was in a revival meeting and was powerfully impressed that I ought to give my heart to Christ. I resisted that impression. I grabbed my hat and left the tabernacle. After I got out, I cried, 'Holy Spirit, leave me! I will never give in to be a Christian.' I determined to blot that desire from my mind. I have never had a desire from that time on to be a Christian. I am lost, and I don't care."

APPEAL:

Men can harden their own hearts until they cannot repent. That is why the Bible puts such emphasis on making one's decision to obey God "today." The Bible never talks about making a decision to obey God "tomorrow." "Today, if you will hear His voice, harden not your hearts." "Today, lest any of you be hardened through the deceitfulness of sin."

It is a solemn thing, but true, whether you realize it or not, that if you fail to act on a call, the next time that call is made, your heart will be a little harder than it was previously. It will be a little harder to yield every time. You can go on and on refusing to yield to the calls of the Holy Spirit, until you become hardened to the most solemn appeals.[35]

---

35. John L. Shuler, *Typical Evangelistic Sermons*, Vol. II, 250-251.

As the Spirit speaks to your heart right now, will you heed His voice? Will you say yes to God? Let us bow our heads. While all heads are bowed, and all eyes are closed, will you lift your hand toward heaven signifying your desire and willingness to hearken to your Savior's calling?

PARDON REFUSED

In Dorchester, England, a prisoner had been convicted of manslaughter and was sentenced to life imprisonment when he was a young man. After several years, Queen Victoria granted his pardon. The world, however, had lost its attraction and after a few days liberty he returned to prison, requesting to be readmitted. His request was granted, and he remained at Halifax until the Maritime Penitentiary was built at Dorchester, and the long-term prisoners removed thereto. When the prisoners were marched from the depot to the penitentiary, all but this man were handcuffed and strictly guarded. He followed the line at a little distance and requested a place in the new institution.

He had been there for several years. By the grace of his sovereign, he could have been a free man entitled, upon request, to a full suit of civilian clothing. Clad in such, the great prison gate would open for him as readily as for the warden himself. Yet, so long as he preferred prison life, he must submit to prison discipline. He must wear that gloomy, prison garb. When the bell rang at six o'clock, he must fall into line with the others and be satisfied with prison fare. At the appointed hour, he must return to his cell where the iron door closed upon him, where again he listened to the heavy bolt grating harshly in the lock, and where night after night the receding steps of the turnkey revived the consciousness that he was still a prisoner.

APPEAL:

Strange, you might say. Why would somebody prefer prison to freedom? Yet, there are thousands living today who, when they could be free from sin, choose its gratification at the expense of enduring its gloomy bondage and final punishment![36] The Scriptures say that men prefer darkness rather than light. Every soul who refuses to give himself to God is under the control of

36. *The Homiletic Review*

another power. He is not his own. He may talk of freedom, but he is in the most abject slavery. He is not allowed to see the beauty of truth, for his mind is under the control of Satan. While he flatters himself that he is following the dictates of his own judgment, he obeys the will of the prince of darkness.

Friend of mine, Jesus came to break the shackles of sin-slavery from the soul. "If the Son therefore shall make you free, ye shall be free indeed" (John 8:36). Is it your desire to be free? Won't you surrender your will to God? Have you become so used to the pleasures of sin that it has fastened on you like shackles? Do you want to be free? Will you raise your hand to heaven by faith, and ask the Lord to deliver you? Will you do it just now?

Chapter 12

CHOOSING CHRIST OVER THE ANTICHRIST

BRUCE THE AIRMAN

Bruce was a Christian in the U.S. Air Force. Having a burden for his fellow soldiers, he offered Bible studies. At the same time in his trailer park, a neighbor's wife had been offering studies to him and his wife. He always had a reason why he couldn't. Then a prophecy seminar began, and the neighbor's wife encouraged them to attend. Again, there were the usual reasons for not being able to attend.

One night while the neighbor's wife went over to invite them to the prophecy seminars, Bruce arrived at home from work with a fallen countenance. "What is the problem?" Asked the neighbor. "It is just too bad that I have something wonderful to offer, and people don't seem to care about it," Bruce responded. "Well, now you know how I feel," responded the neighbor. "What do you mean?" Bruce questioned. "I have been inviting you to this wonderful set of lectures and you have not attended," she said. Looking over at his new bride, Bruce said, "What are we doing tonight?" "Nothing," responded his wife. "OK," Bruce said, "we are going."

As the neighbor happily rushed home to inform her husband of the good news, she froze. "Oh no," she thought, "tonight is the topic of the Antichrist. This couple does not have the proper background to hear such a strong message." When she told her husband of her concerns, they earnestly prayed that the Lord would overrule.

As Bruce heard the message unfold, it seemed as if he was entranced. Then at the conclusion of the presentation, the speaker made an appeal for those present to accept the truth as it was in Jesus and follow Him. Bruce bolted out of his seat, went forward to the altar, and that night requested to be baptized immediately. For the first time in his life, the Bible and its prophecies made sense. The missing link had been found. All the bewilderment about why so many different Christian churches finally vanished. All the confusion as to why there were so many contradictory practices in Christianity that did not go along with the Scriptures finally became unraveled.

APPEAL:

Maybe you are just like Bruce. Many things have not made sense in Christianity. You love the Lord, but you have wondered, why so many contradictions? But tonight, you have found the missing link. It all now makes sense. You desire, like Bruce, to come out of her and not partake of her sins. Is that your desire? Will you come to the altar and signify your loyalty to the Lord and His truths? Will you come just now?

UNCLE JOE

Uncle Joe was a devout Catholic. He went to Mass every Sunday. As he approached the entry of the sanctuary, he would take the "holy water" on the wall and put it on his forehead. Then he would kneel and make the sign of the cross over his chest.

As he proceeded to his pew, he knelt again and made the sign of the cross before sitting. When came the time for the sacraments to be offered by the priest, Uncle Joe would go to the altar with his hands clasped in the form of prayer. Once there, he would kneel before the priest, and the priest would place the emblem in his mouth. With great reverence, Uncle Joe would then get up, return to his pew, and kneel for a moment of prayer. After the service, he would return home.

Sad to say, he went in as a saint, but came out as a devil. He was a hard and miserly man. His wife's nephew had a mother who was poor and raising six children. But when they would visit his grocery store, obviously hungry, he would coldly send them away. He would rather throw the spoiling food away than give it them.

His wife on the other hand was grieved by his actions. When he was out getting inventory for the store, she would make a box of food, send her young son to find the boys, who would quickly run to fetch the box of food and take it to their mother. So, as fast as the legs could carry them, they would grab the box, run through alleys to avoid notice by Uncle Joe, and return home to their mother with the food. Meanwhile, Uncle Joe still went on with his weekly rituals.

One day a young girl appeared at their home "looking for her father." "Is my dad here?" She inquired. Mrs. M., being sure that the girl had knocked on the wrong door, told her that she was mistakenly knocking at the wrong address. "My mother told me that I could find him here," she insisted. "Who is your father?" Asked Mrs. M. "Joe M.,," answered the girl. Struck with horror and grief, she was shocked to discover that her religious husband had for years been living in adultery.

Uncle Joe's two children had made their confirmation and their first communion in the church, while the nephews, being too poor to accomplish the same and not religious, were disdained by him. However unbeknownst to him, his clean-cut, college-attending son had become addicted to heroin. By this time, the nephews had experienced conversion to Christ and feeling a burden for their lost cousin attempted to convert him. Uncle Joe angrily denounced them for their attempts, demanded that his boy be left alone, and insisted that they were the ones who were "banditos" and street kids.

Being unmindful of Uncle Joe's demands, the concerned nephews continued to pursue their cousin until he finally became converted. Angered by his son's change of religion, he denounced the nephews as scoundrels and stated that they were never to show themselves around his house. Troubled by his rash and unreasonable reaction, his son one day approached him and said, "Dad, sit down. I need to tell you something." "Go ahead. Tell me. I don't need to sit down," he insisted. "Oh yes," said his son, "you need to sit down."

Slowly, Uncle Joe took a seat. "Dad, I know that you hate my cousins, but if it were not for them, I probably would be dead." "What do you mean?" Asked the surprised father. "You see Dad, I have been a heroin addict, but I could never overcome the habit.

I kept it from you because I knew what kind of a man you are, and if you knew, you would kill me. You have condemned your nephews' faith, but your religion has never done anything for you. All they ever offered you were indulgences, a confessional, bowing down to statues, and the paying for your sins. But you have continued to be the same. It was because my cousins led me to Christ that I finally gained the victory over the habit and found true forgiveness for my sins and a changed life.

Startled and shocked Uncle Joe sat almost paralyzed. "What?" He exclaimed. "Yes, Dad! Christ even gave me the courage to tell you the truth," his son revealed. Falling off his chair, the grief stricken man fell broken. With tears in his eyes he said, "If their religion has done that for you, I need the Lord to do it for me." Uncle Joe accepted the Lord as his Savior and became a changed man.

APPEAL:

Oh, friend, only Christ's gospel saves. Only His truth can set you free. Have you been following the doctrines of man? Have you been trying by your own works to save yourself, only to find that there is no peace, no power to change? God cries out, "Come out of her My people" (Revelation 18:4).

Have you been taking the wrong medicine—a gospel that cannot save? Have you been following an insipid religion? Why not accept the invitation to eat the true Bread of Life. Come and drink of the waters from which you will never thirst. "And the Spirit and the bride say, Come. And let him that heareth say, Come. And let him that is athirst come. And whosoever will, let him take the water of life freely" (Revelation 22:17). Will you accept Christ and His truth just now?

AVOIDING

One night after the presentation on the beast of Revelation 13, the speaker was bidding farewell to those attending. After all had left, or so he thought, he noticed one lone man still sitting in the pew. His head was bowed down like a bulrush and his shoulders jerked giving evidence that the man was crying. Gently approaching the gentlemen, the speaker asked, "Are you all right?" Still with his head bowed he nodded in the affirmative. "Can I do anything for you?" Was the expressed concern. "No," was the short answer. "May I pray with you?" Again, moving his head up and down he signed in the affirmative. The preacher prayed. Then the man rose up and began making his exit. "I would like to come and visit you. Would that be all right?" Asked the pastor. Turning around the man gave a nod of consent and left.

The next day the evangelist mentioned to the intern pastor that he needed to visit the man. "Oh, we can't," said the intern. "Why not?" Asked the evangelist. "I called him, and he said that he had family problems and preferred that we not visit," was the reply. "I know what he said, but we must go and visit him. The Holy Spirit is working on his heart, and he is strongly under conviction."

When they arrived at the home, all the window blinds were pulled, and the car was parked in the driveway. Approaching the door, the pastor began to knock, but there was no answer. "He must not be home," stated the intern. "No," responded the evangelist. "He is home." He continued to knock. Finally, the door went ajar and the man said, "Alright, come on in." Once they were inside, it was obvious that the man was a bachelor. As they sat down, the man began crying again, and he did so for about half an hour.

Once he gained his composure, he opened his heart to the pastor. He confessed that he wanted to avoid him because he feared that he would have to make a decision; one that he did not want to make. But now, he realized that it was the best thing to do. So together, he, the intern, and the pastor knelt and prayed. He made his commitment to the Lord and was later baptized.

Two years later the evangelist returned to Australia. After the morning sermon, the man met the evangelist at the social hall where they were serving food. He approached the surprised pastor and said, "I just had to come and see you." Then turning to the men standing around he said, "I want you to hear this. Two years ago the pastor was in the adjacent town giving a series of meetings that I attended. At that time I was destitute of my family, had no job, and expected to die from terminal cancer. The only refuge of support and comfort I had was my church. The night I heard the subject on the antichrist, I was devastated. Now, knowing what I heard, I felt that I was being deprived of the only peace that I had.

I was torn. It was then that I decided not to hear any more. When the young pastor called me, I told him not to come. Then to my surprise, the pastor was at my door. I determined not to open, but he kept on knocking as if he knew I was home. I finally gave in and opened the door. He led me to understand that I must place my confidence in God and not in a church. He was right, and I did.

"At my baptism something miraculous happened. My sickness disappeared! I found the greatest peace ever, and I found a church that embraced me with loving arms. How thankful I am that the pastor came after me." And then, turning to the evangelist, he embraced him in a hug and said, "I love you."

APPEAL:

Perhaps, like this man, what you have heard has been earth-shaking. Sorrow and confusion may be racing through your mind. You may be asking, "How can these things be?" But friend, the Holy Word of God is true and history gives evidence to its veracity. Just like on Mt. Carmel where the people of Israel saw the blinding light of the truth that Elijah brought to their attention, so God in His goodness has enabled you to see the light.

The question is what will you do with that light? Jesus said, "Come out of her my people" (Revelation 18:2). God calls you His people. Will you follow Him? Will you cast your lot with Him? Who here will respond to God's call? (They can show their indication by a decision card, the raising of the hand, by standing, or by going forward to the altar.)

ONLY ONE MEDIATOR

A knock came to her door. She was a sweet Catholic lady in an apartment complex and her caller was a young man offering in-home Bible studies. She was very open to study the Bible. After several studies, the topic of the heavenly sanctuary was next in line. As the young man was making the different points, he knew he was getting really close to exposing the fact that Jesus is our High Priest. Knowing her to be a Catholic, in his heart he held his breath as they read these words, "There is one God, and one mediator between God and man, the man Christ Jesus" (1 Timothy 3:5). "We don't need the priest in the confessional!" He said. "We don't need some earthly man to approach our God! There is only one to whom we confess our secret sins—Christ Jesus!" He concluded. Then he stared, awaiting a reaction. He noticed that she glanced to the left and to the right and said, "You know, I haven't told anyone. But years ago I stopped going to the confessional because I felt that I needed to go straight to God. I don't understand why the Catholic Church teaches that."

APPEAL:

Like this dear Catholic lady, many are going through the same experience, anxiously visiting earthly priests to find peace of heart—but to no avail! There is only one "mediator between God and man." Why go through a substitute when you can go directly to your heavenly Father through the One God has ordained? The Scriptures encourage us to "come boldly to the throne of grace" (Hebrews 4:16). Jesus opened the way. In fact, He said, "I am the way."

Oh, friend, do you have burdens that you need to unload? Do you long to go right to your heavenly Father and find peace? Why not come to Him now? Why not turn directly to Him and in faith claim the forgiveness that He alone can give? Will you respond to His invitation now?

Chapter 13

CHOOSING CHRIST OVER THE MARK OF THE BEAST

MARTYRS IN SCOTLAND

Scotland has given many a martyr to the church. Along with others were Mary Wilson and Agnes McClaughlin who perished in the Tyne Tide. They were fastened to stakes, and as the tide rose they were slowly drowned for refusing to give up their Christian faith. The older woman was fastened farther out than the younger one, for they thought the younger would recant when she saw the older one in her death struggle with the water. Quickly the tide swelled, first to the older woman's ankles, then to her knees, then to the waist, then to her neck, and then to her lips. The executioners called out to the younger woman, "Look, what do you see? What do you see now?"

She turned her head a little and saw the struggles of her drowning friend. Then she made this wonderful Christian answer, "What do I see? Why, I see the Lord Jesus Christ suffering in one of His members."

APPEAL:

Ah, friend, what are you willing to sacrifice for Jesus? Many faithful ones have perished in the flames, at the stock, or have been cut asunder for their faith. Is it not time to be wholehearted in our devotion to the Lord? With Peter, let us say, "We ought to obey God, rather than man" (Acts 5:29). But what are you willing to suffer for your Savior? The Lord cries out, "Come out of her my people that ye be not partakers of her sins, nor of her plagues." God calls you My people. Will you obey Him? Are you willing by faith to take a stand on the Lord's side?

Oh, friend, if that is your desire, will you stand just where you are? Will you come out of her? Will you come and stand alongside of those who will overcome by the blood of the Lamb and by the word of their testimony? Please stand now as we make a prayer of commitment to our Lord.

I CAN'T ACCEPT; MY MOTHER WORSHIPED THE DEVIL!

A pastor visited a man whose wife, being a Christian, requested the visit. Simon had been attending church with his wife, but he would not consent to be baptized. As the pastor spent time becoming acquainted with this quiet congenial man, he finally broached the question. "So Simon, how do you feel about the church?" "I love it," was the response. "The people are lovely and the message is right from the Bible. I love that." "When did you become a member?" Asked the preacher. "I am not," he said. "What would keep you from becoming a member?" came the inquiry. "I can't believe my mother was worshiping the devil." Was Simon's cold reply.

Sensing that he had hit a tender spot, the pastor asked, "What do you mean?" "You teach that the beast is the papacy, right? And that the enemy is behind her power, right? Well, if I were to be baptized into your faith, then I would have to admit that my mother was being led by the devil, and I cannot do that." "Tell me about your mother, Simon," the pastor asked.

I was an alcoholic. From among all my siblings, I was the greatest concern of my dear mother. She agonized and prayed for me, but I was hardened in my vice and unyielding. Her greatest desire was to see me get sober. Then she died." Simon concluded, with a tear in his eye, "Are you straight now?" Asked the pastor. "Yes," responded Simon. "How did you overcome?" The pastor asked. "Oh, I could have never done it on my own. God helped me," was his reply. "Well then, who answered that prayer of your mother?" inquired the pastor. Then with a look of amazement, Simon said, "God did!"

"No, Simon. Your mother was not serving the devil. She prayed to God in the way that she was taught and understood. And the One who made mothers' hearts answered your mother's prayer. If your mom were alive today, she would be rejoicing and praising

God for answering her prayer. The God who answered that prayer is calling you to give your entire life to Him."

APPEAL:

Our parents who loved us did the best in their power to lead us in the right path. But unfortunately, they were not privileged to have the knowledge we have of the truth in God's Word. God says, "To him that knows to do right and does not do it, to him it is sin" (James 4:17). While He winks at our ignorance, He now calls us to repent and follow Him. God has been pleased to alert you to the dangers of following a man-made religion in place of His precious gospel.

Satan is constantly at work to wound and poison the soul. In order to withstand his efforts, we must breathe the atmosphere of heaven. We must individually get hold and keep hold of Christ. The truth of God, dwelling in the heart and guiding the life, will be our safeguard. With the truth in our possession, we may humbly and firmly advance from light to a greater light, and we shall be guided into every good and holy way. Unless the truth of God transforms the character, it is of no value to the receiver.

Jesus says, "Come out of her my people." Will you heed His voice? Will you place your Lord above all others and follow Him? Will you stand just where you are?

BEING GYPPED

Thirteen-year-old Johnny had just spotted five-year-old Mary pick up a crumpled green colored paper that he recognized as a ten-dollar bill. As he approached Mary, he had a plan. "What is that you found?" "Oh just a crumpled-up paper." "Well, look what I have!" There in his hand, he had ten brand new shiny pennies. With wide eyes, Mary's face revealed exactly what Johnny had hoped it would.

"Would you like to trade these beautiful shiny pennies for that crumpled-up piece of paper?" Johnny encouraged as he held up the brilliant pennies. Anxiously, Mary grabbed the pennies as she happily turned over the paper. Patting Mary on the head, Johnny exclaimed, "You got a great deal, but you deserve it."

APPEAL:

Oh, friend, what did that young man do? He defrauded that poor child. Does that make your fire burn? Oh, can you see why God issues such strong denunciations. He sent His Son to suffer the cruel death on Calvary to bring you heaven's offer of salvation. But there is a system that is offering a substitute. Friend, "There is no other name given among men under heaven whereby you can be saved" (Acts 4:12). God's heart yearns for you. He is pained to see that so many are accepting the chaff rather then pure wheat. Will you accept His salvation? He has promised, "He that cometh to me, I will in no wise cast out" (John 6:37). Will you take Jesus as your Savior, your Lord, and God? Will you come to Him now?

LSD IN TRICK OR TREAT

The community was outraged to discover that someone had laced candy with LSD, a hallucinogenic drug. Unsuspecting parents were horror stricken as their innocent children became victims. The children had run home to partake of the booty they had collected in their trick-or-treat Halloween spree. Unsuspectingly, they had eaten the candy with glee. Imagine the hot tears of those parents. How could anyone be so cruel? Could the perpetrator even be considered human? Oh, friend, if parents' angers are hot resulting from this terrible atrocity, then how must God feel?

APPEAL:

The Scriptures say that "all the world wondered after the beast" (Revelation 13:3). But, those who will be saved will follow the Lamb wherever He goes. Oh, friend, Jesus invites you. If you are to follow the Lamb in heaven, you must learn to follow the Lamb here. Jesus declared, "He that is not with me is against me" (Matthew 12:30). Will you follow Jesus now? Is it your desire to be loyal and true to Him? Then will you arise, and say, "Yes, I want to make Jesus my Lord and my Savior." Will you lift up your hand now? Amen! Let us pray.

NOT COCA COLA BUT BLACK COFFEE

One summer day Louis was very thirsty. He walked over to the refrigerator to see what was there to drink. He was delighted to discover a large bottle of Coca-Cola filled to the brim. Looking to make sure no one was watching, he put the bottle to his mouth. Opening as wide as possible to ensure a mouthful of this beverage, he turned it up and took a large gulp. He was shocked to discover that it was not Coke at all. Instead, it was black coffee. The beverage in the bottle had the right color. It was also the right bottle. What a surprise!

APPEAL:

Fortunately for Louis it was only black coffee. But here we are dealing with something far more dreadfully dangerous—its consequences fraught with eternal life or death. No wonder the apostle Paul warned,

> I marvel that ye are so soon removed from him that called you into the grace of Christ unto another gospel: which is not another; but there be some that trouble you, and would pervert the gospel of Christ. But though we, or an angel from heaven, preach any other gospel unto you than that which we have preached unto you, let him be accursed. As we said before, so say I now again, If any man preach any other gospel unto you than ye have received, let him be accursed. (Galatians 1:6-9)

This is a very serious matter. Your destiny hangs on your election. Knowing this, you cannot afford to be negligent or indifferent. You must be sure that the gospel you believe in is not another gospel, but the true Gospel. Only in the Holy Scriptures will you find the truth. Jesus said, "You shall know the truth, and the truth shall make you free." Oh, friend, will you accept His truth? Will you choose the truth as it is in Jesus? The church must have the right doctrine.

Remember that before there was a Christian church, there was a Bible. Therefore, let us not judge the Bible by the church, but rather judge the church by the Bible. Remember, God's true church must have those two essential identifying marks. The Bible says, "Here is the patience of the saints: here are they that keep the commandments of God, and the faith of Jesus" (Revelation 14:12). Remember it has these two qualifications: the commandments of God and the faith of Jesus. Not the faith *in* Jesus, but rather the faith *of* Jesus. Will you accept this faith now?

THE MAN TAKEN (FOOLED)
WITH DEAD CHRISTMAS TREES

A man had just built a home. Next, he had to begin landscaping the property. He thought of planting trees, so he went searching for them. He found a man who was selling beautiful trees by the wayside. When asking the price, he was amazed at how cheap they were. Some were six dollars, and others were ten dollars. Some trees were six feet and some eight feet tall. He bought several. The man then told him he need not remove the burlap. He could just plant them as they were. He was excited at his wonderful finding.

He planted all the trees, watered, and fertilized them. Then he sat back and looked at what transformation the trees had made of his landscape. He imagined what the landscape would look like in a few years as the trees grew to a stature of thirty to fifty feet.

A few weeks later, he noticed that the trees were showing signs of wilting on the tips. Anxious, he began to water and dig to help the trees. A neighbor came over and counseled that he was using too much water. He decided to water every other day. But the problem continued. Finally, the trees all died.

Disappointed, he decided that the only thing to do was to dig them up and burn them. When he had dug up a few, he decided to remove the burlap and discovered had what happened to the roots. Upon removal, he discovered that there were no roots. He then realized that these were left over Christmas trees that someone had put dirt around the nailed wood at the bottom, and then wrapped burlap around to give the appearance that the trees had been dug up with the roots. It then dawned on him that he had been taken!

APPEAL:

Perhaps you have sincerely believed that you were on the right course. You have made an effort to be true to God in following what you have been taught. But tonight, you have discovered that being sincere is not enough. One can be sincerely wrong. But our Lord is merciful. You might have been like Saul (who later became the great apostle Paul), and with great fervor and zeal followed, oh, so carefully your particular faith.

But like the man taken with the rootless trees, you now realize that you need to make the decision to follow the light as Christ in His Word has revealed to you. You desire to separate from Babylon and become part of God's true commandment-keeping people. Will you like Paul say, "Lord what will you have me to do?" (Acts 9:6). Will you stand for the Lord and His truths? Will you be loyal to your blessed Savior and be true to Him? Will you stand?

PRINCE EDDINE—THE IMPOSTER

Around the sixteenth century, after Albania had received its independence, a problem surfaced. The freedom fighters did not have their own leader, so they asked for a young man, Prince Eddine, to become their leader. He, incidentally, was from the country from which they had just won their independence. Prince Eddine was not too sure that he wanted to be the king of Albania, so he lingered and hesitated in sending his response.

Finally, within a few weeks, a coach drove up to Durazo, the main city. From the coach, stepped out a young man elegantly dressed. He wore a royal uniform with all sorts of medals and was highly decorated. The Albanians were ecstatic. Prince Eddine had decided to be their king! A great celebration erupted. Everywhere there was festivity because they now had their own king.

They celebrated for a week—until a letter from the Sultan of Turkey arrived saying that Prince Eddine had consented to become their king and would be arriving from Turkey in a week. They couldn't believe it. They went to find Prince Eddine, but he had heard that a letter had come from the Sultan and quickly ran out of town.

He wasn't Prince Eddine after all—it was Otto Witt, a circus actor who greatly resembled Prince Eddine. He had a grand old time for a week being the celebrated king of Albania. What an impostor! And yet the people were taken, as many people are being taken today.

APPEAL:

Just like Prince Eddine's successful masquerade has been the Antichrist's efforts. He has succeeded in leading many to believe that he is the Savior. But there is only one Savior—Jesus Christ. Perhaps you have sincerely believed that the religion you have followed was the true one. But today, the letter from heaven has unmasked the deception. You know that this is the truth, and you want to heed the invitation to "come out of her." Will you stand and cast your lot on the side of Christ?

Oh, friend, as Joshua said to the people in his day, "Choose you this day whom you will serve" (Joshua 24:15). The Lord likewise appeals to you. Will you raise your hand in a demonstration of allegiance to your Lord? Will you raise your hand now?

GHETTO BOYS IN NEW YORK

One day a group of Brooklyn, New York, ghetto boys found a bunch of mattresses discarded in the passageway between two tenement buildings. Excited with the perspective of a make-believe trampoline, they stacked the mattresses and began jumping. At first it was quite exhilarating as they leaped into the air and dropped back down like bouncing balls. It was not long before the fun began to subside as the leaping no longer provided the excitement. Wondering how they could jump higher, the thought struck them as they noticed the staircase window.

Pressing the mattresses against the wall beneath the window, they gleefully scampered up the stairwell. Now the usual bantering took place. "Me first, no, me first!" Out they jumped onto the cushions below. Every leap was thrilling. But again, things got old. Then the thought struck them. If the first floor was exciting, how much more would the second floor be?

Once again up they climbed. When the first boy took a look at the mattresses below him, they appeared much smaller than before and the distance seemed much greater and more daunting. Once again the bantering began. But this time it was, "You go first. No, you go first."

Finally, one reluctantly climbed up on the windowsill. As he was poised to jump, he secretly wished he had a way out. Then all of a sudden the sound of footsteps ascending the staircase were heard. As he looked back to see who was coming, he was surprised to see that it was his mother. Greatly concerned to see her son stand on the windowsill, the mother yelled out a scathing and stern warning. "Get off that window, or you'll wished that you had fallen," she shouted!

APPEAL:

Harsh language, isn't it? She hated him, didn't she? Not so. It was the language of a loving mother, who recognizing the danger that her son didn't and cried out in despair. Yes, my friend, Revelation 14 appears to be a sharp denunciation given by a tyrannical angry God. But no, this is a God in desperation yelling to a world that is about to plunge itself into oblivion. Completely unaware of the danger, people are following a system that will ensure the loss of their soul. Here is a God of love describing the outcome of following an insipid faith.

Oh, friend, will you hear his voice of love in His warning? Will you respond to the warning of love? Will you give your heart to God just now? He calls, "Come out of her my people, that ye be not partakers of her sins and receive none of her plagues" (Revelation 18:2). Will you heed His invitation? Will you hear His voice of utter concern for your wellbeing and salvation? Will you stand for the Lord? Yes, just stand where you are.

RIP-OFF ADS

A Romanian woman approached a visiting evangelist and asked for his advice. She had read an American ad in her country. It offered the opportunity to make a lot of money right from the comfort of home. All it took was seventy-five dollars to get started. Upon receipt of the money, supplies would be sent to make earrings out of beads. The completed work would then be sent to America where it would be sold for a lot of money, and the laborer would receive at least four times the amount of money sent.

The ad was shown to the pastor. Sorrowfully, he read it. It was a ruse. The poor woman had sent $75, which in those days represented $15,975 of their money. At a great loss to herself, she embarked upon a project that she thought would generate much-needed resources for her family. Instead, the pastor had to sadly tell her that she had been defrauded.

APPEAL:

Have you been taken by a false gospel? Do you feel that all this time you have been following a "thus says a man," rather than a "thus says the Lord?" Why not arise and determine to follow your blessed Lord and His Gospel? Will you lift your hand in response today?

Chapter 14

LOYALTY TO CHRIST

THE PURCHASED SLAVE

A black slave was on the auction block. He was young, and his physique made it obvious that he was quite strong. The bidders were waging their bids. Higher and higher went the price. The slave was yelling vehemently that they were wasting their money. "I am not going to work for any man," he shouted. But the bidding continued. Higher and higher the auctioneer cajoled. Finally the mallet struck, "Sold to the highest bidder!"

Angrily the slave kept cursing and raving. "You wasted your money, mister. I am working for no man." The owner did not seem to pay attention to his threats. For miles as the cart carried the slave, his defiant threats rent the air. When the cart reached the owner's property, he went over took the key to the chain, unlocked the lock, and removed the shackles. "Mister, didn't you hear? I am not going to be your slave. I am not working. I told you, you wasted your money," yelled the slave. The owner simply said, "I bought you to set you free. You are free to go."

Taken back by his purchaser's words, the slave said, "What?" "I bought you to set you free." And upon that the owner turned and began to walk away. "Wait a minute. You are telling me I am free?" Enquired the slave. "Yes!" Responded the owner. Being gripped with gratitude, the slave said, "Mister, I'll serve you forever."

APPEAL:

Ah, friend, 2,000 years ago, Jesus paid the maximum price to redeem you from the slavery of sin. The Bible says, "Ye are bought with a price" (1 Corinthians 6:20). Your freedom was purchased at a great sacrifice. Knowing this—"that you were not redeemed with corruptible things as silver and gold . . . but with the precious blood of Christ, as of a lamb without blemish and without spot" (1 Peter 1:18, 19). But remember, "to whom ye yield yourselves servants to obey, his servants ye are . . . whether of sin unto death or of obedience unto righteousness" (Romans 6:16).

Will you choose to give yourself to Jesus and render your obedience to Him? Man may attempt to constrict you to obey Him, but that obedience will only lead to death. As Peter declared, "Is it right to obey man rather than God?" You judge. How is it with you? Who here would rather choose to obey Jesus rather than man? Will you stand to that?

YOUNG MISSIONARY

Two missionaries were traveling through Africa. As they came to a certain spot in the jungle, they realized they were surrounded by a band of armed men. They were commanded to stop the Jeep and get out. Obeying the order, the two stopped the Jeep and stepped out. One of the men was an older missionary, and the other was a young man new to missionary work.

The leader of the band stepped up and immediately demanded to know what they were doing. "We are Christian missionaries," replied the older man. At this, the hardened warlord demanded that the missionary renounce his faith on the threat of death. The older missionary, raising his hand toward heaven, began to explain why he couldn't. At the command of the leader, he was stopped as men jumped at him and cut him down with machetes.

Then looking at the young missionary the leader demanded the same of him. Looking down at the slain missionary, he looked at the bandleader and said, "I just bought this jacket. I paid a good deal for it. It would be a shame to ruin it." Then taking it off, he said, "Here, take it. I am sure one of your men can benefit by the use of it."

Amazed at the sincerity, courage, and love of the young man, the leader turned. "Let him alone. You cannot fight against such love."

APPEAL:

The day will soon come when you will tested for your faith and love of Christ. Where will you stand? Jesus said, "These are they that walk with the Lamb whithersoever he goes." Oh, friend, you cannot walk with the Lord unless you are willing to walk with the Lamb here. Jesus said, "Whosoever shall deny me before men, him will I also deny before my Father which is in heaven" (Matthew 10:33). Like the young missionary, do you love the Lord that much? Are you willing to stand for the truth though the heavens fall? Will you stand on the side of Jesus now? Who here is willing to rise to their feet and say, "Lord, here I stand!" Will you stand just now?

CUBAN EXILES

In 1979 and 1980, Cuba's leader Fidel Castro decided to get rid of its prisoners. He also gave anyone who wanted to leave permission get on the boats. Thousands were placed on the boats. But when they left, Castro allowed them to take nothing except the clothing they were wearing. Stories were told by refugees as to how their mouths were checked for gold. And if any were found, they were yanked on the spot.

Among the exiled prisoners were convicts and criminals. But included in the cleansing were Christians that had been numbered among them. One translator aiding in Fort Chaffee, Arkansas, was informed that among the 20,000 refugees at the camp were fifty Sabbath-keepers. He and his wife proceeded to try and locate them but discovered that finding them among 20,000 other Cubans was like looking for a needle in a haystack. Though he enlisted the aid of soldiers who spoke Spanish, the search was futile.

Then while sitting in their car, they prayed and asked God for His help. When they finished praying, they noticed a group walking on the other side of the fenced enclosure. The husband said, "Let me ask them and see if they might know." Then approaching the fence, he called out to get one of the women's attention. Somehow, having a sense that this was the group, he asked, "Are you a Seventh-day Adventist?" Cautiously, she asked, "Why?" "Because I am a Seventh-day Adventist pastor, and I have been looking for them," replied the pastor.

Caution turned into excitement. Turning to the small group ahead of her,, she yelled, "They're here!" To this the pastor turned to his wife still sitting in their car and shouted, "It's them!" The group turned and hurried back to where he was. "I understand there were about fifty of you?" said the pastor. "We are actually fifty-four," was the reply. "Where are the rest?" the pastor inquired. "They are at the barracks. But tonight, we will have prayer meeting, and all of us will be together," said the woman.

"Do you have a Bible?" asked the pastor. "No, some of us have not seen a Bible for at least ten years. They were taken away from us when we were thrown into prison," was the sad reply. "Well, I have a Bible in the car. I will go and get it," the excited pastor said. Then he fetched the Bible and brought it back to them. Reaching over the fence, he offered it to them. Without hesitation the oldest man in the group (about eighty years of age) leaped forward, grabbed the book, pressed it to his chest, and rocking from side to side, he held it tight to his chest as tears of joy streamed down his face.

APPEAL:

The days are swiftly coming when your faith and fidelity to God will be tested. Just like the betrayal of Christ came from a believer, so your betrayal will not come from those outside, but rather from those who profess to be followers of Christ. America, the stalwart of religious freedom, will make an image to the beast and seek to coerce the conscience.

Just as the Bible was precious and their love for Christ dear to those faithful Adventist Christians, so must the Bible be precious to us and the love of the Savior dear. But where do you stand? Your standing to your faith now will determine where you will stand tomorrow. Do you love the Savior? Is the Word of God that precious to you that you would be willing to suffer for it? Is it your desire to side with your Lord now? Will you show your faith for Him by standing? Will you stand now for your Lord?

JUSTIN'S TURN

Justin was two weeks from being initiated into the Buddhist faith. Though raised in a Christian home, he felt untouched by his religious upbringing. Finding no satisfaction in Christianity, he turned to search elsewhere. He now thought he had found what his soul was looking for. Then one day, he received an invitation in the mail to a prophecy seminar. Justin had never heard of such a thing. "Could the Bible have answers to the future?" he wondered. In his home, the Bible had not been a reference book for his religious upbringing, and it made him curious to see what this meant.

The opening night of the seminar Justin found fascinating. He could hardly believe that the Scriptures were so insightful. For the next several nights, his wife, mother, and sister also attended. In this series of meetings, Justin at last discovered the inconsistencies of Christianity. For the first time, he understood the cross and its meaning. Light seemed to be flashing in his darkened mind concerning all the questions he had about his spiritual needs and how to live a purer life through the power of Christ. This Buddhism never offered. On the night of the appeal to accept Christ as his Lord and Savior, Justin, his wife, mother, and sister responded.

APPEAL:

Perhaps you too have been feeling empty. You have gone from one religious faith to another. But your soul is still not at home. Now, as you have seen the wonderful revelations of the Scriptures, everything has finally fallen into place. You now understand the great controversy being waged, and it is your desire to stand in your lot—on the Lord's side. And just like Justin, you want to accept the Lord and his truth into your heart. Will you rise and say by your rising, "Lord, it all makes sense. I choose to be on your side and for your truth. If that is your desire, will you stand now, just where you are?

Chapter 15

HONORING GOD
REVELATION 13:11-17

NAZI SABBATH-KEEPER

During World War II, a Sabbath-keeper was forced into the army because he was an engineer. Though a Christian literature salesman and married with two children, he was nonetheless constrained to serve his country. Franz Hasel was interrogated as to why being a German he kept a Jewish day. He responded that it was not a Jewish day but rather God's day. He was held suspect and finally told that when the war ended, he would be sentenced to death as a traitor. The lieutenant made this note in his record.

He continued his labor as a bridge builder. At times, while having to go ahead of the team to purchase supplies, he would warn any Jew to leave town. This way, he was able to save some. Finally, the war became more intense against the Russians. Fearing that they would not survive against the odds, the leading officers called Franz in for a secret and private meeting. "Tell us, who do you think will win the war?" With the promise that nothing would be done to him, they pressed him for an answer.

Pulling out the Bible, Franz unveiled the marvelous prophecy of the second chapter of Daniel. He concluded by telling them that Hitler's ambition to reunite Europe was diametrically opposed to the written will of God. Therefore, they were not fighting against the Allies, but rather against God. Convinced of the predicted outcome, they ordered him never to tell anyone of their meeting. They further ordered, since he was the one assigned as the supply purchaser, to buy enough fuel to get them back to Germany on their retreat.

And so it happened. The whole unit was spared based on one man's faith in the unfailing Word of God and His commandments. After being captured, the interrogating American noticed Franz's record.

"Why?" Was the question. "Because I am a Sabbath-keeper, and thus, I was charged with treason." "Are you a Jew?" Questioned the interrogator who happened to be an American Jew. "No," responded Franz. "I am a Christian who believes in obeying a 'thus saith the Lord,' and Saturday is the biblical day of worship." "What is your occupation?" asked the American soldier. "An engineer, but before the war I was a Christian salesman," responded Hasel. "Alright, I am going to stamp 'farmer' on your papers so you can get out quicker," he was told.

When Franz finally returned to Frankfurt, he discovered that all of the buildings in his neighborhood were destroyed. He wondered about the safety of his wife and children. When he neared the building where he left them, it was still standing—the only one in the entire neighborhood. God had protected them and blessed his faithfulness.

APPEAL:

God blesses faithfulness. He promises, "If you turn your foot from the Sabbath, from doing thy pleasure on my holy day; and call the Sabbath a delight, the holy of the Lord, honourable; and shalt honour him, not doing thine own ways, nor finding thine own pleasure, nor speaking thine words: Then shalt thou delight thyself in the Lord; and I will cause thee to ride upon the high places of the earth, and feed thee with the heritage of Jacob thy father: for the mouth of the Lord hath spoken it" (Isaiah 58:13-14).

Oh, friend, it pays to be faithful to the Lord. The Christian world will be following the beast, but whom will you follow? The seal of God is being placed on those who love God and keep His commandments. Will you be among them? Will you choose today to turn your loyalty to Him—your Savior? What is your choice? The call is, "Choose you this day whom ye will serve!" (Joshua 24:15). "How long halt ye between two opinions? . . .if Baal; then follow him" (1 Kings 18:21) If it is God, then serve Him! What is your decision? Will you answer God's call? Will you respond just now?

I MIGHT AS WELL CLAIM BANKRUPTCY

Steve was attending a series of meetings. One night he heard about the importance of the Fourth Commandment. When he met with the speaker, he said, "If I follow what you say, I might as well shut down my business and claim bankruptcy." The evangelist asked him to elaborate. It turned out that his business was tourism. He had thirteen contracts with hotels on the beach front for which provided all the sports equipment. The greatest amount of business was usually on the Sabbath. He also informed the pastor that a typhoon had just destroyed a third of his equipment for which there was no insurance. He also explained that he had a hundred workers and felt responsibile for them and their families.

"What is more important to you, your salvation or your business? This, the evangelist asked to test the level of conviction. He was pleased to hear the response—his salvation. The pastor then encouraged him to follow the conviction the Lord had placed on his heart. Steve decided to surrender his life to Christ and was baptized. The evangelist then moved on to the next place of work.

Two years later, Steve called the surprised evangelist. "Got a minute?" Steve asked. He then began to unfold a wonderful miracle. After his baptism, Steve decided to terminate the thirteen contracts. He talked and explained his new-found convictions with his employees. Their response was not cordial. They felt that he was putting their lives on the line for a stupid religious idea. Steve stuck with his conviction. He closed his main shop on Saturday.

His employees thought he would lose his business to his competitors. But it was not to be. For seven months it rained every Sabbath. His business increased. He said that prior to keeping the Sabbath, he could never keep up with his debts. Once he kept the Sabbath, he was able to pay off $3 million of his debts. He was now far better off financially then ever.

APPEAL:

Perhaps you are faced with similar challenges. To obey the voice of the Lord, do you think it would cost you too much? But God will never ask you to do that which it is impossible to do. The disciples pled, "Lord, increase our faith!" (Luke 17:5). Why not offer that plea just now? You sense deep inside that God wants you to. The problem is, how? Remember, He that opened the Red Sea and dried up the Jordan can certainly make a way of escape for you. But you must take the step forward. Will you obey the voice of the Lord? Will you do it just now?

BENEDICT ARNOLD

At age fourteen, he ran away from home and fought in the French and Indian War. At the outbreak of the Revolutionary War, he joined the American army as a colonel, and in 1775, he shared a command with Ethan Allen in the capture of Ticonderoga. Later, he led 1,000 men into Canada where he fought in the battle of Quebec. His courage in battle won him a promotion to brigadier general. But something went wrong.

Thoughts of compromise ate away at his patriotic zeal. Soon the unthinkable happened. He offered his services to the British, and in 1780, he devised a plan to surrender West Point to British control. Today, instead of being remembered as a national hero, Benedict Arnold is synonymous with "traitor."[37]

APPEAL:

We are living on the brink of eternity. Mankind has sought to usurp the place of God. The beast has already made his attempt to change the "times and laws" of God. God's Sabbath has been replaced by man's doctrine of Sunday-keeping. Jesus declared, "But in vain they do worship me, teaching for doctrines the commandments of men" (Matthew 15:9). Who will you serve? Joshua of old demanded of the people of Israel. "And if it seem evil unto you to serve the LORD, choose you this day whom ye will serve; whether the gods which your fathers served that were on the other side of the flood, or the gods of the Amorites, in whose land ye dwell." Then he exclaimed, "as for me and my house, we will serve the Lord" (Joshua 24:15).

We are standing on Mount Carmel. The same challenge that Elijah gave to the people of Israel is before you today. "How long

---

36. *Today in the Word* (Chicago, IL: Moody Bible Institute, June 1990), 10.

halt ye between two opinions? If the Lord be God, follow him: but if Baal, then follow him" (1 Kings 18:21). Will you choose the God of heaven—the Creator of heaven and earth? Or will you choose the god of this world? If your choice is for the Lord of heaven, will you stand?

THE MOST UNLIKELY HERO

Desmond Doss was a medic in the army during World War II. He had two counts against him as far as his fellow soldiers were concerned. He was a Sabbath-keeper and a conscientious objector— he would not carry weapons. He was always subject to ridicule and harassment for his odd faith. But in spite of his oddity, they could not help but respect him. He eventually endeared himself to his company. Often, they would not move because Desmond would not go on his Sabbath. This served on several occasions to "just be missed" by the enemy.

Finally, the day came when his faith paid off. His entire company was caught under heavy enemy fire. Many fell wounded. The embankment was steep and difficult to climb. Desmond saw many of his friends being cut down by the hostile fire. He sent up a prayer and began to climb the hill. Under heavy fire, Desmond grabbed a wounded soldier, dragged him to the edge of the hill, and with rope lowered him to help. Though wounded himself, this he did, not for one or two, but for seventy-five who were wounded. Desmond became the unlikeliest hero and was decorated with the Congressional Medal of Honor, two Bronze Stars, and three Purple Hearts.

APPEAL:

Because he was willing to stand for his God, God was willing to stand for him. What about you friend? Are you willing to stand for your Lord in the face of ridicule and harassment? Are you willing to live for your Lord, and are you willing to die for Him? Remember, Jesus said, "Whosoever therefore shall confess me before men, him will I confess also before my Father which is in heaven" (Matthew 10:32). Will you stand for Him now? Will you confess Him before this congregation by lifting your hand? Will you now follow your hand and rise to your feet? Will you do that now?

COURT MARSHALED

Bruce had become a Sabbath-keeper while in the U.S. Air Force. Being zealous for his Lord, he began to share his faith with the other airmen. One by one, they became believers and began to keep the seventh day of the week as the Sabbath. Before long, there were six airmen who became Sabbath-keepers. This created a big problem for the Air Force. Having six men not working on the Sabbath made the flight line come to a halt.

They were ordered to work or else face consequences. The crisis came to a head when all six decided to obey God's commandment rather than that of men. This resulted in a military Court Marshal. Needless to say, the men were all very concerned about their futures. Would they be sentenced to time in prison? Would they all have to face a dishonorable discharge? What would be the outcome? Those days of waiting were intense. Was it worth all this trouble? Were they really willing to loose all to follow their conviction? Yes! They determined to stand at whatever the cost.

On the day of the Court Marshal, earnest prayers were lifted to the Lord in behalf of those brave faithful men who were willing to risk all in order to be true to their commitment. When the charges were brought forth, the only fault found was that they refused to violate their conscience. Oh, friends, God wrought in a marvelous manner. Instead of being sentenced to prison and being expelled from the military with a dishonorable discharge, all were given honorable discharges with full military credit and study privileges.

APPEAL:

Perhaps like those men, you are worried about your finances or your future. You can't see beyond the problems and calamities. But, friend, the same Jesus who delivered those men can deliver you like He did the three boys who faced execution if they did not bow down to the golden image erected by Babylon's King Nebuchadnezzar. Their response to the king's demand was, "O Nebuchadnezzar, we are not careful to answer thee in this matter. If it be so, our God whom we serve is able to deliver us from the burning fiery furnace, and he will deliver us out of thine hand, O king. But if not, be it known unto thee, O king, that we will not serve thy gods, nor worship the golden image which thou hast set up" (Daniel 3:16-18).

My friend, when Christianity follows the beast, will you follow the Lamb? But can you follow the Lamb then if you are not following the Lamb now? Who here will stand in your place now and be counted for the Lord? Is there one who will stand for the right though the heavens fall? If that is your desire, will you stand right now?

Chapter 16

CHOOSING TO BE TRUE TO GOD

BURNED AT THE STAKE

Hugh Latimer was now a frail eighty years of age with a failing memory. But he refused to recant and stood firm for his faith. The Martyrs Memorial in the university city of Oxford hallows the spot where Hugh Latimer and Nicholas Ridley were burned at the stake on October 6, 1555.

Before they were burned to death, they knelt together and prayed. Then they were fastened by chains to an iron post, and a bag of gunpowder was hung around each of their necks. The fires were then lit. Latimer encouraged Ridley by saying, "Be of good comfort, Master Ridley, and play the man. We shall this day light such a candle, by God's grace, in England, as I trust shall never be put out!" Both men were burned to death.

APPEAL:

When Latimer was called to answer for his faith in Christ, he gave his life rather than reject the Lord who had saved him.[38] What about you? God has in mercy revealed the wonderful truth of His church. You had been wondering with confusion as to why there are so many Christian denominations, when there is only one Bible. Now you have seen through the Word of God that the enemy has been at work. But God declared, "Come out of her my people" (Revelation 18:4). Jesus said, "In vain do they worship me, teaching for doctrine the commandments of men" (Mark 7:7). Oh, friends, in spite of the devil's decoys, God still has his remnant faith. He is calling you to join His ranks; are you willing to risk all for

---

38. Erwin R. Gane, *Jesus Only*, 167-168.

your Savior? Are you willing to follow Him wherever He may lead you? Will you take your stand on the side of God's true faith now?

IT DOES NOT MATTER

One evening after the presentation, a well-dressed man approached the speaker and requested a visit in his home. The speaker, having to communicate through a translator, said yes. After the man was gone, the translator asked the speaker if he knew who that man was. "No, should I?" Was the answer. "He is the secretary of the Communist party. He is a ruthless man, and I have personally suffered at his hands," the translator informed. "Well, I have already given my word. So, we will have to go," said the speaker.

On Sunday morning, the men made their way to the town of Cumpaniza. They arrived at the house and knocked on the door. After a little while, a woman answered the door. "Come in," she commanded. After stepping inside, the woman once more ordered, "Sit down." Once seated, she began with, "What are you doing down there?" Not sure as to what she was asking and being careful with his answer, the evangelist answered the question with a question. "What do you mean?" he asked. "I want to know what you people are doing down there?" She demanded again. "I am still not sure what it is you are asking," said the preacher.

Then the woman began crying and said, "I do not understand. I cannot tell you how often I have had to go out in the middle of the night to look for him. Oftentimes more than not, I have found him in a drunken stupor, lying in the middle of some road. I have had to drag him from the street so that some vehicle would not run over him.

On many occasions, he has come home so drunk that he could not find the door. If he has fallen and wounded himself, I would have to get up and take care of him. But this past Friday, he said, 'Get my clothing ready; tomorrow I am going to church.' 'What church?' I said, 'Tomorrow is Saturday; there is no church tomorrow.' 'Just get my clothing ready,' was his response. In the morning he got up, dressed, and left the house. I don't understand. What is going on; what are you doing down there?"

"Now I understand," replied the evangelist. "We are preaching the Gospel of Christ. That's what we are doing." Just at the time that the speaker said these words, the man of the house stepped into the living room. Sitting next to his troubled, weeping wife, he placed his arm around her. Then adding his tears with hers, the man said, "Pastor, something wonderful has happened to me, and I want to be baptized. Is this possible?"

Surprised, the pastor responded with, "Do you believe with all your heart?" "I do," he replied. "Well, we will have to prepare you for the occasion. Is that all right with you? The pastor here will help you. Do you know him?" continued the evangelist. "Oh yes," he said. "OK then, we are going to have a baptism next weekend, and if you are ready, you can be in it," the pastor encouraged. Then they had a prayer.

Just prior to his baptism, the former Communist asked if he could say a word to his people. "Yes," said the pastor. When it came time for his testimony, the secretary stood up and said, "You know me and know who I am. I have something to say to you. I have been a Communist, an atheist, and a drunkard for fifty years. And what communism and atheism could not do in fifty years, the Gospel of Christ has done for me in three weeks. Therefore, today I seal my decision for Him."

APPEAL:

For fifty years, he was a slave to alcoholism as well as the other "isms." But all the "isms" had no power to deliver the man from his addiction. Friend, there are a lot of "isms" out there. There are many gospels being offered. But there is only one true gospel that has all of the necessary ingredients to save. Paul warned:

> I marvel that ye are so soon removed from him that called you into the grace of Christ unto another gospel: Which is not another; but there be some that trouble you, and would pervert the gospel of Christ. But though we, or an angel from heaven, preach any other gospel unto you than that which we have preached unto you, let him be accursed. As we said before, so say I now again, if any man preach any other gospel unto you than that ye have received, let him be accursed. (Galatians 1:6-9)

Yes, there is only one gospel. Jesus left us all the identifying marks so that you and I should not be deceived. Have you been confused and bewildered, thinking to yourself, "It is impossible to determine who is right?" Or maybe you have thought, "All roads lead to Rome, it does not matter." But now you see that it does matter. God does have a message, a faith that saves, and it is the one that "keeps the commandments of God, and has the faith of Jesus." Is it your desire to accept the true message and faith of Christ? God calls you to walk in His light. Will you stand in your place? Will you give your heart to Him? If it is your desire to become part of Jesus' last-day faith, will you lift your hand?

Chapter 17

CHOOSING TO BE READY

HARRY R. TRUMAN

Harry R. Truman (not the former President of the United States) was warned of the impending doom. He had lived on Mount St. Helens most of his life. Yes, the mountain at times shook and quaked, but nothing substantial happened. Irrespective of the storms that had assaulted his domain, he had been able to weather them. Again, the authorities insisted on his evacuation. And again, Mr. Truman refused. He did not believe the admonitions given him. Defying all warnings, he settled in for the worst thinking, "This too will pass."

Then it happened. With the power of several atomic bombs Mt. St. Helens blew its top spewing ash for hundreds of miles. The entire top of the mountain disappeared along with Harry Truman.

APPEAL:

So it is today. There are many "Harrys and "Marys" who despite all the signs linger in indecisiveness. "Yes," they say, "there have been storms, earthquakes, and wars, but all things continue the same from the beginning." Ah, friend, soon Jesus will come. How will you be found? Will you be found among those who believe and make every effort to heed the warnings and signs? Or will you be among those who will be taken by the Lord's coming? Where will you stand? Your standing then can be fixed by your standing now. Will you rise to your feet and say, "Lord, I want to be ready for Your glorious appearing." Will you stand now?

Jesus warned His disciples to pray that their flight would not be on the Sabbath or in the winter. Only those who heeded His words were saved when Jerusalem was destroyed. And only those who believe His Word will be saved when He comes. Do you want to be saved when He comes? If that is your desire, will you raise your hand now?

SLEEPING WHEN THE WINDS BLOW

Years ago a farmer owned land along the Atlantic seacoast. He constantly advertised for hired hands. Most people were reluctant to work on farms along the Atlantic because they dreaded the awful storms that raged across the ocean, wreaking havoc on buildings and crops.

As the farmer interviewed applicants for the job, he received a steady stream of refusals. Finally, a short, thin man, well past middle age, approached the farmer. "Are you a good farmhand?" The farmer asked him. "Well, I can sleep when the wind blows," answered the little man.

Although puzzled by this answer, the farmer, desperate for help, hired the man. The little man worked well around the farm, busy from dawn to dusk. And the farmer felt satisfied with the man's work.

Then one night the wind howled loudly in from offshore. Jumping out of bed, the farmer grabbed a lantern and rushed next door to the hired hand's sleeping quarters. He shook the little man and yelled, "Get up! A storm is coming! Tie things down before they blow away!" The little man rolled over in bed and said firmly, "No sir. I told you, I can sleep when the wind blows."

Enraged by the response, the farmer was tempted to fire him on the spot. Instead, he hurried outside to prepare for the storm. To his amazement, he discovered that all of the haystacks had been covered with tarpaulins. The cows were in the barn, the chickens were in the coops, the doors were barred, and the shutters were tightly secured. Everything was tied down. Nothing could blow away. The farmer then understood what his hired hand meant, so he returned to his bed to also sleep while the wind blew.

APPEAL:

Soon the winds of this earth's destruction will blow. The Lord shall return with a tempest to render judgment on all who do wickedly. The Scriptures tell us that the islands will disappear and the mountains shall be moved out of their places. Will you be able to repose in the Lord when the wind blows? Now is the time to get ready. Like the hired hand, I want to be able to "sleep when the wind blows," don't you? Is your faith anchored in the Lord? Have you made your peace with Him? How is your standing with your Lord? Do you desire to be ready? If that is your desire, will you lift a hand of faith up to the Lord? Will you do it just now?

PACKED AND READY

When the great explorer Shackleton was on his quest for the South Pole, he was at one time driven back and was compelled to leave some of his men on Elephant Island, though he promised that he would return for them.

When he endeavored to get back, he found a sea of ice between him and the island. But he must keep his word! He tried to reach them, but failed. He tried again and again without success. Beyond the ice were his companions, who had every confidence in him. They had only scant supplies with them. At that time of year, it seemed folly to hope for any favorable change in the weather. He was told that there was absolutely no hope of getting his little boat, the "Yalcho," through the great ice barrier to Elephant Island.

He could not be inactive. He must reach his men. So at the risk of losing his boat and his crew he pushed nearer to the island; unexpectedly, there came an opening in the ice. He hurried in, rescued the waiting men, and in an hour was back again with all on board. Had they been delayed only a few minutes the crushing ice could have destroyed the frail vessel as it closed around it.

When they were sure they were beyond danger, and the nervous tension had passed, Shackleton said to one of the rescued men, "Well, you were packed and ready, weren't you? "Yes," came the reply, "we never lost hope. We believed you would come for us, even though circumstances were unfavorable. You had promised, and we expected you. So each morning we rolled up our sleeping bags and packed all our equipment that we might be ready."[39]

---

39. C. L. Paddock, *God's Minutes*, 315-316..

APPEAL:

According to His promise, Jesus will soon come. Though it appears that He has lingered, His promise is true. He will keep His Word. When He does come, He wants to find us ready. There will not be a second chance. Just like in Noah's day and in Lot's, there will not be two groups remaining alive after He comes. In Noah's day, "all flesh died." In Lot's day, only he and his daughters were left alive. When the Master returns, only those who have "loved His appearing" will be ready to be saved.

Are you ready for Jesus to come? Do you long for His appearing? If you do not feel ready now, would you like to be ready? If that is your earnest desire, would you raise your hand to say, "Lord Jesus, help me to be ready." Yes, raise your hand up high!

I AM READY

A farmer who had been a faithful deacon in Jacksonville, Florida, had an accident. While he was on his tractor, somehow the plow got stuck. The tractor rose up and turned upside-down on him. He was pulled from underneath the tractor and taken immediately to the hospital because his wounds were life-threatening.

When the pastor arrived to see him, Eric was hooked up to every medical device conceivable. When the pastor asked, "How are you doing, Eric?" Eric could not reply because of the tubes in his nostrils and throat. Then lifting up his arm, which was in a cast, he pointed to the wall ahead of him. The pastor turned to see where Eric was pointing. There on the wall was a sign which read, "There is nothing that can happen to me that the Lord and I can't handle together." Eric was ready to meet his Lord. He died, but he did so with the blessed hope.

APPEAL:

There is nothing like being at peace with the Lord. Eric had that peace and felt ready for whatever the Lord had for Him. And so at this time, are you ready to meet the Lord? If the Lord were to come today (or tonight) would you be ready to meet Him in peace? Perhaps the better question is do you want to be ready? If that is your desire, will you respond to the Lord?

TRAVELING TOO FAST

A boy who lived on a large farm got a great deal of pleasure from driving with his father in a wagon or buggy the seventeen miles between his home and town. Here, they often went to sell produce and do the family shopping. Every trip to town and back meant thirty-four miles. The boy probably asked many questions during the ride. To keep him occupied, the father suggested that the lad count the billboards, the telephone posts, and, later, the fence posts along the road.

If he counted the billboards going into town one time, he was encouraged to count them again the next time to be sure his first count was correct. It made the trip a little shorter for the boy and gave the father some time for thought. It was a simple matter to do the counting in the horse-and-buggy days, but when the automobile came, the counting was not so easy. They talked about the change of speed, and the father gave the lad some good advice. "Son," he said on one of the trips, "you will live much longer and much better, too, if you always drive so that you can count the signs on life's highway."

We have done a lot of speeding up in the last few decades. Some trains travel more than 200 miles per hour. Cars are being made with more powerful engines. On the German Autobahn, people can go as fast as they want to drive. However, these are a bit too slow for some of us, so we take to the air. Computers have to go faster and faster. Everything seems to be accelerating. Everything is geared to top speed. We are traveling so fast that we do not have time to read the signs on life's busy highway.

APPEAL:

What are the signs all around us? There are disasters by land, air, and sea. Storms are becoming more frequent, earthquakes are more numerous, and diseases are more virulent. Millions of people are dying from various causes. The end is near, but could it be true that we are traveling so fast in our busy lives that we are having trouble counting the signs on life's highway? Perhaps just now it is dawning on you that you need to change your priorities. Jesus is coming and now you realize it more than ever.

Will you choose just now to make an alteration in your life? Do you want to be ready? Or will you be among those that just like in Noah's day were too preoccupied? They noticed not the events around them until, "Noah entered into the ark, and they knew not, and the flood came and took them all away." Oh, friend, why not ask the Lord to help you slow down and count the signs on life's highway? Why not determine to make your commitment to Christ just now? Will you do that? Will you raise your hand (have them kneel as they make the commitment, or stand, or go to the altar)?

"I WILL RETURN!"

During World War II, General Douglas McArthur fled the Philippines declaring, "I will return!" Pearl Wilcox; her sick, ailing mother; her son; and her missionary husband were now prisoners. Pearl was allowed to stay in one of the abandoned houses to care for her sick mother. Her son and husband were interned in the prison camp.

As time passed, hope began to wane. Three years elapsed and still no deliverance. Then one day, while all looked bleak and hopeless, Pearl heard the sound of engines in the air. She first thought they were enemy planes. But as she looked up, she saw paratroopers jumping out. Could it be? Yes, it was! American paratroopers were floating down from the sky. They looked like angels come down to deliver the prisoners of war.

The thrill of deliverance swept over her being—what joy she felt! When it appeared the darkest, deliverance came. It was later discovered from captured documents that the day of deliverance was to be the day of death. All the prisoners were to be killed, but instead, the keeping of the promise saved them.

APPEAL:

Almost 2,000 years ago, Jesus promised, "I will come again" (John 14:3). Just like Pearl Wilcox who had almost come to wonder if they would ever be delivered, so it will be in this earth's darkest hour. It may appear hopeless out there. But Jesus promised, "I will come again." Friend, Jesus will keep His promise. He declared in another passage: "When these things come to pass, then look up and lift up your eyes, for your redemption draweth nigh" (Luke 21:28). Oh, friend, there is no doubt. What Jesus predicted, we are seeing with our eyes and hearing with our ears. Jesus is coming! And He is coming soon! Won't you meet Him in peace?

He is coming to rescue you from this world of toil and trouble. Look at the suffering mothers, the starving, the violence, nature itself being weighed down by the weight of wickedness and pollution. Jesus is coming! Are you among those who will, like Pearl, be excited to see Him come, or will you be among those who will be crying to the rocks saying, "Fall on us, and hide us from the face of Him that sits on the throne?" Oh, friend, will you accept Him now as your Savior? Will you respond to His call now? Will you raise your hand (stand, or come down to the altar)? Will you respond to His call now?

I HAVE TIME

The women were attending a series of meetings. On this particular night, the evangelist began to make an appeal. The subject was on the glorious appearing of Christ and the need to be ready to meet Him. As the speaker adjured the listeners to make their lives ready, he appealed to them to show their response by standing. The older woman rose to her feet.

As the appeal continued, the mother noticed that her daughter was still sitting. Turning to her, she bent low and whispered, "Sweetheart, why don't you stand with me in this commitment?" "No mother, not now. You need to do it. You are old and do not have much time. I am young and still have things I want to do before I make this kind of commitment. I am glad you are doing it." The anguished heart of the mother pained as she heard those words. The appeal came to an end. The pastor had a prayer, and then the meeting came to its conclusion.

At the exit, the pastor was shaking hands and bidding the attendees good night. When the mother went through the door, she pled with the pastor to pray for her daughter and shared with him her sorrowful response to the appeal. Assuring the mother of his prayers, he encouraged and commended her for her decision.

The women made their way to their car. On the way home, while on the highway, something terrible happened. A semi-trailer went out of control. It crashed into the car and fell on it. The car was crushed, and both women died.

APPEAL:

Friend, we do not know how much time we have on this old earth. Some of us will meet a time of departure sooner than we think. Life is unpredictable. And knowing this, how can you procrastinate in your decision? The Lord says, "Now is the day of salvation. Today, if you hear my voice, harden not your hearts."

Oh, friend, Jesus will come. Don't you want to be ready? When the end of all things comes, don't you want to find yourself safe in the arms of your Savior? Don't put off that decision. As the Spirit speaks, yield yourself to Him. Accept His invitation of salvation now. Will you lift your hand toward heaven? Will you do it just now?

HOW CAN YOU SERVE A COWARD

A visiting pastor went to visit an interest of one of his friends who was another pastor. When they arrived at the home, the man of the house graciously welcomed them. Once seated, they began to get acquainted. Pastor Price informed him that the visiting pastor was from America and was just in the area giving some lectures. Everything went well until they entered into the topic of God.

"How can you serve a coward?" There was obvious contempt in the tone of his voice. "What do you mean," asked the visitor. "I would not let my son take the rap for me." What kind of God do you serve who was not man enough to take care of the problem himself?" responded the man.

Pausing for a moment to gather his thoughts, the visiting pastor asked the man if he had any children. "Yes," he replied, "I have one son. Why?" "If you had to make a choice between you taking a beating or watch your son take the beating, which one would hurt the most?" Asked the pastor. The man was silent. There was no reply.

APPEAL:

Oh, friend, when Jesus was hanging on the cross of Calvary, He was not the only one suffering. Having to watch while His Son was going through the shame and agony of the cross, and letting His Son feel as if He had forsaken Him, I am sure was far more than any human could bear, and to think that He suffered it all for you. He loves you!

The question is do you love Him? He could do nothing more than He has done. Can you serve a God like that? Will you give yourself to Him? If that is your desire, will you raise your hand?

A NEW YORK GANG MEMBER

Early one morning, a gang member went and rapped on his brother's door. Upon opening the door, the surprised brother asked, "What is the matter?" His countenance gave witness that his gang member brother was greatly stirred by something. "What's the matter?" "Louis, Louis, I had a strange dream. While asleep, I thought I was awake," he said. He saw a bright light flooding the window.

Fearing that the police were searching for him, he crouched down and slowly approached the window. To his surprise, the light was not coming from police floodlights on the ground, but rather from the heavens, for in the sky were myriads of bright shining beings. In the midst there seemed to appear the form of One sitting on a throne. "I saw God," he declared, "I saw God." "What happened?" asked his brother.

"Fearful that God was coming, and that I was not ready, I ran down the steps into the street. Buildings swayed and trains fell from the elevated tracks. Everything was in commotion. I began to yell out Gene's name (an older brother who was a Christian). I kept running, but there was nowhere to hide. Then I woke up and found myself drenched in sweat. Louis, what does this mean?"

APPEAL:

Just like the gang member who found himself unprepared to meet the Lord, perhaps you are in the same predicament. Your own heart tells you that you are not ready. But you want to be ready. You would do anything to meet the Lord in peace. But you must go to the Savior. You cannot make yourself ready apart from His help.

Oh, friend, why delay? Why not rise to your feet and come to Jesus? Come just as you are, and He will make you what you ought to be. Will you come just now?

OR:

Tonight, I wonder, how many of you here really feel in your heart that you long for Jesus to come? Would you raise your hand? You long for Jesus to come. Amen. What a wonderful thing! And I wonder also, there may be some of you here tonight who for the first time have realized that like those people in the antediluvian world, those people outside the ark, you too find yourself outside the ark of safety. And your heart is beating. Tonight you sense in a new way that Jesus is inviting you to make your commitment to Him. I wonder, is there anyone here tonight who would like to say, "Yes, I have not really understood this before, but tonight I see it; by God's grace, I want to be ready for Jesus when He comes?"

Is anyone here like that tonight? You'd like to raise your hand and say, "I want to be ready. I didn't know this, but tonight I want to commit my life to Him. I raise my hand in faith saying, 'Lord, I want to be with that group that will be ready in that day.'" God sees your hands. Anyone else? Would you like to lift your hand to heaven and say, "I want to be ready for that day?" Is there anyone else tonight? Just lift your hand and say, "By God's grace, I want to be ready." Yes, God sees your hand. What a wonderful thing!

Chapter 18

DELIVERANCE FROM THE
FEAR OF DEATH

AFRAID TO SLEEP

A visiting pastor was invited by a doctor friend to go with him on a visit. "Since you are going with me, I would like you to present the study to my client," suggested the doctor. "On what?" responded the pastor. "I'll let the Lord lead you," replied the physician. When they arrived at the house, it was obvious that this family was financially comfortable. When they entered into the home, there was quite a spread prepared for them. The husband invited them to the table, and after the repast, they were led to the living room.

After a few words, the doctor announced that his visiting friend would be leading out in the study. The pastor still pondering with what subject he should begin, started into the Scriptures. It wasn't long before they were deep into the subject of the whereabouts of the dead. As the topic continued to nearly the conclusion, the lady of the house began crying. "How did you know?" she questioned. "How did I know about what?" questioned the pastor. "Did you tell him?" she questioned, as she stared at the doctor. "No," he said, "I told him that he would have to let the Lord lead him." "Then how did you know?" she again asked the pastor. "I didn't know, but God did," he declared.

"I have been living in torment of death all of my life. I can't sleep unless the lights are turned on. Then oftentimes while sleeping, I have terrifying nightmares that I am dying. I awake drenched in sweat. I have been so terrified that I fear to go to sleep," the women revealed. "Oh how thrilling to know the truth! At last I can sleep in peace!" And yes, two days later she joyfully announced to the doctor and pastor, "I have had such wonderful sleep for the last two days."

APPEAL:

The Bible says, "Forasmuch then as the children are partakers of flesh and blood, he also himself likewise took part of the same; that through death he might destroy him that had the power of death, that is, the devil; And deliver them who through fear of death were all their lifetime subject to bondage" (Hebrews 2:14-16).

Listen, have you been in torment over this subject? Have you been tortured by the thought that you would end up in some dark, dreaded abyss? Perhaps you have been confused as you have attended a funeral, and the attending minister declared, "May he rest in peace." Yet, they proceed to declare the person to be walking into the pearly gates or perform a Mass to extricate the dead out of purgatory.

Tonight, we see that it is Jesus who has the keys of death. The Scriptures declare, "He that hath the Son hath life; he that hath not the Son of God hath not life." Oh, friend, will put your destiny in the Lifegiver's hand? Remember, He said, "I am the resurrection and the life: he that believeth in me, though he were dead, yet shall he live" (John 11:25). Do you want life? Will you accept the Lifegiver?

LADY IN HUNGARY WHO LOST THREE LOVED ONES IN ONE YEAR

A lady in Hungary, the principal of a school, was attending a Bible seminar. One night the subject of the dead was presented. As the speaker looked in her direction, he noticed tears running down her face. At the conclusion of the meeting as the pastor was shaking the hands of the attendees who were leaving the meeting hall, the lady approached him. "How are you?" asked the speaker. "I am relieved," she replied. "Relieved about what?" asked the speaker.

"This year has been a very hard year for me. First, I lost my husband. Then I lost my daughter, and finally my granddaughter died. I feared they were either suffering as they saw me suffer my great losses, or suffering in purgatory or hell. In either case, I was greatly troubled. Thank you so much." Having said that, she left.

The next night, she returned. Gone was the troubled look, and a sense of peace pervaded her. After the meeting, the speaker said, "I see that something is different about you." "Yes," she said, "last night was the first night I was able to sleep for several months. I am comforted to know that my loved ones are not suffering, but rather resting in peace."

APPEAL:

Have you lost a loved one? Have you been troubled wondering what has happened to him or her? Maybe you have been led to believe that your loved one is in heaven, looking down on all the misery, pain, and turmoil on earth. Or, are you tortured by the thought that your loved one is in eternal torment. Jesus declared, "Blessed are the dead which die in the Lord from henceforth: Yea, saith the Spirit, that they may rest from their labours; and their works do follow them" (Revelation 14:13).

My friend, your hope and mine is in the one who can restore to life. Jesus invites you. Will you accept Jesus, your hope of life and the resurrection?

MOTHER'S SON IN HELL

A lady walked into a store one Saturday morning. When she was inside, she noticed a group of people sitting on chairs in a circle. The owner noticing her, approached her, and said, "Lady, I am sorry. We are not open for business today. I neglected to lock the door." "Oh," she said, "I am sorry." As she was about to turn and leave, a thought came to him. "By the way, we are just having a Bible study, and if you would like, you can join us." Looking at her watch, she said, "Okay, I have some time."

As they proceeded with the Bible study, the owner noticed the lady crying. "Oh, I am so sorry for offending you," he said, "This is the first time that I am doing this, and I am sure I said something that offended you. Please forgive me."

"You haven't offended me," she said, "You comforted me." "How so?" asked the owner. "You see," she said, "I had an only son. I raised him as best I could, but no matter what, he continued in his own way. Then last week he committed a crime. The police gave chase. As he was speeding away, his car went out of control, crashed, and he died instantly. But that was not the worst of it. On Sunday, as I went to church, some of the ladies approached me and said, "Oh, we are so sorry that your son is in hell. We are praying for him. I was devastated. It was bad enough that he suffered so much while living. To think that he would be in torment forever was more than my heart could bear. I was distraught. No, you did not offend me. You brought me comfort. Thank you!"

APPEAL:

How many are tormented with the fear that their loved ones are suffering! Others are bewildered by the contradiction of what is practiced and what is taught. "May he rest in peace," they say. Yet, the uncertainty of the hereafter leaves you with no peace. Perhaps you have been a victim of this dreaded thought. Friend, your destiny can be secured in Jesus. He said, "I have the keys of death and of the grave." Will you make Him your life insurance tonight? In Him is life; will you have life? If that is the longing of your heart, will you lift your hand to heaven just now?

LITTLE GIRL KILLED IN CAR ACCIDENT

A beautiful little golden-haired girl of five or six was playing in the street when she was hit by an automobile and killed. Her mother was a dear Christian woman, but she had never been well since her child had been born. The father, a strapping specimen of American manhood, had never given his heart to the blessed Savior, so he did not have the trust that his wife had.

Finally, the hour came when they had to say goodbye to their darling and lay her to rest. The father came to the side of the casket with a minister and relatives gathered around. He just stood there and sobbed as only a strong man can. He put his hand on the little forehead and entwined his fingers in those golden curls. Then with great shaking sobs, he clutched his breast, and as the sweat poured from his brow, he said "Goodbye, little tot—forever!" He then turned and walked away.

The mother then neared the casket. She was not well and strong like the father, but she stood there alone by the casket in the midst of her great sorrow. The father just couldn't stay any longer. She put her hand in her child's curls and patted the little head, while she said, "Mama's so glad you were with us for a few short years. Mama's so glad you were here for a little while. Goodbye, darling, goodbye!

Mama will see you again, beyond the sunset and the night."[40]

APPEAL:

What made the difference, friend? Jesus did! In Christ there is hope beyond the tomb. Jesus declares to you, "And if Christ be not risen, then is our preaching vain, and your faith is also vain. . . . For if the dead rise not, then is not Christ raised: And if Christ be not raised, your faith is vain; ye are yet in your sins. Then they also which are fallen asleep in Christ are perished. If in this life only we have hope in Christ, we are of all men most miserable" (1 Corinthians 15:14, 16-19).

Oh, friend, will you accept Him? Will you make Him your Savior? Who here would like to respond to this invitation? Will you do it just now? Will you stand?

---

40. H.M.S. Richards, *Revival Sermons*, page 234-235

Chapter 19

FAITH

THE LITTLE GIRL CAUGHT IN A FIRE

A father had left his daughter home asleep while he went to the store to buy something. While he was doing his shopping, he heard the fire trucks' sirens sounding. Curious to see where and what was the fire, he stepped out of the store only to discover that they were heading toward his house.

Dropping what he was doing, he raced home. When he arrived, the house was engulfed in flames. There was no way he could get inside. Then from the window on the second floor, he heard his little girl's frantic cries. "Daddy, daddy, where are you?" she cried. Running toward the window where she was, he shouted, "Jump!" Blinded by the smoke the little girl cried, "Daddy, I can't see you!" With reassurance he shouted, "I can see you, jump!" She stepped on the windowsill and jumped. Her father braced himself and broke the fall as he caught her in his arms.

APPEAL:

Yes, there are times in our lives when it seems that God is not there. In our darkest moments, we can't see through the smoke of our trials. But, friend, put yourself in His care. You may not be able to see Him, but He sees you. Is there someone here who has been struggling with your faith? Perhaps you felt that you needed to see Him before you believed. But Jesus says to you like He said to doubting Thomas, "Thomas, because thou hast seen me, thou hast believed: blessed are they that have not seen, and yet have believed" (John 20:29).[41] Why not trust Him now? Will you raise your hand toward heaven and by faith accept Him?

---

41. The King James Version (Cambridge: Cambridge), 1769

MAN OBSERVING PAINTINGS IN STORE WINDOW

A man was strolling along the sidewalk, and his eye caught the display of paintings in a store window. He stopped to admire them. In the center of the display was a scene of the crucifixion. He was deep in thought. However, while he stood there gazing at the paintings, his meditation was interrupted. A little boy had joined him.

"See that man on the center cross, that's Jesus," the boy began. "And see that man over there," the little boy said pointing to the painting. "That is John, Jesus' best friend. And you see that lady over there, that's Jesus' mother," the little boy replied. As the little boy continued, the man's long-forgotten thoughts came to him from his childhood. He felt a knot welling in his throat. Not willing to give into his feelings and without saying a word, he abruptly turned and left the little boy. As he was walking away, he felt a tug on the back of his coat. Turning around, he heard the little boy say, "Mister, I forgot to tell you that He died for you."

APPEAL:

Yes, friend, He died for you! Perhaps you have wandered away. Something happened. Maybe you became enamored with the things of this world. Before you realized it, you had no more desire for spiritual things. You had pleasure in sin for a season. Now you long to come back, but like the prodigal, you feel unworthy. Maybe you feel that you have done too much—you've gone too far.

Friend, there is no sin so black that God can't forgive. Remember! He has promised, "If we confess our sins, He is faithful and just to forgive us our sins, and to cleanse us from all unrighteousness" (1 John 1:9). Like that prodigal, you must come to yourself and arise. Come to the Lord just as you are, and He will receive you and do for you what you in your own strength cannot do for yourself. Will you arise? Will you come?

LITTLE BOY AND BISHOP

One day there was a little Christian boy anxious to tell others about Jesus. He came across a man and took the opportunity to share His Jesus. "Mister," the boy began, "Do you know that Jesus loves you, and that He died to save you?" The man responded and said, "Why, little boy, I am a bishop." Not knowing what that was, the little boy said, "That's alright sir. Jesus can save a bishop too." Yes, friend. It does not matter who you are. Jesus can save you.

APPEAL:

Yes, He can save a bishop too! And friend, if Jesus can save a bishop, then He can save you. He says, "I stand at the door and knock, if any man hear my voice and open the door, I will come into him and sup with him and He with me" (Revelation 3:20). Will you let Him save you? He can if you will. Are you willing to invite Him? Why not do it now? Will you respond to His invitation?

TWO GYPSY YOUNG MEN

While holding an evangelistic meeting in Tirgu Mures, Romania, a young Gypsy man approached and pleaded, "Do for him what you did for me." Surprised at the request, Pastor Torres said, "Young man, I have not done anything for you. It was God who did it!" "I don't know how you say it, but what was done for me, I want to have done for my friend," the Gypsy responded. "What has been done for you?" asked Pastor Torres.

"When I came here two weeks ago, I was a desperately lost man." Then rolling up his sleeves, he showed the pastor his many scars from street fights. "I am only nineteen," he said, "But as far back as I can remember, I began drinking. From bad I went to worse. Though I got married, I was constantly in the streets drunk, and when at home, I was abusive to my wife. I had reached the end of my rope until I came here. Today I am a changed man! Do for him what has been done for me."

Then turning to the young friend of the Gypsy, Pastor Torres looked him over. His hair was matted, his eyes bloodshot, and his alcohol breath filled the air. "Do you want to be free?" Inquired Pastor Torres. "Yes," he replied, "yes." "How badly do you want to be free?" the pastor asked again. "I would give anything," replied the drunken gypsy. "Alright. Let us kneel together. You make a fervent plea for help, and then I will pray for you that God may deliver you," Pastor Torres suggested. All present knelt. With anguish, the young captive made his plea. Then Pastor Torres lifted his voice on behalf of the young man. When the prayers were finished, the pastor grabbed the hand of the young man and said, "Go in peace. Never touch liquor again." With this, the two young men went on their way.

What a transformation the Lord wrought for those boys! On the day of their baptism, these two husbands along with their wives stood before the more than 4,000 in attendance and testified to the power of Christ in their lives.

APPEAL:

There is power in the blood! No sin or habit is so strong that the Lord Jesus Christ cannot give power to overcome. Is there some habit in your life? Do you feel that the devil has you in shackles? Have you felt hopeless—feeling that there is no hope? In Christ, you can become a new creature. The Scriptures say, "If any man be in Christ; he is a new creature. Old things are passed away, behold, all things become new" (2 Corinthians 5:17). What a wonderful hope we have! Praise the Lord! We are not stuck in the mud forever. Through His power, you can be an overcomer. Is that your desire? Troubled heart, do you long to be free? Then do as that young Gypsy man. Be willing to do anything, and you can receive His grace to overcome. Will you be free? Will you lift your hand toward heaven?

Chapter 20

CHOOSING TO HEED THE WARNINGS

LUTHER WARREN

Luther Warren was invited to speak at a meeting in Jamaica. He was to demonstrate to the students of theology just how an evangelistic meeting was to be held. The students were anxious to participate and learn how to preach the gospel more successfully. The local leaders had advised the preacher concerning what sort of exemplary teaching was needed. They wanted the seasoned evangelist to demonstrate how to stick to one subject per night and how to build a progression of topics.

The opening night arrived to a buzz of activity and great anticipation. Luther walked onto the platform and began delivering his message. But contrary to the instruction given, he did everything unconventionally. Rather than sticking with one subject, he seemed to give all the subjects. Besides this, he did something unusual. He made an altar call the first night. Hundreds of people went to the altar to commit their lives to Christ.

Filled with mixed feelings, the leaders asked, "Why did you do that? This was not what had been the plan for the instruction." Luther said, "I don't know. Something seemed to take over me. It seemed like I was compelled to do it. I was not in control."

That night as they went to sleep, and while the city slept, the answer came. A terrible earthquake shook that city, and many who had come forward that night died. Little did they know that night was the last opportunity to accept salvation—the last chance to prepare for eternity. And fortunately for them, God in His mercy gave them that last opportunity.

APPEAL:

How important it is to be ever ready! When is a warning a good thing: after the event happens or before? All the signs are omens of an imminent appearing of Christ. The question is if Christ were to appear tonight, would you be ready to meet Him in peace? Let me ask another question. If the Lord were to appear, would you want to be ready? Would you lift up your hand if that is your desire?

HURRICANE IN NEW YORK CITY

A man living in Long Island, New York, made a mail order for a barometer. How excited he was when the mailman brought him the expected package. He quickly opened it and hung it on the spot he had prepared for the instrument. But as he looked at the mounted apparatus, he became dismayed. The readings pointed to weather conditions for a hurricane.

Taking it off the wall, he shook it and tapped it to see if the instrument would correct itself. "This thing is not working," he said, "Hurricanes don't happen in New York." Shaking it once more and tapping it, he hoped that the jarring would cause the needle to get loose. He concluded it was futile. They sent him a malfunctioning instrument. Angry and left with frustrated expectations, he put the thing back in the box and drove to the post office to ship it back. While at the post office, the winds gave evidence that the barometer was right, and shortly thereafter the storm struck.

APPEAL:

It is clear that the signs all around us give evidence that the coming of Christ is near, even at the door. Maybe you have thought, as the apostle Peter wrote concerning those in his day, "Where is the promise of his coming? For since the fathers have fallen asleep, all things continue as they were from the beginning of creation" (2 Peter 3:4). But now you see that the day of the Lord hastens and is even at the door. Are you ready to meet the storm when it hits? Do you desire to prepare yourself for that eventual climatic appearing of the Lord? If it is your desire, will you raise your hand just now? Let us pray.

Chapter 21

SEEKING THE LOST

SCOTT O'GRADY

Thoughts on Luke 15:4—"What man of you having one hundred sheep, if he loose one of them . . . goes and find the lost sheep?"

Bosnia, June 8, 1995: Scott O'Grady had waited six days. He had been praying and waiting for rescue. His F16 was shot down—hit on its under pass and blind spot. In twenty seconds, he ejected. When he landed, the enemy went to capture him. In minutes Serbians surrounded him, but they could not find him.

He put his face in the dirt. He ate ants and grass. He drank water from his drenched socks. Special Forces were dispatched with a Naval Fleet of forty planes. The whole shooting match was garnered for one soldier.

APPEAL:

If the whole support system was put together for just one who pleaded, "Help, I am alive, send help!" Then the great God of heaven is also preparing a team for the rescue. There was one lost. Christ came and searched. He did not give up easily. He forgot all about Himself and went searching inside enemy territory. He came at great expense.

Jesus did not ask, "Why did the sheep leave? What happened?" Instead, He found it and placed it on His shoulder. When Captain O'Grady was rescued, the whole nation rejoiced. How much more will God rejoice over you? "There is more joy in heaven over one sinner that repents more than over one just man" (Luke 15:7). Heaven is concerned for the lost—God is concerned for you. Why not let Him save you today?

Chapter 22

STORIES FOR IMMEDIATE DECISIONS

TWO INDIAN HUNTERS

It was near the end of winter, and the lake was completely frozen. Two Indian hunters were on their way back home. Then suddenly, the ice where they walked broke apart. The older Indian immediately jumped to safety. The younger one feared to jump across the opening gap. The older Indian encouraged him, but the fear of jumping held him frozen. The block of ice continued to float away from shore. "Jump," cried the old man, but the young man continued to hesitate as the opening gap continued to widen. Sad to say, the young man never did jump and was lost.

APPEAL:

Oh, friend, when Jesus calls us, it is not safe to hesitate. We ought to follow when He calls. When He called the disciples, the record states, "And they straight way left their nets and followed Him" (Matthew 4:20). Jesus said to a certain man, "Follow me." He said, "Lord, suffer me first to go and bury my father" (Matthew 8:21). Jesus said unto Him, "Let the dead bury the dead" (Matthew 8:22). Another said, "Lord, I will follow thee; but let me first go bid them farewell, which are at home at my house. And Jesus said unto him, No man, having put his hand to the plow, and looking back, is fit for the kingdom of God" (Luke 9:61).

There is a time to delay, and there is a time to act. "Today, if you will hear His voice, harden not your heart." Is there anything that will keep you from following your Lord? Will you come just now?

MAN WITH GANGRENE

A man went to a doctor to check his infected finger. Unfortunately, he had waited too long. "It must be amputated," the doctor said. "Oh, no!" the man argued, "I don't want my finger amputated. How can I live without my finger?" "But you must, or it will get worse," the doctor replied. "No, it won't." And with that, the man left. The condition worsened, and the man returned to the doctor. Now the gangrene had moved to his arm. "We must amputate your arm," the doctor told him. "No! Never! How could I live without my arm?" Responded the patient. "But you must, or it will take your life," the doctor said. The man loathed to have his arm amputated and died.

APPEAL:

So it is with our sins. You must be willing to let Jesus remove them from you or else you will die. Oh, why will you die? God tells us that He has no pleasure in the death of the wicked. Why not give Him your sins? Why not arise and come to Him just as you are? Will you come?

GOD WILL NOT FORGIVE THE SINS OF MY YOUTH!

A pastor visited a man in a Hungarian hospital who was suffering from terminal cancer. As the minister approached the bedside, the man lay with his eyes closed. The pastor greeted him, and he opened his eyes. "How are you?" the pastor asked. The man began to cry. He was just skin and bones. The worst of it was that the man had no hope for the hereafter. "God will not forgive the sins of my youth," he wept.

Moved with compassion, the pastor asked, "Are you a Christian?" "Yes," he said, "but I have been too great of a sinner, and God will not forgive the sins of my youth." "Oh, friend, do you believe the Bible?"

Then he turned to the Scriptures and read the verse: "If we confess our sins, He is faithful and just to forgive us our sins and cleanse us from all unrighteousness" (1 John 1:9). "Oh, my brother, God has promised, but you have doubted Him. You have believed the enemy of your soul—accepted his suggestion. But there is no peace in his suggestions. There is only torment of mind and soul. If God so promised, will you accept Him? Will you believe Him?" Seeing his dilemma, he said, "I see, I see."

APPEAL:

Oh, friend, do you see? Have you thought your life too vile, too wicked to be forgiven? Why not turn to Him just now? God waits to receive you. He will not coerce you. He longs to heal you, but you must decide to go to Him. Will you respond to His invitation today?

THE URGENCY OF THE APPLICATION

A Christian physician had for some years tried to win a friend and patient to Christianity. He urged him to believe the Bible and to accept God's Word in faithful obedience. He had always been put off with the reply, "Some other time."

One day the doctor was hurriedly summoned, for his friend felt that mortal sickness had overtaken him. On diagnosis, the condition was discovered to be trivial, but the doctor hid the fact and offered some medicine with the instruction that it was to be taken in six month's time. "But," cried the patient, "why wait so long? I may be dead in that time." "Ah, well," said the doctor, "take it in a month's time." "But, why wait even so long as that?" queried the anxious patient. "Then take it in only a week," said the doctor. "Why not take it at once?" the patient insisted. "I may not live even a week. I need to take the medicine now."

APPEAL:

You see the analogy. Why be so insistent for an immediate need for the body that will perish anyway and so indifferent to the need of the soul when eternity is at stake? The Great Physician comes to our aid and longs to heal us from the malady of sin. He says that if "we turn away our ears from hearing the law, even our prayer is an abomination" (Proverbs 29:8). Our attitude toward God's law determines His attitude toward our prayers. Do not wait until some more convenient time to give your heart to Him and be found obedient to His Word. It may be fatal to wait even a week before taking the cup of salvation. Dare we wait a moment when the case is so serious and the need so great? The Master has come to you now with His Word. Why hesitate? Behold, now is the hour of salvation. Oh, sinner, why delay? Who here will respond to the calling of the Lord?

THE EAGLE

One day a spectacular event took place in Niagara Falls. A large, bald eagle swooped down on a large floating chunk of ice to feast on carrion. As the chuck of ice drifted toward the falls, the eagle unconcerned continued to gorge itself. Nearer and nearer was the approach to the edge, but the eagle looked unconcerned.

Then as the block of ice reached the edge, the eagle spread it huge wings to take flight. But it could not. Unbeknownst to the eagle, its claws had become frozen to the ice. With desperate efforts the bird attempted to lift, but with feet frozen to the ice, the eagle plunged to its death.

APPEAL:

Its confidence in its ability to spread its wings and flee death, allowed that eagle to procrastinate until it was forever too late. Could it be that you are doing the same. You know the Lord says, "For he saith, I have heard thee in a time accepted, and in the day of salvation have I succored thee: behold, now is the accepted time; behold, now is the day of salvation" (2 Corinthians 6:2). How long will you wait until it is too late? The Lord calls, will you respond? Will you accept His mercy while He makes the offer? Why not say, Lord I will not gamble any more with my salvation. I will come now.

Chapter 23

SPIRITUALISM

GOD'S ADMONITION

And when they shall say unto you, seek unto them that have familiar spirits, and unto wizards that peep, and that mutter: should not a people seek unto their God? For the living to the dead? To the law and to the testimony: if they speak not according to this word, it is because there is no light in them. (Isaiah 8:19, 20)

There shall not be found among you any one that maketh his son or his daughter to pass through the fire, or that useth divination, or an observer of times, or an enchanter, or a witch, or a charmer, or a consulter with familiar spirits, or a wizard, or a necromancer. For all that do these things are an abomination unto the LORD: and because of these abominations the LORD thy God doth drive them out from before thee. (Deuteronomy 18:10, 12)

KING SAUL DIED FOR ASKING COUNSEL FROM A MEDIUM

The first earthly king of Israel was unwilling to follow God's counsel. Finally, God forsook him. The Scripture says, "And the Spirit of God departed from Saul" (1 Samuel 16:14). What a terrible condition to be in! There is no darker moment in a person's life than to be abandoned by God. But why did the God of great mercy forsake Saul?

So Saul died for his transgression which he committed against the LORD, even against the word of the LORD, which he kept not, and also for asking counsel of one that had a familiar spirit, to inquire of it; And inquired not of the LORD: therefore he slew him, and turned the kingdom unto David the son of Jesse. (1 Chronicles 10:13, 14)

APPEAL:

Oh, friend, you can see the great hatred that God has for this evil delusion. God pleads with you to turn from darkness unto His light. The prince of darkness is working with all manner of deceitfulness to ensnare as many as he can. Will you turn to God? Will you put your trust in the God of truth?

DEAD MOTHER TALKING ON THE PHONE (McMINNVILLE, OREGON, 2006)

"My wife's mother died," stated a man. "However, prior to her death, she was into spiritualism and anything that had to do with the occult. She had also told my wife that if anyone would dare to get close to her casket upon her demise, she would sit up and cast fire on the person. Obviously, at the funeral, my wife was very anxious and frightened, expecting that the bizarre would occur, but the wake passed without anything unusual happening.

The funeral ended as undisturbed as is typical of a resting cemetery. Several days after her death, the phone rang. When my wife picked it up, it was the voice of my deceased mother-in-law. This went on for a while. It was when my wife studied the Bible and discovered the truth that the "dead know not anything," that the calling ceased.

APPEAL:

The Scriptures clearly state, "Put not your trust in princes, nor in the son of man, in whom there is no help. His breath goeth forth, he returneth to his earth; in that very day his thoughts perish" (Psalm 146:3, 4). Oh, friend, believe in the Word of the Lord. We live in days when spiritism is rife. Great delusions are attempted by the enemy. But if we put our trust in God, we shall not be deceived. Will you today place your confidence in a "thus saith the Lord?" It is your only safety. Let us pray.

IF THERE IS A DEVIL, THERE MUST BE A GOD

An elderly gentleman walked into a church during the mid-week service. As he sat to listen, he was entranced with the whole presentation. The subject that the visiting minister presented was about spiritualism's spread in these last days. At the conclusion of the sermon, the man approached the speaker and requested an audience. After the speaker had dismissed the people, he sat with the man and listened.

"I grew up as a Christian," he began, "but when I was about nineteen years old, I left the church and turned my back on religion. After I finished college, I got married and went into business. I became successful and have lived a full life with my wife. After fifty years of marriage, my wife passed away two weeks ago. It was the greatest loss of my life. While still in deep grief, just yesterday something strange happened.

"As I was sitting on the edge of my bed thinking over my life and my great loss, suddenly I felt a strange sensation. It seemed as if someone sat next to me—I could feel the mattress giving way. Cautiously and slowly I turned my head. As I looked at the spot next to me, there was a depression on the bed that took the shape of a human impress. Trembling, I jumped off the bed and moved quickly away from it. Looking back, there was the impressed form still on the bed.

"Then suddenly, a Bible text came to my mind that I had forgotten for years. "The dead know not anything.' So I thought if there is a devil, there must be a God. As a result, I decided, after all those years of my wilderness wanderings, to come back to God."

APPEAL:

Have you been like this man? Have you been wandering here and there? Maybe you have even turned to the mediums or psychics? "Why seek ye the living among the dead?" (Luke 24:5). Have you been distant from God and now desire to return to Him? Will you come to Him? Remember Jesus said, "Him that comes to me, I will in no wise cast out."

PASTOR'S DEAD SON

A pastor's thirteen-year-old son contracted leukemia. He happened to be an only child. Upon knowledge of the condition, the pastor began to pray and fast. The pleadings were heartfelt to God that the child could be healed. Unfortunately, the boy's health continued to get worse. "Oh, God," pleaded the pastor, "he is my only son; please don't let him die." The pleading seemed to go unheard until finally the boy passed away.

Grief-stricken, the family laid the lad to rest. The unheard petitions haunted the pastor. "Why did God let my boy die? I have committed my life to serve Him. Why did He let this happen?" He thought.

Three weeks later while the pastor was by himself grieving in his bedroom, he heard a familiar voice. "Dad, it's me. Look Dad, I am okay. You do not have to worry about me any longer." Raising his eyes toward the direction of the voice, he was amazed to see before his very eyes the son he loved. There he stood in perfect form. "But how can this be my son? My son is dead," thought the pastor. Then while a vicious battle raged in his heart—the longing to run and clutch to his bosom his departed son, or believe what he had taught his people about the dead. Then, a text came to him. "The dead know not anything" (Ecclesiastes 9:5).

Pulling his resolve together he demanded, "Get thee behind me Satan." Immediately at the command of his voice, the apparition disappeared.

APPEAL:

How cruel is the archenemy! What advantage he takes of the ignorant and unwary! Many are led to believe in the first lie of the devil—"ye shall not die." But God's Word unmasks the villain and reveals that the wages of sin is death, not perpetual living. Oh, friend, Jesus is the only hope of life beyond the grave. "He that has the Son has life; he that hath not the Son has not life." Do you want life? Why not turn to the Lord just now? Have you been misled? Have you had fear and trepidation concerning death? You can find peace in the Lord. Remember, He died to destroy him that had the power over death—to say, the devil—and deliver them who through fear of death were all their lifetimes subject to bondage.

JANET AND THE APPARITIONS

Janet was on a spiritual quest. Because she had no inhibitions, she became involved with everything considered spiritual. She got into macrobiotics, rebirthing, astro-traveling, and the Native American practices and beliefs. When she moved to New Mexico with her two children, she and a would-be prophet began to live together. Strange happenings started to occur in her home. Demons visited her lodging on a frequent basis. Wanting to divest herself of these frequent harassers, she asked her live-in prophet what to do. The counsel was that she needed to be baptized, and then the spirits would leave her alone. "But by who and where?" She asked. He directed her to a church.

Feeling her urgency, Janet insisted she and her "prophet" find and visit the church immediately. Saturday morning, they showed up. After the service, they approached the pastor, revealed their desire, and the man insisted on Janet's immediate baptism. "I would love to have the honor of baptizing her, but first I need to get better acquainted," he said. "Besides, this coming week I must go to the Indian Reservation. I will not be able to do anything until I return." With an obvious look of consternation, the man said, "Let's go."

Two weeks later the couple attended the church service again. After the worship service, they again approached the pastor. "You need to baptize me," Janet demanded. Pointing at her "prophet," "He baptized me, and it did not work. The demons are still harassing me and my kids." "Alright," said the pastor, "let me visit with you tomorrow. We can discuss the matter and prepare you for baptism." With this, the couple left.

During the visit, the pastor became acquainted with the man's background as well as hers. It was obvious that she was an honest seeker, and he wasn't. Bible studies began. Janet drank of the living water as soon as she heard it. Her life began to change. This troubled the man.

Finally, being concerned that he was loosing his spiritual grip on her, he demanded that she choose between the pastor and him. The pastor replied, "The choice is between Christ and you." Janet made the right choice; she chose Christ and was baptized. Once she was baptized into Christ, she was delivered from the demonic harassments, never to be annoyed again.

APPEAL:

Maybe you are like Janet—an honest seeker. Perhaps while in search for truth, you have delved into the occult and dabbled into areas that you now know are of the devil. You long to be free but do not know how to free yourself. Jesus is your answer. He cleansed the lepers, delivered the oppressed, and cast out demons from those victims of possession.

Do you long to be set free? Christ said, "If the Son therefore shall make you free, ye shall be free indeed" (John 8:36). Will you turn to Him? He has the power to break the shackles of the evil one. Only in Christ will you find deliverance. Will you accept Him now? Will you raise your hand toward heaven and say, "Lord Jesus, I want to be free." Will you come to Him now? Listen! There is no question that the foe is strong. But "greater is He that is in you, than he that is in the world" (1 John 4:4).

Remember that the Lord promises us that we "can do all things through Christ" (Philippians 4:13) who strengthens us. Why not then turn to the Savior? He has promised to save you to the uttermost. Will you accept Him now?

JANE—BEING OPPRESSED

Jane had been happily taking Bible studies. Oh, how she looked forward to learning all that she could concerning the prophecies. God marvelously unfolded the future in a way she never imagined. All went well until she began to sense that knowledge brought responsibilities. It was not enough to know. There seemed to be a dawning realization that she must live in harmony with what she now knew; however, she was not inclined to do this.

Finding fault with the church's simple worship service, she stated that she preferred to find a church "filled with the Spirit." Her sister happened to attend such a church, so Jane decided to attend. During the service, she saw the people caught up with a Spirit that she had not encountered in her Catholic services. As she saw the people seemingly enraptured with holy joy, she began to feel left out. Worried that she was missing something, she approached the pastor with the complaint.

Then it happened. The pastor told her to kneel down. While facing him, he hit her with the palm of his hand on her forehead. Jane fell back and began rolling around the church. This uncontrolled rolling frightened her. When whatever possessed her, ceased rolling her around, she rushed to the pastor for help. The pastor told her she was oppressed and needed to be delivered. Taking her to a back room, the elders of the church surrounded her. They all began to talk in a strange way. She felt eerie, so she opened her eyes to see what was happening. Horrified at seeing demons instead of people surrounding her, she got off her knees and bolted out of the church.

By the time she arrived home, she felt hungry. Fetching food from the refrigerator, she sat at the dining table and began to eat. While sitting, something shoved her off her chair. Feeling terrified and not knowing what to do, she went to her bedroom and laid down on the bed. As she was lying down, she felt something pulling her legs. Springing off the bed, she knelt and tried to pray. Again, something shoved her off her knees. She then grabbed the telephone, called the pastor, who had been studying with her, and asked for help. She begged to see him. By the time she arrived at the pastor's home, she was frantic.

After revealing all that had just recently transpired, she asked, "What's happening to me? Am I going crazy?" "No," responded the pastor, "you have become possessed." "No!" She cried, "What must I do?" "Repent from your unwillingness to live in harmony with God's will. Confess your sins, and accept Him not just as Savior, but Lord of your life," the pastor told her. At this, Jane knelt down and with sorrow lamented her unwillingness to follow the light Jesus had given her. She determined to align her life in harmony with God's truth and was delivered.

APPEAL:

There is a real battle raging for the soul. Our only safety is in the protection of the Lord, but you must be willing to walk in harmony with the light that He sheds on your path. Jesus said, "Walk in the light while ye have the light, lest darkness come upon ye." Oh, friend, is there something holding you back from accepting the light heaven has been pleased to give you? Either you are in the Lord's tender protection or the tyrannical control of the enemy. Are you willing to walk in that light? Will you lift up your hand to heaven saying in your heart, "I want to serve only you Lord." Will you do that just now?

THE APPARITION AT THE DORM

During a week of prayer held in Palau Mission Academy in the Palauan Islands, something strange took place. After the speaker made his presentation on the second night, the students went to retire in their respective dorms. The boys' dorm was above the girls' in the same building. As the girls were getting ready for bed, an old woman dressed in white appeared. Frightened at the sight, the girls began to scream. The boys upstairs laughed at the silly girls' cries.

The following morning, none of the girls were awake enough to study seeing they spent the night petrified of the apparition. The following evening the pastor spoke again, and once more the students went to their respective dorms. This time the pastor's wife stayed with the girls through the night. While it was quiet in the girls' dorm, that was not the case with the boys. Yelling and screaming erupted from the boys' location—this time the apparition appeared to them.

This was very troubling to the school. The next night, the pastor's wife once again slept with the girls, while the pastor slept with the boys. The following morning the pastor met with the student body and announced to them that this evil presence was present because someone was either knowingly inviting it or inadvertently inviting it. So he suggested that a fifty-gallon drum be placed outside the dorm, and anyone who had something they knew needed to be discarded should do so.

Opportunity was given to the students to surrender willingly whatever items or relics might be held that Satan could claim as his. One by one, the students disappeared into the dorms and appeared with all manner of cultic artifacts. Eight balls (supposedly able to give answers to the tests), rock-n-roll records, drugs, and other symbols of witchcraft were brought. Each dispensed their items into the barrel.

Then a prayer was offered, and gasoline was poured into the barrel and ignited. Up in smoke it all went, ascending toward heaven as a sweet incense. After this, a great revival took place, and many of the students committed their lives to Christ.

APPEAL:

Have you been harassed by apparitions? Do strange things happen in your home? Do weird things that take place in your dwelling frighten you? Could it be that unknowingly you have substances in your home that are inviting evil presences? Are there times that a paralysis hovers over you when you sense an evil presence, and though you try to cry out or call for help, you can't?

There is only One power that can overcome this influence. That is the presence of the only One who conquered the devil. That is Christ! Do you want deliverance? Christ can free you. But you must come to Him. Only through Jesus can you find power to overcome the evil one. Do you want peace in your heart and home? Are you anxious to divest yourself of the fears that come from evil presences? Then come to Christ. Will you come to Him now?

NEW AGER

Anne's phone rang. It was her niece who had just attended a spiritual emphasis weekend for youth. She was weeping with joy over what she had just experienced in her life. While at the meeting, she had experienced a conversion. Elated with her encounter with Christ, she thought she would call her auntie and appeal to her to turn her life to Christ. Anne became enraged. She was into the New Age movement, and was quite steeped in it. Incensed that her closest niece had been brainwashed, she tried to dissuade her, but to no avail. After failing to persuade her to reconsider, she hung up the phone.

Anne had grown up as a Christian but had turned away from Christianity feeling frustrated about its control over her life. There were things she wanted to do but couldn't because of the perceived pressures from others. Never having experienced conversion herself, or the power of Christ in her life, she went seeking for something else. So she became deeply entrenched in the New Age movement and became an ardent advocate of it.

The appeals of her concerned niece troubled her, and they kept ringing in her ears. When she got home, she was still distraught. In her anger she tried to shake the conviction she felt from her niece's words, which angered her more. She could not sleep. Desiring to distract herself from her thoughts, she decided to find something to read. Turning to her night stand next to her bed, she opened the drawer and checked to see what she had to read. To her surprise, there was a book there entitled *Steps to Christ*. She tried to recall where this thing came from. How did it get in her drawer?

She decided to open it and begin reading. As she got into the book, the conviction intensified. She wanted to lay the book aside but felt an overwhelming drive to continue. As she read of Christ and his matchless love, she began to weep. By the time morning dawned, Anne could resist no longer.

Yielding to her niece's appeals, Ann slipped over the edge of her bed and decided to fight no more—she knelt and invited the Lord into her life. What a peace came over her—a peace she had never previously experienced. Rejoicing over her conversion, she went to her library and throughout her home, gathered everything she had from the New Age, and cast it in the garbage.

That same morning she had an appointment with some of her practitioner friends. They were supposed to have a session in her home. When they arrived at her door and knocked, she opened it, and they were taken aback. Something was different about her. She invited them to enter for she had something wonderful to share with them.

Feeling tremendously uncomfortable with her presence, they refused. Then sensing that they would not accept her invitation, she told them about her newfound faith in Jesus Christ. They could not retreat fast enough. They left fearing fleeing from a power they had never encountered, and one that generated fear in them.

APPEAL:

There are those that can relate to Anne's experience. Perhaps like she, you have never experienced the converting power of Christ in your life, so you have gone searching. As you have heard the testimony of this woman, you, like she, are sensing an overwhelming power appealing to your heart to give yourself to Christ.

My friend, there is nothing like the drawing power of the love of Christ to change your heart. Yes, magical power pervades all of these practices for they stem from the great enemy of Christ.

But there is no power to bring peace into your life—no power to change your heart like the power of Jesus.

Have you been resisting the drawing power of the love of Christ? Yet, deep inside you know there is none like Him. Why not do as Anne did? Why not just slip to your knees and yield your heart to Him? Though you have wandered far away from Him, He will receive you. Will you do that just now? Will you allow Him to change you?

Chapter 24

CHOOSING TO BE OBEDIENT
LAW AND GRACE

FATHER TAKING SON'S PLACE

It was July 1794. The dungeons of Paris were crowded with men and women destined for the guillotine. On one particular night, an old gentleman who had just been taken there that day, began to roam and look at all who were there. As he was looking, he couldn't believe what he saw. He came across a young man who looked very, very familiar. Sure enough, as he got close to the sleeping young man, it was his own son.

He thought about the terrible ordeal that lay before each of them. "How can I help my boy escape this terrible ordeal?" He thought and thought as he sat by his sleeping boy. "Ah, I know what I'll do! When they call his name, I'll answer." They both had the same name.

He sat by his son until early the next morning when three soldiers came and called out the name. The father said, "Here I am." "Well, come this way." They took him out past a soldier who was recording the names and who called out his name, Jean Simone, and he said, "That's me." "Age 37?" He said, "Nope, 73." To this the soldier muttered, "Eh, stupid mistake," and made the correction. The old man then was taken to the guillotine where he died.

When the son woke up, he wondered how come they hadn't come for him. He waited and waited, and no one came. Finally, someone approached him and said, "There was an old man who was sitting by you last night. He sat there and when they called your name, he responded and went to his death for you." It was only three days later that the ringleader Robespierre of the great Reign of Terror was himself taken to the guillotine, bringing his reign to an end. That young man was able to walk out alive, owing his life to the one who was willing to take his place.

APPEAL:

That reminds me of our Savior, Jesus Christ. What do you say? He was willing to die and take your place and my place on the Cross of Calvary. Are you willing to give your life to Him? Are you willing at this time to give your heart to Him? He gave His all for you. He longs to save you, if you would have Him? Will you respond to Him now?

LAW AND JUSTICE

In a discussion about keeping the Ten Commandments, a man commented, "I've done pretty well. I think I deserve a passing grade." That sounds fine, but what is a passing grade? In school, it is about seventy percent. Does that mean that if we keep seven out of the Ten Commandments, we pass? I doubt it. Most people who are in jail have obeyed seventy percent of the laws. It's the one law they broke that got them into trouble.[42]

APPEAL:

Is it enough just to obey seventy percent? The apostle James says, "If we keep nine yet break one, we are guilty of breaking all" (James 2:10-12). Is it your desire to follow all that the Lord has commanded you? Oh, why not give your total allegiance to Christ? Will you respond to His calling today? He is asking you for a total consecration, not part. He gave His all for you. Will you give your all to Him? Will you respond by lifting your hand (standing, etc.)?

A MOTHER ABANDONED BY HER HUSBAND

Elsa and her husband had six children: one girl and five boys. They were very poor, living in a shanty. This woman's best friend

---

42. Albert P. Stauderman, *Let Me Illustrate*, 113.

did not have anywhere to stay. So the mother, feeling sorry for her, invited her to come and stay in their already tight quarters. The woman was so grateful to her. However, before long that woman began to be interested in Elsa's husband. The mother didn't realize it. Sad to say, the day did come when the father abandoned the family for the woman.

Elsa was heartbroken. Betrayed and abandoned, poor and destitute, she was left with six children, and to think that that's the way her friend repaid her kindness. She cursed that woman and prayed that God would visit her with cruelty wherever she might be. Not long after, the little girl became gravely ill. Due to the impoverished conditions, the mother could find no help, and the little girl died. Again, with hot bitter tears that mother cursed the woman. Oh, she was filled with rancor and hate.

Elsa married another man. In a short time another boy was born. The new husband decided to take the family to New York City. There they could begin a new life. Only able to afford the trip for three of the children, the man returned back to his country to earn enough to have the entire family together.

Misfortune struck again. In a few months the mother received a telegram announcing the death of her husband. Again Elsa bemoaned her life. Bereft of her husband, three children on the other side of the ocean, the miserable living conditions, the sufferings, and bitter lot brought to bear by the cursed woman. "Oh, my God, curse that woman wherever she is," was her hurtful cry.

Finally, she became very sick, developed cancer, and was told that she was going to die. She begged God for mercy and to allow her to live to see her children raised. She lived, but even though God answered her prayers, she still could not forget. She could not forget the fact that she was in her dire situation because of the treachery of that friend.

Meanwhile, the father had gone to Chicago with the second woman. There he forsook her and found another one named Lolita. Soon after he found the third, she began to study the Bible. He liked to dance, drink, and live a riotous life, but Lolita began to change. She encouraged him to help her with her studies, so he did. Before long, he too began to change. The grace of God converted him. In the end, both Lolita and the father gave up their sinful ways and were baptized. Then he confessed to Lolita the fact that he had left six children, and now he was convicted that he had to make things right. Oh, thank God for His grace.

They both left Chicago and returned to New York to find those children. But the children were now in their adolescent years, and they had no interest in Dad. In fact, they tried to do everything they could to get rid of him. He would visit and talk about religion. But they remembered their mother's words: "That man, not even God himself, can forgive him for what he has done." Those boys thought, "Now that he's old, he's afraid he's going to die, and he has to find some way to salve his conscience."

The father kept witnessing. It took ten years before he would see any results for his efforts. God's grace began to work. One of the boys became a Christian. He was baptized and began to witness to the other boys. Before long two of those other boys accepted the Lord and their lives changed. They left all the things that they were doing and before long two other boys turned their lives to God. God's grace was working, pulling them out of drugs, out of gangs, and out of evil.

Elsa was still bitter. She still didn't like that old man that came around her home. She despised him even more because the children were changing and were becoming like him. She couldn't stand that. She fought it, but it wasn't long before God's grace began to work on her heart. One time there was an evangelistic meeting being held. Ron Halverson, an evangelist, was preaching and made a call, and what do you suppose? That dear mother and one other boy went forward on the altar call and gave their hearts to Christ. They accepted the same religion that father had. But how could it be? God's grace!

Lastly, just to let you see what God's grace can do, two of the boys became preachers. One day, one of the boys was scheduled to preach in Chicago. The oldest of the brothers happened to live in Chicago. On one occasion, while knocking on doors, he found his first stepmother. When he knew that his brother was going to preach in Chicago, he invited the woman to the church, and at the same time, he invited Mother to listen to her boy preach for the first time. Elsa, of course, wanted to be there, so she traveled from New York to Chicago.

On the morning of the service, the other boy disappeared and went to get that lady, never telling Mother what he was planning. While Elsa was standing in the foyer, in walked the woman. The first person she saw was her old friend, and she turned pale. She couldn't believe it! They recognized each other.

Thirty years had passed, but that woman's face had been engraved in the mother's heart. She could never forget her. Now was her chance to get back. The woman froze, expecting the mother to lash out at her. But the mother had been changed by God's grace. She stretched out her arms, and with tears streaming down her face, embraced the woman and kissed her. Friends, only God's grace can do that. What do you say? Only God's grace can do that.

ADDENDUM:

When the older brother's daughter was getting married, he decided to invite all of the family: Dad and his new wife, that woman and the two girls that were a result of the second relationship, and Mother with all her kids. That's faith, isn't it?

Elsa, one of the girls, the dad, as well as all the boys attended. What a joy it was to see the mother walking hand in hand with the girl as though they were mother and daughter. I can tell you, friends, only God's grace can do that.

I know the story well because that's my mother and my father, and it's because God's grace reached my dad's heart that I'm a preacher of righteousness today. It's because of God's grace transforming my father, my mother, changing my brother, changing my own life that I stand before you today. I couldn't stand before you, friends, and talk about these things if I thought that it was not possible for a man to change.

APPEAL:

Oh, friend, do you have bitterness in your heart? Is there someone who wounded you that you have not been able to forgive? God's grace can give you the power. Is there a sin in your life that has such a grip on you that you have not been able to overcome? God offers His abundant grace. Have you felt that it is hard to live in harmony with God's law?

God's grace can enable you. Will you accept His grace? Will you give him your weakness? Will you come to Him just now?

OR:

We, as humans, struggle with all sorts of things. Some of us are black and racists, just as some whites are racists. You know what I'm talking about? You don't mind if I talk frankly with you, do you? Some of us have bad tempers. Some of us have drinking problems. Some of us have lust. Some of us have dirty minds. Some of us have all sorts of problems that we don't want to share with anybody. We lack faith. We think we can't accomplish anything. We have inferiority complexes; we're never any good. We can't reach to any great attainments.

Friends, I'd like to tell you, God's grace is sufficient for you. God's grace will empower you to obey God's law. Oh, sinner, weak as you are, God will strengthen you! Drunkard, you who have a problem with alcohol, God can take it away. I know. One day I committed my life to Christ (I know God works in different ways, and I know that God doesn't do this for everyone), and since then, I have had no more desire for drink, marijuana, smoking, etc. Now I know that I serve a God who can make miracles. I know that and I'm preaching to you of hope, a message of courage, a message that you can accept because God's grace is sufficient for you.

Yes, the Scriptures declare that "sin abounded, grace did much more abound" (Romans 5:20). Grace is more powerful than sin. Thank God! What do you say?

Oh, I can tell you story after story. I remember a young girl who was a drug addict; in fact, she got hepatitis from a contaminated needle. She came to our home. We studied with her, and the girl changed. Today, she's a worker for God.

I can tell you about another girl who was 19 years old and a prostitute—sold her body to get drugs. She was brought to our home, and we prayed with her. We studied the Word of God with her. God's grace reached her. She's married today and settled.

Thieves and robbers become honest people. People who have impure thoughts become pure. God's grace, friends, is still working today—it didn't stop there on Calvary. But we must take advantage of God's grace.

I wonder tonight. I wonder if there's anyone here who can relate to what has been presented. In your heart you recognize that you've tried—you've struggled against sin. You've tried to overcome, you've tried to do this, and do that. You feel as if you are sinking in quicksand, going in deeper all the time. Tonight, there's a glimmer of hope as you see that God can do great things, but your faith is not strong. Maybe like the man in the Bible who came to Jesus, you'd like to say, "Lord, I believe; help thou mine unbelief" (Mark 9:24). Friend, if you do that, God will never turn you away. But you must come to God. Give your heart to Him and say, "God, I want Your grace."

BIG TOM AND LITTLE JIM—THE UNRULY SCHOOL

George Brown had come to fill the vacancy created when the teacher had left because the behavior of the students had become too tough for him to handle. As Mr. Brown stood at the table that served as a desk in the front of the room, he looked the students straight in the eyes. Hank Landeen, a husky boy of 18, whispered to the boys across the aisle, "I won't need any help; I can lick him myself."

"Good morning students," Mr. Brown greeted the group. The response was glares, giggles, and malicious glances. "I want this to be a good school," but his remarks were interrupted with yelling from the students. When they quieted down, Hank shouted, "But what, teacher?" "But it won't be a good school unless you help me. Perhaps we should have a few rules. You tell me what rules we should have, and I will write them on the blackboard."

One boy called out, "No stealing!" Another shouted, "On time!" In a few minutes there were ten rules on the blackboard. "These rules will be no good unless there is a penalty for breaking them," said the teacher. "What shall we do with one who breaks any of them?" "Beat him across the back ten times without his coat," one of the boys called out. "That is very severe. Are you ready to stand by it?" asked Mr. Brown.

There was another yell, and Mr. Brown said, "School now comes to order." George Brown had made a wise beginning in this mountain school. There on the board were the boys' own rules, followed by the penalty that they had recommended.

Day after day went by until the cold winds of late fall whipped around the hills. School had been in session for about a month under the new teacher. He hadn't taken the beating that the president of the school board had been so sure he would get.

Then one day in November, Big Tom found that his dinner had been stolen. He let it be known in loud tones. There on the blackboard the first rule stood, "No stealing," and beneath it the penalty stipulated, "To be beaten ten times across the back without wearing a coat."

Throughout the noon recess, the afternoon, and after school, Mr. Brown tried to discover who had stolen Big Tom's dinner. The following morning he announced the thief had been found, and he must be punished according their rule—ten stripes across the back.

"Jim, come to my desk." A hungry little boy of ten years came slowly forward, trembling from head to toe. The coat he wore was much too large and was fastened up to his neck. "Please sir," he pleaded, "you may lick me as hard as you like, but please don't make me take my coat off." "Sorry, Jim, you helped make the rules," was Mr. Brown's reply. "Take the coat off." "Please, Sir! Don't make me!" "You must!" Jim began unfastening the coat. When it dropped from his shoulders, the teacher saw that the boy's body was bare except for his trousers and the two strings over his shoulders that held up the trousers. His body was so thin that his bones seem to be covered only with skin with no flesh beneath.

To himself Mr. Brown was saying, "How can I whip this poor hungry child? But I must do something to hold the school together." Aloud he said, "Jim, why aren't you wearing a shirt?" "My father is dead," began the boy's story. "Mother is very poor. I have only one shirt, and Mother is washing it today. I borrowed my brother's coat to keep warm."

Mr. Brown raised the rod slowly, hoping that something would prevent him from using it on this poor little child of the hills. At that moment, Big Tom jumped to his feet and said, "Sir, if you don't object, I will take Jim's beating for him." Mr. Brown's hand came slowly down. Then to the students he said, "There is a law which says that one man can substitute for another. Are you agreed?"

Off came Tom's coat, but after five hard strokes the rod broke. Mr. Brown bowed his head in his hands and thought, "How can I finish this awful task?" When he raised his head, he saw that all the students were sobbing. Little Jim was standing in front of Big Tom with both arms about his neck. "Tom, I so sorry I stole your dinner, truly I am. I was very hungry. Tom, I'll love you till I die for taking my beating for me." [43]

APPEAL:

Back long ago, Jesus knew that you and I would break all the rules, and that according to that law, we would deserve severe punishment. But there on that cross, He took the beating for us. "Christ was treated as we deserve, that we might be treated as He deserves. He was condemned for our sins, in which He had no share, that we might be justified by His righteousness, in which we had no share. He suffered the death which was ours, that we might receive the life which was His. 'With His stripes we are healed.'"[44]

Oh, friend, will you love Him forever? Will you give your heart to Him now? He died that you might live. Will you accept that gift now? If that is your desire, will you accept His invitation? Will you stand?

ANYTHING THAT CAN BE BROKEN?

A college student discovered that he needed a Bible for a course and wrote home asking that his Bible be sent to him. His father wrapped it carefully and took it to the post office and mailed it to his son.

The postal clerk took the package and shook it. "Anything in here that can be broken?" he asked. "Only the Ten Commandments," the father replied.[45]

APPEAL:

Yes, the law can be broken. It was because of the broken law that Christ's heart was broken. And it was broken for you and for me. Oh, the love of the Savior! But the same One who died, lives

43. Elva B. Garner, *Junior Guide,* Vol. 4, No. 49; 3, 19, 22
44. E. G. White, *The Desire of Ages,* 25.
45. Albert P. Stauderman, *Let Me Illustrate*, 154.

in heaven for you. The Scriptures say, "He ever liveth to make intercession" (Hebrews 7:25) for you and me. He lives to atone for your sins and my sins, which are the transgression of that holy law. Is it your desire to heed the request of Christ—"If you love me, keep my commandments" (John 14:15). Is it your desire to keep those commandments? But you cannot keep them in your own strength. You must have Jesus living in your heart in order to be in harmony with His will. I ask you, will you accept Him now? Just raise your hands where you are!

RULES BY LOVE

A husband and wife didn't really love each other. The man was very demanding, so much so that he prepared a list of rules and regulations for his wife to follow. He insisted that she read them over every day and obey them to the letter. Among other things, his "do's and don'ts" indicated such details as what time she had to get up in the morning, when his breakfast should be served, and how the housework should be done. After several long years, the husband died.

As time passed, the woman fell in love with another man, one who dearly loved her. Soon they married. This husband did everything he could to make his new wife happy, continually showering her with tokens of his appreciation. One day when she was cleaning house, she found the list of commands her first husband had drawn up for her tucked away in a drawer.

As she looked it over, it dawned on her that even though her present husband hadn't given her any kind of list, she was doing everything her first husband's list required anyway. She realized she was so devoted to this man that her deepest desire was to please him out of love, not obligation.

APPEAL:

Yes, it is love that makes the commandments of God not grievous. When you love, you are not thinking how little you can do for your loved one. No, no! You are desirous of making that person happy. And so it is with the Lord. If you find yourself chafing at the law of the Lord, could it be that your love is not what it ought to be? Listen, "Great peace have they which love thy law: and nothing shall offend them" (Psalm 119:165). "O how love I thy law! It is my meditation all the day" (Psalm 119:97). Oh, friend, Jesus wants you to obey Him because you love Him.

Maybe you realize that you need greater love for the Lord and desire for Him to place greater love in your heart. If that is your desire, will you come to Him just now?

THOU SHALT NOT KILL

Angered by the presence of a sect in his Communist community, one man determined to do something about it. After getting his courage up, he purposed to carry out his scheme. Arming himself with two grenades, one in the left coat pocket and the other in the right, he left his home on Saturday morning.

Planning to wait until everyone was already inside the sanctuary, he lingered in the foyer. But latecomers continued to arrive. The pastor began preaching, and still more latecomers walked into the church. The homily's main text was, "Thou shalt not kill" (Exodus 20:13). The angry murderer was gripped by the message. Strangely, he forgot all about his purpose. Instead, a feeling of guilt began to creep over him as he stood and listened. Overwhelmed with conviction, he turned and left the church. As he walked over the Tirgu Mures River, he pulled out the grenades and threw them into the river.

Overcome with remorse, riddled with guilt, and bothered with a troubled conscience, he thought over the terrible atrocity he almost perpetrated. The text and message he heard that day kept ringing in his ears, "Thou shalt not kill." Not able to stand it any longer, he returned to the church and sought an audience with the speaker.

Amazed with what the visitor revealed of the confession of the would-be assassination, the pastor asked, "What stopped you?" "As I stood there listening to those words, they seemed to be like arrows piercing through my soul. I saw myself as a terrible lost man. I went home and began to consider my lost condition and realized that if it had not been for those words, I would have committed a crime for which I would never be able to forgive myself. I need forgiveness and a changed heart. Will God forgive me and accept me?"

APPEAL:

What about you tonight? As you have heard the Word of God, have you experienced conviction of your sinful life? Has there awakened in you a sense of things you have done that give you remorse? You have broken His law and desire to be at peace with Him. You want to turn from a life of sin and live in harmony with His divine law. Will you come to Him with your contrite heart?

Listen! God said, "Yea, I have loved thee with an everlasting love: therefore with loving-kindness have I drawn thee" (Jeremiah 33:3). Will you arise and say, "Oh, Lord, forgive me." Remember He has promised, "He that cometh to me, I will in no wise cast out" (John 6:37). Will you come? Will you humble yourself and surrender yourself to Him? Why not do it now?

THE KLEPTOMANIAC

One summer day as a woman was walking by a church, she heard through the opened window the words; "Thou shalt not steal!" Strangely, the words seemed to penetrate to the depths of her soul. She was a kleptomaniac. Never before had words made such an impression on her. Rushing home as if her dealings had become transparent to all she rushed inside. Before her, as if standing before the judgment, came all of the times she had stolen. But why was she feeling badly about it now. The words kept ringing in her ears, "Thou shalt not steal."

Unable to sleep, she decided to visit the church the following day in hope of relief. When she visited with the pastor and discovered it was his voice she heard, she told the story. Surprised and amazed at the woman's confession, he could not doubt but that it was not he, but God who had spoken to her. "If you want peace of heart," the pastor counseled, "you must make matters right." "But if I do," she responded, "I will probably spend a long time in jail." "God has spoken to you," the pastor replied, "Therefore, you will not have peace until you make restitution." With this, the woman left.

When at home, she began to calculate the amount she had taken through the years. Though fearful of the consequences, she made her way to the stores from which she had been stealing.

Surprised and shocked, the store owners listened as she unfolded her story—tracing her conviction to that walk by the church window. Greatly relieved that the loss from this astute thief had finally come to an end, they gladly pardoned her. Returning home greatly thankful, and at peace, the converted kleptomaniac realized God's great mercy and forgiveness.

APPEAL:

Perhaps you are not a kleptomaniac, but you can identify with her experience. As you have listened to the message the Lord has given to you, wrongful deeds and acts of God's violated law have been brought to your attention. With a troubled conscience, you long for peace. Why not turn to the Lord just now? Why not accept your guilt in the matter and beg God's forgiveness?

Remember, "if we confess our sins, He is faithful and just to forgive us our sins, and to cleanse us from all unrighteousness" (1 John 1:9). If you turn to Him in contrition, God will not only forgive you but also cleanse you. Do you long for peace? Will you come to Him? Will you raise your hand to Him, and accept His pardon? Will you do that just now?

UPHOLDING THE LAW

In the early days of Australia, during the British colonization stealing became a great problem. To stem the tide of such a problem, the governor ordered that the next person caught stealing would be punished with forty stripes on the back. This threat, seemed to work for awhile.

One day, it was reported that a perpetrator was apprehended in the act. The thief was locked in temporary confinement, and the next morning ushered before the governor to be punished. To the governor's amazement and chagrine, the offender was his aged mother. As he pondered his dilemma, he recognized that his frail mother would never survive the lashing. But what could he do? He knew full well that to deliver her without punishment would throw the law and state of things into chaos. Yet, he feared that to suffer her to be punished would be her end. The governor stepped off his bench, placed himself in her place, and took the forty stripes.

APPEAL:

As you and I stand before the Great Judge of the universe, the evidence declares us guilty. We have all violated God's holy law and deserve punishment. But your loving Savior knew that your frail, sinful condition could never tolerate the consequences of your sin. So, stepping down from his throne, He came to this earth to take what you and I deserve. Yes, He died that you may live. "He was wounded for our transgression, he was bruised for our iniquities: the chastisement of our peace was upon him; and with his stripes we are healed. All we like sheep have gone astray; we have turned every one to his own way; and the Lord hath laid on him the iniquity of us all" (Isaiah 53:5, 6).

Oh, friend, have you sinned? Do you deserve punishment? Remember! "The wages of sin is death" (Romans 6:23). But why will you die? Why not accept your loving Savior's offer to have his death pay for you? Will you come to Him by faith? Will you accept His offer? He died for you! But you cannot avail yourself of this offer unless you are willing to take Him as your Savior. Will you take Him now? Will you lift your hand toward heaven and by so doing, say, "Thank you Lord for taking my place. Here I am. I give myself to you." Will you do that just now?

Chapter 25

HONORING GOD'S SABBATH

Usually on the completion of this subject, I do not make a direct appeal, but rather an indirect one. I have found that people who hear this for the first time are not ready to make a decision in favor of keeping the Sabbath. If pushed to make a decision, because the keeping of it requires (for some) great changes, they may not have enough faith to decide in favor of it. In the pressure of the moment, they may feel forced to make a decision and opt to not respond. This may lead them to prematurely reject the message.

Therefore, I usually present the following scenario to show them the seriousness of the message without the pressure of having to make an immediate decision. This way, when they attend the meetings, they avail themselves with more faith-building messages that hopefully will increase their faith to the level that enables them to make the commitment.

AT THE JUDGMENT BAR

Let us suppose that you and I were taken to the judgment bar of heaven, and God were to ask us, "Why did you go to church on Saturday?" I would have to say, "Lord, in the beginning of Genesis, the first book of the Bible, You kept the first Sabbath on the seventh day. Then You gave Your Sabbath to Adam. After that, Noah, Abraham, Isaac, Jacob, and Joseph kept Your Sabbath. Then when You delivered the children of Israel out of Egypt, before You even wrote the Ten Commandments on stone, You gave them the same Sabbath. Then You pronounced the unchangeable nature of the Sabbath by inscribing it on stone to be a perpetual decree.

Moses kept it. The Israelites kept the same Sabbath for centuries. Even after they went into Babylon and after they returned to the land of Canaan, You instructed them to keep the Sabbath through Nehemiah, Your servant. Then You came, Lord, to this earth, and as Your custom was, You went to the synagogue on the Sabbath. Your disciples Matthew, Peter, John, and even Paul kept the same Sabbath that You gave them. Then in the book of Isaiah, You stated that the same Sabbath would be kept throughout eternity. Lord, that's why I kept the seventh day as the Sabbath."

APPEAL:

Now suppose God turns to you and asks, "Why did you go to church on Sunday, the first day of the week?" Who in the Bible will you turn to as your example? (Pause; then have a prayer and leave them with this provocative and haunting thought.)

A BUSINESSMAN'S SURPRISE

Steve attended an evangelistic series of meetings. Though his wife was a Sabbath-keeper, and faithful Christian; while respectful to her, Steve was preoccupied running his business. While at the meetings, he heard a stirring message on the importance of Sabbath-keeping. Though deeply impressed with the soundness and logic of the message, Steve could not see his way to obey this commandment. Surely the Lord can overlook the negligence of one. But the text rang clearly in his ears: "For whosoever shall keep the whole law, and yet offend in one point, he is guilty of all" (James 2:10).

How in the world would it be possible to keep the Sabbath? The recent typhoon had wreaked havoc on his boats, storage garage, and equipment. He was having problems paying his creditors, and to keep the Sabbath would demand canceling thirteen contracts with the beach hotels that rented his sports equipment—his bread and butter. This move would cause his financial demise, or so he thought. But conviction lingered, so he decided to speak with the evangelist.

One day, the evangelist visited him at his office. Steve presented his ordeal and insurmountable challenges. After listening, the speaker responded, "If you will put your trust in God, He will never let you down. God has promised, and he will be true to his word." "But it will take me some time to get out of the contracts," Steve replied, "First, I need to make sure that I can get some other company to fill my place. I don't think it would be right just to drop my customers without providing them a back up."

Nevertheless, Steve decided to place his trust in the word of the preacher, so he went ahead and was baptized. Steve was amazed by what happened next. He was able to get out of his contracts that had weekend obligations. Then, in keeping with the commandment, he kept the Sabbath.

Two years later, Steve called the pastor and said, "I took you at your word and everything you said was true. Prior to my commitment to God, I could never keep up with my debts. In the last two years I have paid off more than two million dollars. My business is secure, and I am far better financially set than in all my previous business experience. Thank you, pastor, for encouraging me to trust in the Lord. He is faithful."

APPEAL:

Perhaps you are troubled and concerned just like Steve. But listen, Jesus said, "And every one that hath forsaken houses, or brethren, or sisters, or father, or mother, or wife, or children, or lands, for my name's sake, shall receive an hundredfold, and shall inherit everlasting life" (Matthew 19:29). Oh, friend, it takes faith and trust to follow your Lord but it is worth it. Who here would take a step forward in faith and say, "Yes Lord, I will obey and trust you." Will you raise your hand just where you are?

GOVERNOR ETPISON

Governor Etpison of Palau had just received a letter from his former pastor. The pastor wrote that in a dream he was shown that the governor would become president of his island nation. This brought great concern to the perplexed governor. "If I become president, how will I be able to keep the Sabbath?" He wondered.

Troubled over the certain future reality, he continued to pray and wonder how he could keep the Lord's Sabbath. Finally, in his devotional time, it finally struck him: "If I become president, I can set my own schedule." At last peace came over him.

The dream did come true, and Governor Etpison did become president. As his custom was, he went to church on the Sabbath. At his funeral, the succeeding president testified concerning the witness Etpison bore of his faithfulness to his faith in the Lord. In all of his presidential tenure, Etpison never veered away from his commitment to keep God's Sabbath.

APPEAL:

Yes, you may be concerned about your future if you decide to step out in faith and keep God's holy Sabbath. Like President Etpison, you may be struggling with the quandary as to how to follow God in obedience and survive financially. My friend, the Lord, says, "Seek ye first the kingdom of God and all these things shall be added unto you" (Matthew 6:33). Will you step out in faith? Remember He said, "If you love me, keep my commandments" (John 14:15). Will you, like President Etpison, struggle with your God over how you will obey Him? Who here needs prayer for strength over this? Will you raise your hand?

STOREOWNER

A storeowner was enjoying attending the prophecy seminars held in the tent. Every night she sat in the front row enraptured by the presentations. She had never heard anything like it. Then one night she heard a topic that troubled her; nonetheless, she continued to attend. She believed everything she heard, for it came from the Bible.

One day the speaker visited her in her store. "Now is the opportunity to ask about that troubling subject," she thought. "I am confused. Which day is the Sabbath day?" The pastor asked if she had a Bible. She happened to have one under the counter. However, she cautioned that it was her late husband's Catholic Bible. "That's fine," encouraged the pastor. Then turning to Luke 23:54-57, and 24:1-2, she read for herself the answer to her question.

"Oh, I have been wrong all this time. I need to try and close my store on the Sabbath." Then correcting herself, she said, "No! I need not try. I must close my store on God's Sabbath and somehow God will take care of me." Not only did she decide to keep the Sabbath, but to demonstrate her faith in God, the following Sabbath, not only did she close the store, she was also baptized.

APPEAL:

It takes faith to step out and make a decision like that. But perhaps you are thinking, how can I do that? Friend, there is only one way. That is to do as the storeowner did. She decided not to try, but to do it. The Bible says, "Not the hearers of the law are just before God, but the doers of the law shall be justified" (Romans 2:13). Oh, friend, do you want to stand justified before the Lord? I know this is a big decision, but if God has brought you to it today, He will bring you through it. Will you say yes to the Lord? If that is your decision, will you stand?

IT'S MY OWN CONVICTION

During the 1970s, Salem Farag worked as the director of public health for Governor Jerry Brown in California. One Sabbath morning, just as the family was getting into the car to go to church, the phone rang. Salem was hesitant to answer it, but then thinking it might be someone from the church he went back inside and answered the phone. On the other end was Governor Brown asking him to attend an emergency meeting right away. Salem's heart sank as he explained to Governor Brown that he would not be able to participate as he was just leaving for church.

"Don't worry," Brown told him, "I'll write a note for your bishop or priest, I am sure he'll understand. This is a very important meeting, and we need you here." Mr. Farag then explained that he didn't attend church for his pastor or priest. It was his own convictions and beliefs, and he would not be able to go to the meeting. After a long pause on the line, the governor said, "Okay," and hung up. Salem returned to the car where his wife and three little girls were waiting and told them that he would most likely not have a job when he went to work Monday morning.

Monday morning arrived and Salem went to the morning meeting. He fully expected to have to look for a new job to support his family because of the decision he made to keep the Sabbath. He sat down next to a coworker who was a Jew. "Where were you on Saturday?" the man asked, "We really needed you at that meeting!" Salem replied, "I was at church. Why weren't you at the synagogue?" "You're right," the man said. "I should have gone."

As the meeting was getting started, Governor Brown looked over at his secretary and said, "Make a note that we will never call Dr. Farag in on a Saturday again." That was all that was ever said about the incident.

APPEAL:

What the world needs today are women and men "who will not be bought or sold, who in their inmost souls are true and honest, men and women who do not fear to call sin by its right name, whose conscience is as true to duty as the needle to the pole, who will stand for the right though the heavens fall."[46] Oh, friend, are you that kind of man or woman? Is your love for God and His truth more important to you than your job or profession? Are your convictions about the Sabbath stronger than the consequences you fear? Who here will stand and say, "Lord, I love You more than these. I want to be true to You. Whatever the cost, I choose to serve You." If that is your decision, will you stand?

I WONDERED WHY

Larry and his wife were invited by a visiting couple to attend a series of Bible lectures on prophecy. Because of their fondness for the couple, they graciously accepted the invitation. They gained so much from the first presentation that they decided to attend every night. From night to night, they were enthralled with what they heard. The Scriptures came alive for them. Larry was the professor and choir director for the local college. He was also the choir leader for a prestigious church in town. But he admitted he had never learned as much in all his years of church attendance as he learned in a few short weeks at this series of meetings.

One evening, the speaker visited with Larry and his wife in their home. After the usual getting acquainted, the evangelist asked if they had any questions that needed some clarity from the presentations made during the meetings. "No," Larry said, "it is all so clear. You see, when I was young, I was raised Lutheran. In our church we would have Bible competitions. So I read and read through the Bible to win the competitions. However, I noticed that throughout the Scriptures, it says, the Sabbath, the Sabbath, the

46 E. G. White, *Eduction,* 57.

Sabbath. So, I went to my pastor and asked, "Why do we go to church on Sunday when the Bible says the Sabbath?" The pastor simply told me it was because Jesus was resurrected on Sunday.

Larry then shared that though he accepted the answer, he still felt unsure that this was completely satisfactory. Though not completely satisfied, he did not question his pastor. But for years, though he wondered at the discrepancy, he continued his Sunday-keeping. "Well," asked the pastor, "what do you think now?"

"Now," said Larry, "I completely see that God's day of rest is not Sunday but Saturday—the true Sabbath." "Is there anything that would keep you and your wife from obeying our Lord's command in honoring Him on His day?" asked the pastor. Then glancing at his wife, and looking back at the pastor, he said, "Nothing." Then his wife spoke, "I feel like I am coming home at last."

APPEAL:

Perhaps, you too have been given by others the usual reasons for Sunday-keeping but have not been satisfied. Something inside of you has led you to feel uncomfortable. You have not understood the reasons why; you just know that something has not been right. But as you have listened to the truths presented from the Word of God, like Larry and his wife, you too are convinced that God's Sabbath is not Sunday, but Saturday—God's true holy day. Like Larry's wife, you now feel that you are, "Coming home."

As the Lord speaks to your heart, and the question is posed, is there anything that would keep you from honoring your Lord on His day? What is your answer? Will you say like Larry's wife, "I feel like I am coming home!" Will you raise your hand at this moment, and by so doing signify your decision? Will you do that just now?

Chapter 26

CHOOSING GOD'S TRUE FAITH

TRUTH CARRIERS

"We are made a spectacle" (1 Corinthians 4:9). Throughout biblical history, God has kept His attention focused where His truth carriers were. The camera of heaven zoomed in on Enoch, and then Noah. Wherever Abraham dwelled, whether temporarily or permanently, the place of his sojourn or country is mentioned. From Canaan, his truth-carrying descendents went to Egypt. When God's children left Egypt, then wandering in the wilderness is mentioned. From there, the Bible records their wanderings until they settle in the Promised Land.. From the Holy Land, we are introduced into Babylon. Why? God's children were in exile there. There we find Daniel and the three worthies.

The Medes and the Persians then arrive on the scene. Finally after centuries, the Bible focuses on Jerusalem from where the Son of God—the true truth carrier—came. Then we are taken through the scattering of the disciples, and the varied kingdoms, nations, and towns where the disbursed believers made their influence. The countries they impacted are mentioned until we are brought to the wilderness of Revelation 12. From the wilderness, the truth was transported to America from which shores the gospel will be proclaimed to the world.

APPEAL:

Here we stand today. We are at the end of earth's history. All that the Holy Writ has described will take place concerning America has come to pinpoint, accurate fulfillment. We now face the remaining chapters of the role that the United States will play in the closing scenes of earth's history. God has raised up a people to proclaim the final warnings and to reveal to the world why there are so many different denominations. Simply put, He has his true faith.

God is calling you out of the multitude of faiths into the true one. His invitation is: "Come out of her, my people, that ye be not partakers of her sins, and that ye receive not of her plagues" (Revelation 18:4). Notice, He is calling you "My people." This invitation is now given to you. Will you heed His calling? Will you accept His invitation? Will you respond to Him now?

SUNDAY SCHOOL TEACHER

An evangelist was visiting a lady who had been a Sunday School teacher for fifty years. She had been attending his prophecy seminar. Her piety stood out. Her demeanor was saintly, and her walk with Christ quite obvious. As the pastor became acquainted with her, he discovered her ministry and burden. "How do you feel about what you have been hearing?" He asked. "Oh," she said, "it is wonderful to see how easy it is to understand the book of Revelation."

"Have you learned anything new?" questioned the visiting preacher. "Oh yes," she replied. "How do you feel about the Ten Commandments?" "Well," she responded, "I believe that any true Christian should obey all of them." "Then what about the Fourth Commandment? Do you believe it should be kept by Christians today?" "Oh yes," she answered. "Then why are you still observing Sunday?" the speaker inquired.

"Well, you see," she said, "I have been teaching the children in Sunday School the truth about God's holy day. But I have met some resistance from parents who do not want me to teach their children about the Sabbath. Some have already removed their children from my class and will not allow them to return. I can't understand why people choose to avoid knowing what Jesus wants to reveal to them. It makes me grieve over the determined effort to shut out the light that heaven bestows."

Then the preacher asked a troubling question. "Have you ever thought that you were doing your children more harm than good?" "What do you mean?" the surprised woman questioned. "Jesus said in His Word, 'For not the hearers of the law are just before

God, but the doers of the law shall be justified' (Romans 2:13). The apostle James wrote, 'But be ye doers of the word, and not hearers only, deceiving your own selves' (James 1:22). By your teaching them the truth and not practicing it, you are teaching the children by your example that it is not important to obey the Lord. You can know the Lord's will, but you do not have to comply with it. Is this the lesson you want to teach your children?" "Oh no!" she exclaimed, "I did not realize I was doing that." "Then why not step out in faith and decide not only to be a hearer, but a doer of the Word of God?" requested the preacher.

"Alright," she said. So that night she entered the watery grave of baptism and publicly declared herself among those who keep the commandments of God and have the faith of Jesus.

APPEAL:

Yes, Jesus said, "If you love me, keep my commandments" (John 14:15). Love for God removes all fears of whatever consequences the enemy may be placing in your heart right now. Jesus declared, "He that loveth father or mother more than me is not worthy of me: and he that loveth son or daughter more than me is not worthy of me. And he that taketh not his cross, and followeth after me, is not worthy of me" (Matthew 10:37, 38). Yes, it is possible that we place our church, friendship, or even family above the Lord? Remember the words of Christ:

There is no man that hath left house, or brethren, or sisters, or father, or mother, or wife, or children, or lands, for my sake, and the gospel's, but he shall receive an hundredfold now in this time, houses, and brethren, and sisters, and mothers, and children, and lands, with persecutions; and in the world to come eternal life. (Mark 10: 29, 30)

It may be a hard decision for you. But remember, Jesus left the glories of heaven for you. What will you give for Jesus? Is it your desire to take up your cross and follow Him? Who here will raise your hand to heaven and say, "Lord, I will follow you?" Will you do it just now?

Chapter 27

THE BIBLE

THE WIDOW AND THE SKEPTIC

One day there was a skeptic in Piccadilly Circus, London, denouncing faith and God. A crowd had gathered to listen to him. At the conclusion of his speech, he dared anyone to come forward and debate him. He had a commanding appearance and was quite apt in speech, so no one was willing to take his challenge. Finally, after repeated dares, an old widow pressed to the front from the back of the crowd.

"Mister," she said, "I have something to say." "Say on," the skeptic answered confidently. "When I was a young wife, my husband died and left me with eight children. I did not know what to do. All I had was this Bible. So I took it and read it. I prayed to the God of the Bible. It gave me hope and comfort. Not one day passed that I did not pray and ask for His provisions and strength. Through His help, I was able to raise my children. Today, all are well. Now I am old and do not have long to live. But I am so happy and so thankful for all His has done. That's what my belief has done for me."

"Now tell me, what has your unbelief done for you?" The skeptic was speechless.

APPEAL:

God has given you this book—this sacred book. In it are the words of life. They are also the words of destiny. Will you take it as the inspired Word of God? Will you accept it as God's Holy oracles? Jesus said, "It is the spirit that quickeneth; the flesh profiteth nothing: the words that I speak unto you, they are spirit, and they are life" (John 6:63). Through this Word we are sanctified or made holy. Will you now accept His Holy Word tonight? Would you now make it the rule of your life? What is your choice tonight? Will you lift your hands to heaven, and say, "Oh, Lord, I believe in Your Word and accept it as Your divine counsel"?

THE CONVERTED CONVICT

A certain man had been sentenced to prison. He vowed that he would get even with the attorney who prosecuted him.

One day, news came to the family of the attorney that the man had escaped. One evening, the mother and wife of the attorney were alone at home when it came time for evening worship. They sat at the kitchen table and read passages from the Bible. Then they prayed for the attorney's safety and for the man who had escaped. They made sure that the doors and windows were all secure and went to sleep. Later on that night the attorney got home, checked all the doors, and went to bed.

Next morning, when the ladies went to make breakfast, they found the Bible they had left on the table missing and a dagger left in its place. They were sure that before they went to bed all the doors and windows were secured. Where did the Bible go, and where did the dagger come from?

Later on, war broke out in that country, and the attorney was called into its armed forces. In one of the battles, there were many left dead. The attorney, now turned captain, was seriously wounded and left for dead. The day after the battle, a fisherman happened to go to the battlefield strewn with the dead when he heard the sound of someone moaning.

It was the captain. Feeling compassion for the wounded man, the fisherman dressed the wounds and carried him home. Several days passed, and the captain finally regained consciousness. The fisherman sent a message to the wife to come and fetch her husband. Upon the day of departure after the wife had arrived to take him home, the captain offered to pay the fisherman.

"No," the fisherman said, "you have already paid me more than you know." "I have not given you a cent," replied the captain. "You don't recognize me?" asked the fisherman. "No," responded the captain." "I am the man who swore I would kill you. One night I slipped into your home. While I was hiding, I heard your wife and mother read from a strange book, and then they prayed for me. I was captivated by what I heard. I had to have that book. So, when the ladies went to bed, I took the Bible and left the knife as payment for it. I read it, and it changed my entire life. You have paid me far more than I could ever repay you."

APPEAL:

The Lord said, "Is not my word like as a fire? saith the LORD; and like a hammer that breaketh the rock in pieces?" (Jeremiah 23:29). Oh, how many go on in their lives aimlessly without a compass? Perhaps, in your own wisdom, you have done the best that you could, but you realize that human wisdom is not sufficient to meet the challenges of life. Here, in this book (hold up the Bible), you find an unerring guide. Many great men have found this Book to be the answer to all of their unsatisfied questions. Will you accept it as your guide—your source of strength—your comfort in trouble—your source of wisdom for all your perplexities? Will you stand, and by standing signify your longing, desire, and acceptance? Will you stand just now?

THE LIGHTHOUSE AND THE NAVY

October 1995: Conversation between an U.S. Naval ship and Canadian authorities off the coast of Newfoundland.

CA: Please divert your course to the south to avoid collision.

US: You divert your course 15 degrees to the north to avoid collision.

CA: Negative, you divert your course 15 to the south to avoid collision.

US: This is the captain of a U.S. Navy ship, I say again divert your course.

CA: No, I say again, you divert your course.

US: This is the aircraft carrier USS Lincoln, the second largest ship in the Atlantic fleet. We are accompanied with three destroyers, three cruisers, and numerous support vessels. I demand that you change your course 15 degrees north. I say again that's one five degrees north or countermeasures will be taken to ensure the safety of this ship.

CA: This is a lighthouse. Your call!

APPEAL:

Some go on stubbornly through life attempting to defy God's word. They give no heed to its admonishing and warnings. Perhaps you have found yourself heading in the wrong direction and you desire to turn your life in God's path. Will you turn now?

Oh, sinner, will you accept God's counsel now? The Bible is the lighthouse that can direct your path and lead you through the darkness of this world. The psalmist declared, "Thy word is a lamp unto my feet, and a light unto my path" (Psalm 119:105). And Jesus said, "Search the scriptures . . . and they are they which testify of me" (John 5:39).

As you have listened to the spoken Word, you recognize that these are not just normal words. Perhaps like the man in the days of Christ, who, coming to Him with tears, said, "Lord, I believe; help thou mine unbelief" (Mark 9:24). Maybe you can identify with this man. You desire to believe, but you still have questions and doubts. If, just now, you can identify with that plea, would you like to say, "Lord, I too believe, but help Thou mine unbelief"? Is that the cry of your heart? Will you lift your hand to heaven, and by so doing, demonstrate your desire for the Lord to help you? Will you raise your hand just now?

AUDREY, A CONFUSED YOUNG WOMAN

Audrey was a young woman who was confused. She didn't believe the Christian faith, but neither could she accept atheism. While studying secular philosophy in France, she had given up her belief in the Bible, but she had nothing to fill the void that remained. "I guess I'm an agnostic," Audrey reasoned. "I'm not sure there is a God, but then again, I'm not sure that there isn't." Life had no meaning for her. She thought, "*If* it is true that there is no life beyond this one on earth, then what does it matter how I live now?

Then one night Audrey locked herself in her bedroom determined to discover what she believed. In the darkness, she went to the window and threw it open. Looking up to the heavens she cried out, "God, if there be a God, if You will give me some philosophy that makes reasonable sense to me, I will commit myself to follow it."

She paced the floor, mulling over the philosophies she had studied in college. Then the words of Jesus came to her mind, "Whosoever liveth and believeth in Me shall never die. Believeth thou this?" (John 11:26). "Of course not!" Audrey thought. "I've already settled that question. Bible stories don't make sense. I can't believe those miracle stories—the virgin birth, Jonah and the whale, and Noah and the flood. The Bible is not reasonable."

But she couldn't get the words out of her mind, "Whosoever liveth and believeth in Me shall never die. Believest thou this?" She later wrote, "Suddenly God's mysterious revelation was given to me. I could not reason out the mystery of the incarnation, but God caused me to know that it was a fact. I knelt in tears of joy and worshiped him as Savior and Lord."[47]

APPEAL:

Are you struggling with your doubts? Do you sense a void in your soul that nothing has been able to satisfy? Oh, friend, only believe! That's what faith does. God's Holy Spirit will convince you that Jesus is indeed the Savior of the world if you will let Him. He died for your sins, and He lives today as a risen Savior. Your faith will transcend human reason. God will increase it if you will only believe.

Why not slip to your knees just now and cry out as Paul cried out, "Who art thou, Lord? . . . And he trembling and astonished said, Lord, what wilt thou have me to do?" (Acts 9:5, 6). If you do this, He will never turn you away. Will you do this just now?

MAN IN BOLIVIA

An Aymara Indian man was a heavy drinker. One night his aim was to get drunk and then return home, his usual habit. But on his way home he fell from his horse and lay there on the trail all night in a drunken stupor. His horse remained standing beside him.

When the man awakened early the next morning, he noticed a black object sticking out of the dust. Wiping away the dust, he found it was a Bible and wondered who could have left it there. He began reading the book immediately and felt God speaking to him. He returned home and told his wife what had happened.

47. Erwin Gane, *Jesus Only: Paul's zletter to the Romans*, 162.

"I am giving my life to Christ!" he said. He had never heard the gospel preached, but he continued to read the Bible out loud. Some time later his wife also accepted Christ. Together they decided to contact a mission station, the address of which they found on the inside cover of the Bible. They traveled 120 miles to meet one of the missionaries. Later, the couple confirmed their new-found faith by being baptized.[48]

APPEAL:

Paul said, "I am not ashamed of the gospel of Christ for it is the power of God unto salvation" (Romans 1:16). Yes, the Word of God is sharper than any two-edged sword; able to pierce to the very marrow. Do you need power to change? Do you need victory in your life? Listen: "Whereby are given unto us exceeding great and precious promises that by these you may become partakers of the divine nature having escaped the corruption that is in the world through lust" (2 Peter 1:4).

Through the Word. your faith can increase. Paul wrote, "So then faith comes by hearing, and hearing by the Word of God" (Romans 10:17). Yes, there is power if you will receive it. God's Word can change your life if you will believe. Who here will accept the Bible as the inspired Word of God? Will you lift your hand toward heaven? Maybe you would like to believe and would like to lift your hand for prayer that God will increase your faith in His Word. Will you likewise lift your hand now?

YOUNG ATHEIST

During the reign of the Communist regime in Romania, many thousands of Bibles were confiscated and stored in warehouses. After the fall of Communism in 1989, the government began to distribute the Bibles to the public. Even as a staunch atheist, a young man got a job working in one of these warehouses distributing Bibles.

He disappeared one afternoon, and his fellow workers eventually noticed he was gone. They looked around for him and finally found him sitting at the feet of a huge stack of crates reading a Bible with tears streaming down his face. When asked

48. Erwin R. Gane, *Jesus Only: Paul's Letter to the Romans,* 106-107.

what was wrong, he told them that he had picked up a Bible and decided to thumb through it. When he did, he saw that it had his grandmother's name written in the front. He had picked that one: one out of thousands. It touched his heart and began a transformation in his life.

APPEAL:

Yes, the reading of the Scriptures has changed thousands of lives. It is not just another book; it is the Word of the living God! As you listen to its teachings, it can change your life too. A three-fold blessing is pronounced in it. It says, "Blessed is he that readeth, and they that hear the words of this prophecy, and keep those things which are written therein" (Revelation 1:3). Do you need to know more about God? Do you feel that your faith needs to be strengthened? The Word says, "Faith comes by hearing, and hearing by the word of God" (Romans 10:17). Is it your desire to know the Lord? Will you lift your hand toward heaven and say, "Lord ever more give me this water that I may drink and never thirst again." Will you lift your hand just now? Amen! Let us pray.

Chapter 28

CHRISTIAN STANDARDS

HOW COULD YOU EMBARRASS ME THAT WAY?

Patricia was attending a series of evangelistic meetings. From night to night she would encourage her sister, brother-in-law, and husband to attend. As God's truth was unveiled, she could be heard saying, "Amen." As the series neared the end, several topics were scheduled that she was looking forward to hearing, until the one on Christian standards. That particular night there were no "Amens" from Patricia.

At the end of the presentation, she made her way to the foyer and waited for the speaker. Fortunately, another attendee delayed him. Not wanting to wait any longer, she left. When the speaker finally arrived at the foyer, the Bible instructor said, "Am I glad you did not get here any sooner."

"Why?" asked the surprised evangelist. "The lady was livid," he informed the pastor. "She said, 'when I get a hold of that black-haired, beady-eyed preacher, I am going to slap him in the face.' Then she turned and stormed out of here." Recognizing what was taking place, the evangelist determined to visit her the following day.

When he arrived at her home, her husband gave entrance but then disappeared. When the woman saw him, she burst into a tirade. "You!" She said. "How could you do that to me?" "What did I do?" asked the speaker. "You knew I was the only one wearing jewelry. How could you embarrass me in front of all those people?" she complained. Then the evangelist asked, "Did I single you out by pointing at you?" "No," she responded. "Did I call out your name? "No," she said. Then if it wasn't me, then who was it?" he asked.

Left to her thoughts, she awakened to reality. Awestricken, she said, "God!" Her anger quickly turned into reverence and submission. Humbled by what she now understood to be the real case, she no longer blamed the pastor. "Pat," said the pastor, "the Lord has placed his finger on your idol. Will you, for His sake, forsake it?" No longer angry, but in a pensive mood, Pat surrendered her life to the Lord.

APPEAL:

Many like Pat do not know or understand that the Lord wants his children to dress in simplicity and without outward adornment. Sometimes they do not realize how much of an idol it is to them until the issue comes into sharp focus. Then, supposing that their conviction comes from the pastor, they get upset. But if you sense conviction, it is no one else but the Holy Spirit who is troubling your heart about the issue. The Word says, "When he is come, he will reprove the world of sin, and of righteousness, and of judgment" (John 16:8).

Oh, friend, if you are experiencing uncomfortableness about this issue, it is because God is speaking to you. If you hear the voice of the Lord, will you be willing for him to put off your ornaments? Who here will say, "Lord, I am willing to surrender all to you." (Then, having the song "I Surrender All" sung, make the appeal.) Are you willing to put all on the altar? Will you come to Him now?

RAMONA

Nineteen-year-old Ramona volunteered with her mother to participate in an evangelistic effort in the Philippines. She was very excited to be a part of a group that wanted to share Christ with these people. They both participated in the day-to-day activities.

From night to night, she heard the Word of God preached and witnessed people responding to the altar calls to commit their lives to Christ. But, there was one thing lacking. While she rejoiced and was excited to have a part in encouraging others to make their decisions, she had not made a decision. She had too many questions and reservations.

Feeling uncomfortable from a sense that others may be wondering what was holding her back, she began to voice her objections. Later, one of the girls suggested that she study with one of the participants who, being a pastor, might help her with her objections. Believing that her points of objection were unanswerable, she agreed.

As they sat together, she threw out her first objection, feeling quite smug in her position. But her level of comfort was unsettled as her objection melted away. Determined to remain in her uncommitted condition, she raised another objection. This too was gently explained. Feeling that she was loosing ground, she decided to end the discussion planning to bide time to prepare herself for the next encounter.

Feeling more prepared with what was supposedly her strongest objections, she met once more with the pastor. Again, her objections were removed one by one. Then out of frustration she said, "I don't want to make the decision. I don't want to wear long skirts or take off my jewelry. And besides, you cannot prove from the Bible that it is wrong to wear it." At that point the pastor noticed her tears welling up, and Ramona was making a desperate effort to hide them.

"Ramona, you are under conviction," the pastor said. "Do you really want to know God's will?" He continued. "But it is such an insignificant thing, why would God even care about it?" She retorted. "If it is as insignificant as you just expressed, then it should not be any problem for you to give it up." The pastor gently responded.

After a long pause, and as tears ran down her face, she said, "You are right!" Then the pastor opened the Bible, and from Genesis to Revelation, she heard God's will concerning ornaments and Christian adornment; Ramona surrendered right then and there. She decided to put away anything that would keep her from a complete surrender to her Savior.

APPEAL:

Perhaps, like Ramona, you have been struggling over this exact issue. But as you have heard God's Word clearly outlining His will in this matter, you recognize that it is true. Just now you would like to make the surrender that you know your Lord is asking you to make. You desire to put away the strange gods, change your garments, and be washed. If that is your desire, would you kneel where you are and say, "Yes, Lord." Will you do it just now?

MY HUSBAND JUST GAVE ME A DIAMOND NECKLACE!

Kathy was excited because from night to night, she found herself learning more about the Bible in three weeks than in all of the rest of her life. Then, on one particular night, she heard the subject on Christian standards. She sat spellbound as she listened to the presentation. First ,she slipped off her bracelet, and then stealthily reaching up to her ears, she pulled off her earrings. The more she heard, the more her heart throbbed with excitement.

When the speaker completed his sermon, he began to make his way to the dhurch exit to bid the people good night. But Kathy was so excited that she caught the pastor before he could leave the sanctuary. "I need to talk with you." she said. "Sure," said the pastor.

Then Kathy revealed her excitement. "I have been addicted to jewelry all my life. In fact, I have a chest with every drawer full of necklaces, rings, earrings, and bracelets. No matter where I went, I had to buy jewels. But tonight, I am free. Praise the Lord! I just have one challenge. Just this morning my husband surprised me with a diamond necklace. I am going to have to find a way to let him know that the Lord has delivered me."

APPEAL:

Have you, like this rich lady, been addicted to jewelry? Have you found yourself having to purchase some ornament as often as possible. But now, as you have heard the subject, there is in your soul a responding chord to this lady's experience. Like her, you want to rejoice in the liberty these Bible truths have brought you. Just now, will you lift your hand to heaven, and by doing so demonstrate your joy in your soul's freedom? Will you lift your hand just now?

JEWEL-A-HOLIC

Every night she came, took her place, and waited for the meetings to start. She sat right in the front row. The speaker took notice of her because of her tenacious and deep interest in spiritual matters. He also noticed that each night she attended she wore a different dress with a matching ring, bracelet, and necklace. It was obvious to the speaker that her jewels were neither common nor inexpensive.

One evening, after presenting the message on Christian standards, he noticed the lady still sitting in her seat. She seemed dazed by what she had heard. Coming closer to her he inquired if everything was all right. Looking at the speaker she said, "Pastor, I am a jewel-a-holic." Never hearing that term before, and not certain as to what she said, he asked her to repeat it. "I am extremely addicted to jewelry," she responded. Asking the pastor to sit next to her, she told her story.

As a young woman, she always felt deprived. Having to wear hand-me-downs, she determined to change that. She became successful in business. Due to her success, she began to amass jewels—all sorts of them. So much so, that she became obsessed with them. But as she heard the message from God's Word, she recognized her condition. Yes, jewelry had become a god to her. Now she felt trapped. How could she let them go?

APPEAL:

Oh, how many persons get hooked by what society claims make them beautiful, acceptable, or attractive. Some spend their lives obsessively in pursuit of what is supposed to make them happy, but to no avail. Then when they come to the Word of God, they are rankled when they discover that what should be strange to them they see as normal. What should be normal, they consider strange.

God's Word is clear, and if you, as you have heard God's Word, find yourself with tentacles wrapped around you, and today you want to be free, then why not ask the Lord for help? Who here will raise his or her hand and say, "Lord, free me from this obsession." Maybe it is an obsession for something else in your life, and just now you want victory, will you lift your hand?

I LOVE THE LORD, AND WILL
DO ANYTHING TO PLEASE HIM!

As she attended the meetings, great delight came to her. For the first time, she was hearing teachings directly from the Bible, it was also her first time to experience a meeting where the Bible was the only textbook that was used. The church she regularly attended never took their worshipers from page to page for a "thus saith the Lord." Her heart throbbed as the subject unfolded.

The topic one evening was on "those things that pleased the Lord." Conviction sank deep as she heard about what the Scriptures said concerning the evils of alcohol and tobacco as well as the body being the temple of the living God. Then when the speaker passed on to the subject of Christian adornment, she began to feel uncomfortable. Never had she any idea about this topic. But as the reality struck her that the Lord Jesus did not wear any jewels, she reached and pulled off one earring and then the next.

By the time the meeting was over, she had removed all ornaments from her person. When she approached the exit and greeted the preacher, he took note of the difference. "You have taken off your jewelry," he said. "Oh, yes. I love the Lord and will do anything to please him," she said.

APPEAL:

Many are like this woman. They love the Lord, but they have no idea that there are things in life that are not pleasing to Him. But when they hear the Word of God, they sense the convicting voice of God speaking to them. They joyfully yield and are willing to do anything to please Him. As the Spirit of the Lord speaks to your heart, is it your desire to do anything to please Him? Can you say like the Lord, "I delight to do Thy will!"

Maybe there is something in your life you had no idea displeased the Lord. But as you have heard the Word of God outlining His will, you desire to obey Him. Will you lift your hand high and demonstrate that you long to please Him? Do you long to please Him by putting your practices aside? If that is your desire, will you lift your hand now?

THEY ARE MEANINGLESS!

A woman invited a pastor and his wife to visit her in her home. After the brief getting acquainted period, she related her conversion story. She had been in the top ranks of Playboy. While living the luxurious life, she had spent thousands of dollars on jewelry. Then she went to her dresser and began laying expensive jewels before them that were worth thousands of dollars. Handing one of the rings to the pastor's wife that was worth around $40,000, she said, "In the past, these meant a lot to me. I sold my body and soul to have them, but now they are meaningless in comparison to my Jesus."

APPEAL:

Maybe like this woman you feel you have sold your soul for some earthly treasure. But now your eyes have been opened. You have now found the Pearl of Great Price, and for Him you are willing to surrender all. Just like the woman, the flash of the jewels has faded. You no longer care for those things—they have lost their luster. Now you desire nothing more than to follow your Lord. Is it your hearts desire, like this woman, to turn from your earthly treasures? Do you long to be free? Why not decide to follow your Lord and Master? Will you do it now?

IF YOU TAKE OFF THAT RING, WE ARE THROUGH!

Diane and her husband had been attending the most exciting series of Bible lectures they had ever heard. Though changes in their ideas concerning Bible truths needed to be made, they gladly accepted them, for they could see what the Word of God suggested. Eagerly they went to each lecture anxious to discover more light in God's holy Word. They felt they were learning more in a few short weeks than in their entire lifetimes. As soon as they saw and understood God's truths, they adopted them.

Everything was going great until one night when the excitement turned to bitterness for Diane. The presentation was on the subject of Christian standards. Wihle she did not have any problems with changing her ideas about doctrines that dealt with knowledge, she had a huge problem with anything that seemed to dictate how to dress, or anything that suggested lifestyle changes. That night her husband could see her bristling against the message. Suddenly, Diane lost her relish for the meetings. Though they had made a public commitment to follow the light God revealed to them, she was going no further.

When the pastor visited them to confirm their decision for

baptism, the resistance became obvious. Diane was determined not to part with her jewelry. Her husband could not understand what was taking place. Why would she rescind her commitment to follow God? Then it came out. She was not going to stop wearing jewelry.

She admitted that the Scriptures enjoined such a teaching, but the air became tense when, in agitation, Diane firmly said to her husband, "You take off that wedding band, and we are through." With that, she stomped out of the house and slammed the door. With a broken heart, her husband bowed his head in dismay. How could she place a piece of gold above their marriage and following Jesus? The he and the pastor knelt and prayed.

Diane returned weeping. She then acknowledged that she never realized what a strong hold jewelry had on her. She couldn't believe that she would rather choose the ring over her Lord and her husband. Jewelry had become a god to her, and the fact that she was willing to place it above her Lord shocked her. Repentant of her rash decision, Diane took off her jewelry and felt a great freedom from its strong hold on her.

APPEAL:

Yes, very few realize the unyielding grip that jewelry has on them. They are led to say, "God is not interested in this small matter." Little do they realize that if it were a small a matter, as they claim, they would easily be able to put it aside. But when the Spirit of God, through the Word, reveals light concerning the topic, then it is that the battle ensues. When the believer is faced with the truth from the Word, the struggle begins.

Oh, friend, have you been unaware of the standard that the Holy Word of God enjoins upon you to lay aside your jewelry. Your example, Jesus Christ, never wore it. Neither did He give counsel in His Word for his followers to wear it. As light from heaven has shone upon you relative to this subject, are you willing to follow your Lord and Savior's? Are you willing to lay it all on the altar? Has it been a struggle for you? Right now, are you willing to say, "Lord, help me. Give me the strength to overcome." Will you raise your hand to heaven now? Will you ask the Lord to give you the victory? Let us pray.

Chapter 29

OTHER STORIES

GRATITUDE FOR CHRIST

Gratitude prompted an old man to visit an old broken pier on the eastern seacoast of Florida. Every Friday night, until his death in 1973, he would return, walking slowly and slightly stooped with a large bucket of shrimp. The sea gulls would flock to this old man, and he would feed them from his bucket.

Many years prior, in October 1942, Captain Eddie Rickenbacker was on a mission in a B-17 to deliver an important message to General Douglas MacArthur in New Guinea. An unexpected detour hurled Captain Eddie into the most harrowing adventure of his life. Somewhere over the South Pacific, his plane, known as the Flying Fortress, became lost beyond the reach of radio.

Fuel ran dangerously low, so the men ditched their plane in the ocean in favor of the life rafts on board. For nearly a month, Captain Eddie and his companions fought the water, the weather, and the scorching sun. They spent many sleepless nights recoiling as giant sharks rammed their rafts. The largest raft was nine by five feet. The biggest shark—ten feet long.

Of all their enemies at sea, one proved most formidable: starvation. After eight days, their rations were gone or destroyed by the saltwater. Only a miracle would sustain them, and a miracle occurred. In Captain Eddie's own words, "Cherry" (the B-17 pilot Captain William Cherry) "read the service from his pocket devotional that afternoon, and we finished with a prayer for deliverance and a hymn of praise. There was some talk, but it tapered off in the oppressive heat.

With my hat pulled down over my eyes to keep out some

of the glare, I dozed off. Then, something landed on my head. I knew that it was a sea gull. I don't know how I knew, I just knew. Everyone else knew too. No one said a word, but peering out from under my hat brim without moving my head, I could see the expression on their faces. They were staring at that gull. The gull meant food . . . if I could catch it."

And the rest, as they say, is history. Captain Eddie caught the gull. Its flesh was eaten. Its intestines were used for bait to catch fish. The survivors were nourished, and their hopes renewed because a lone sea gull, uncharacteristically hundreds of miles from land, offered itself as a sacrifice.

So now you know why he never forgot and was forever grateful. Every Friday evening about sunset, on a lonely stretch along the eastern Florida seacoast, the old man walked—white-haired, bushy-eye browed, and slightly bent. His bucket filled with shrimp was to feed the gulls—to remember that one that, on a day long past, gave itself without a struggle like manna in the wilderness.

APPEAL:

Are you grateful for what Christ has done for you? Have you given Him your heart? As you and I come to understand more fully the cost of the cross, our hearts will be filled with gratitude for our salvation. Are you grateful? Will you give your heart to Him in grateful response for your salvation?

DUTY

The time was the 19th of May 1780. The place was Hartford, Connecticut. The day has gone down in New England history as a terrible foretaste of Judgment Day. At noon the skies turned from blue to gray and by mid-afternoon had blackened over so densely that, in a religious age, men fell on their knees and begged a final blessing before the end came. The Connecticut House of Representatives was in session. As some men fell down, and others clamored for an immediate adjournment, the speaker of the house, Colonel Davenport, came to his feet. He silenced them and said these words, "The day of judgment is either approaching or it is not. If it is not, there is no cause for adjournment. If it is, I choose to be found doing my duty. I wish, therefore, that candles may be brought."[49]

APPEAL:

Ah, friend, as the day of judgment draws near, don't you want to be found doing your duty? Don't you want your name registered in the Book of Life? Don't you want to be found faithful and true? If that is your desire, will you lift up your hand just now?

INDIFFERENCE

Kitty Genovese was the young woman who was murdered in a New York residential section while at least thirty-eight neighbors watched from their windows. During the course of the thirty-minute assault, no one even telephoned the police. Studies have uncovered some surprising facts about these people. Interviews revealed that they were not totally indifferent as many had suspected. The main reason nobody did anything was that each person thought someone else would take the initiative to get help.

APPEAL:

Sad to say, many are waiting for someone else to take the initiative. But why wait for somebody else to take the first step? If God is speaking to you, then why not take that step toward the Lord? Why wait for someone else? God speaks to you and waits for you to make that decision. Why not stand in your place? Will you respond even if no one else will?

GOING IN THE WRONG DIRECTION

Two young men traveled through the back roads of Maryland one day. They were anxious to get to their appointment, but they drove on unfamiliar roads, finally coming to the end. They could turn only right or left. The driver, Glen by name, felt strongly that north was to the right. The passenger, however, was not sure. Glen was certain that he needed to turn right, but the passenger suggested that in the interest of time they consult the map.

49. Robert P. Dugan Jr., *Winning the New Civil War*, 183.

Fortunately, as they searched, they discovered a map of the area. Upon observation, the map pointed out that left would take them north, not right. The feelings were strong, but the direction was wrong. So it is with the Word of God. The feelings may strongly suggest one direction, but the Bible may suggest the complete opposite.

APPEAL:

Our feelings may serve us to take the right course in some matters, but when it comes to our spiritual lives, the Scriptures must be our guide. Feelings in these matters can be misleading. Just like the driver who was so sure that his feelings were dictating the right direction, and the opposite was true, so it is with our spiritual lives. The Scriptures say, "There is a way that seemeth right unto a man, but the end thereof is the way of death" (Proverbs 14:12). God has given us His Word to be our comfort, guide, and compass. Our only safety is to depend upon a "Thus saith the Lord."

Will you make the Word of God a light unto your feet and a light unto your path? Will you ask God to help you to believe in His counsel over your feelings? How many of you will lift your hand toward heaven and tell the Lord, that by His grace, you will take Him at His Word? Will you respond now?

MANUEL CABRAL THE PRIEST

Eight monks studied at a monastery in Puerto Rico. When they finished, they were sent to work at a university in Central America. One day, Giovanni, one of the monks, walked by a door and noticed a sign, "Entrance forbidden." With aroused curiosity, he decided to venture in and determine why the prohibition was put into place. He found a Bible. He decided to take it, and as occasion permitted read, all he could to discover what was so terrible about this forbidden book.

As he read, he found answers to the many questions that his faith did not permit to be asked. It was a sin to doubt! But the more he read, the clearer became the solution to all his disturbing, haunting questions.

He shared his wonderful discovery with another friar and then with all eight of them. Together they would gather to read and search the Scriptures, until one day they got caught. Immediately all were summoned to trial.

On the day of trial, Manuel's mother, unbeknownst to him, was invited to persuade him to recant. Manuel loved his mother dearly, but recant he could not. He told the church dignitaries that he would recant if they could show him from the Scriptures his errors.

At this, his mother stepped forward and slapped him in the face, demanding his yielding to the fathers. Looking with tender regard at the mother he loved, he said, "My dear mother, I love you more than life itself, but my loyalty must first be to God." At this his mother said, "As far as I am concerned, you are dead! Don't you ever call me your mother again." Brokenhearted, he saw his mother turn from him, but he had determined that Christ must have first place in his heart. Manuel and the seven friars were excommunicated.

APPEAL:

Oh, the heartbreaking choices that some people are forced to make. In the moment, things look bleak and hopeless. Often sacrifices are made that are painful. Is it worth it? Several years later, Mrs. Cabral confessed to her son that she had made the wrong choice, but he the right one. "Would you baptize me?" she asked. What joy came when Cabral, then a minister of the Gospel, had the privilege of baptizing his mother.

Only the Lord knows what sacrifice you must make to follow Him. But He promised, "And every one that hath forsaken houses, or brethren, or sisters, or father, or mother, or wife, or children, or lands, for my name's sake, shall receive an hundredfold, and shall inherit everlasting life" (Matthew 19:29). Do you love the Lord more than others?

Oh, friend, it pays to follow Him, who gave His all to save you. Will you give Him your heart? Will you come to Him? Will you trust Him with your future, your loved ones, and your life? Why not come to Him now?

MADE HER HUSBAND MISERABLE

To a wife's dismay and anger, her husband changed religions, so she determined to get even. On the day that he went to church and worshiped, her plan was to make it as miserable in their home as possible. They had both been raised Orthodox and married in the Orthodox Church. Now there was a split in the family, and he was the cause of it.

The situation was extremely difficult for the husband, for he often arrived at church with obvious signs of crying. But his love for both the Lord and for her, enabled him to endure. This continued for quite a while.

Subsequently, she was invited to a meeting held by an evangelist of her husband's faith, so she attended only to prove the error of his faith. Night after night she attended; the more she heard, the more convinced she became that the error was not with her husband but with herself. His forbearance was a mystery to her. "I am treating him so cruelly, yet he treats me so kindly," she thought. The more she looked in her Bible to prove the error, the more she realized that she was fighting a losing battle.

When she invited the evangelist to their home for lunch, she posed what she supposed were answerable questions. She was amazed to hear the answers directly from the Bible. Finally, she could fight no more. With weeping she confessed her determined resistance and spitefulness. But finally she said, "You cannot fight against love and truth. I give up. I too want to follow this faith that has transformed my husband and now me."

APPEAL:

Yes, there are those who, like the apostle Paul, "kick against the pricks." The light shines in their path, but pride, rebellion, or fear of the unknown keep them resistent to complete surrender. Perhaps you are in the same condition. Your heart tells you that it is God's truth. He is the one calling. However, your fears keep you determined not to surrender. You hear the voice of the Lord say, "My son, my daughter, give me your heart." Why not surrender now? Why not say like the resisting wife, "I can't fight love and truth." Will you come just now?

PATTY

She was a young wife with a strong faith. She kept herself very active in the church. Her husband however was an unbeliever. Patty tried her best to get him to believe but to no avail. One day, there was a knock on her door. The man inquired as to whether the young man who had sent a card requesting Bible studies was at home. Looking at the card, she recognized the handwriting. "This is my husband's handwriting," she said, "but it must be a mistake. Someone must be playing a joke."

"It is his handwriting?" inquired the man. "Yes," she said, "but I am sure he did not send it. He is an unbeliever." The man suggested that he would leave the first lesson for her husband and would return to see if he was serious about the studies.

Upon his return, Patty informed him that her husband had no interest. Then the man asked, "Will you take them?" She consented and began the weekly study. When she began to put into practice the light that she was receiving, it aroused opposition. Three ministers showed up to see her on different occasions. Strangely, no one had ever visited her previously. They gave her literature to dissuade her, but when she compared it with what she had read herself in the Scriptures, she could see their error.

Patty loved the studies, and all she was learning about her Lord. Finally, the day came when she arrived at the church to be baptized. Her mother also arrived unannounced. Right in the midst of the service, her mother stood up and railed her and the Bible worker. She did everything to embarrass Patty. But though frail in stature, Patty was strong in spirit and determined to follow her Lord whatever the cost. Contrary to all opposition, Patty went ahead and was baptized.

APPEAL:

Perhaps you are going through the same experience as Patty did. No one has paid much attention to you until you decided to study the Scriptures and walk in the wonderful light that God has unfolded before you. The opposition of loved ones is always painful. Jesus was also opposed by His family. He well understands the struggle. But if you will determine to make Him first in your life, He will strengthen you just as He did Patty. That young woman was an eloquent testimony of the courage God can give even to the frailest. Are you determined to follow Him, come what may? Jesus will strengthen you. He says in Isaiah 41:10, "Fear thou not; for I am with thee: be not dismayed; for I am thy

God: I will strengthen thee; yea, I will help thee; yea, I will uphold thee with the right hand of my righteousness." Will you rise to stand on Christ's side? Will you do it now?

WHEN I AM GOOD AND READY

A young man sat on the edge of the sidewalk. A minister who knew him spotted him, decided to stop, and talked with him. "A meeting is taking place tonight, and I would love to see you there," said the minister. "Naw!" was the response. "When I am good and ready to go to church, I will go."

"Young man," responded the minister, "you don't have to wait until you are good and ready to look for God. Why don't you come tonight? I am sure you will enjoy it." "No thanks, preacher. I have plenty of time before I begin to think about church. I will go sometime, but not now." "Alright, but I hope you change your mind. I would love to see you there." The minister then went on his way.

In the morning news, there was a terrible story. A car had gone out of control, hit, and killed a young man sitting on the edge of the sidewalk. To the minister's shock, it was the young man who thought he had plenty of time.

APPEAL

Many like this young man feel they have plenty of time before they need to think about God. But the Lord says, "Remember now thy Creator in the days of thy youth, while the evil days come not, nor the years draw nigh, when thou shalt say, I have no pleasure in them" (Ecclesiastes 12:1).

Oh, friend, don't put off your preparation. No one knows precisely how much time he or she has on this earth. The young man thought he had plenty of time—did he? Felix said to the apostle Paul, "Go thy way for this time; when I have a convenient season, I will call for thee" (Acts 24:25). The sad thing is that a convenient season never arrived. Oh, friend, don't put off your commitment until later. Don't consult convenience. Give yourself to God now! Will you come?

THAT'S IT

One morning a visiting minister was preparing his sermon. He had spent a long time on it, and when the following day arrived, he planned to preach it at the church. However, as he sat and listened to the discussion during Bible class, he felt deeply impressed that the prepared sermon was not suited for the occasion. When he got up to preach, he announced that though he had spent much time on the sermon, he was impressed that it was not the right one, so decided to preach a sermon he had preached elsewhere.

After the delivery and farewells, the preacher went home. The following year, he was invited again to preach to the same congregation. This time, he preached the prepared sermon. After the usual greetings at the exit door, he was invited to stay for lunch. While he was eating, a couple visited his table and asked if they could share something with him.

Upon giving his consent, the wife began, "Do you remember when you were here last year? Do you recall that you felt the sermon you had prepared was not the right one?" "Yes," responded the speaker. "Well as my husband and I were walking home, he said out of the blue, 'That's it!' I looked at him and said, 'What's it?' Again he repeated the same thing, 'That's it!' Once again, I asked, 'What's it?' 'I will never drink again. I had no idea that God loved me that much. If God loves me that much, I am going to live for Him! That's it.'"

APPEAL:

You see my friend; this man had been an alcoholic for twenty-five years. Though his wife was a Christian, he was not. The problem was that he never understood the personal love that God had for him. When the light finally penetrated and reached his innermost soul, he was able to grasp for the first time how much he meant to God.

Yes, that's it. When the love of Christ breaks through your hearts and you realize how great the love of God is for you, you too can say, "That's it!" God says, "I have loved thee with an everlasting love: therefore with lovingkindness have I drawn thee"

(Jeremiah 31:3). Will you accept the love of God? Will you also give your heart to Him and say, "That's it?" Will you do it now?

YOUNG DRUG ADDICT

One evening a young man attended a Bible prophecy seminar. He appeared to be as normal as the others attending. At the conclusion of the presentation, the young man approached the speaker and asked for a private interview. After the speaker was through with dismissing the rest of the attendees, he and the young man went into a side room while his sister waited in the sanctuary.

Once behind closed doors, the young man revealed his urgent need. "I am a drug addict," he began. "Right now I am suffering great physical pain. I am going through withdrawals, but I don't want to continue living this way. I have tried to quit, but I can't. Can you help me?" "Do you believe in God?" asked the preacher.

"I do, but I have turned away from him. Oh, help me!" cried the young agonizing addict. "The Lord has promised, 'Him that cometh to me, I will in no wise cast out'" (John 6:37). And with this, the pastor asked him to kneel, first to offer his own prayer asking for forgiveness, and to plead for the help he needed. With agonizing cries, the young man pleaded with God for deliverance. Once the supplicant made his confessions and request, the pastor likewise beseeched the Lord in behalf of the young man.

At the conclusion, they left the small room and entered back into the sanctuary where the sister was still waiting. As they were standing together and the pastor was talking with the sister, the young man cried out, "It's gone!" And again more strongly, "It's gone!" And once more he exclaimed, "It's gone!"

APPEAL:

Yes, my friend, when you come to Jesus, just as you are and place all your sins in His care, they will be gone. You may have struggles in your heart that you have not been able to overcome. At times you wonder whether you'll ever be set free. But you need not trust in your feebleness any longer. Come to Jesus. He alone can set you free. Jesus said, "If the Son sets you free, ye shall be free indeed!"

Do you want the victory? Come to the Savior now. Will you raise your hand and say, "Lord, I can't help myself. I believe, but help Thou my unbelief." If you do this, He will never turn you away. Will you stand where you are? Why not just rise where you are and thrust yourself toward the helping hand of Jesus?

I AM NOT SERVING ANYBODY

Reluctantly Freddy attended a church service. To save face with the young winsome men that invited him, he went but secretly determined never to return. "I know what they are after," he thought, "but it's not going to happen." His brothers had already become Christians and were excited to see him attend. Freddy found just the place to sit; it was the last row in the back of the auditorium. This way, he could make a quick exit if necessary.

Toward the end of the sermon, the preacher made a strong appeal for those who wanted to serve Christ to respond to the invitation. Freddy's brothers were gathered together in room where they could watch the goings-on and pray without being noticed.

But as the appeal wore on, they noticed that Freddy was not moving. Then one of the brothers decided to approach him. Silently, he walked over to Freddy and said, "Freddy, why don't you decide to serve God?" "I am not going to serve anyone!" Freddy responded. His brother then said, "If you are not serving God, you are really saying that you want to serve the devil."

With that, his brother went back to the room to continue to pray with his brothers. They determined to continue to agonize with God until the appeal came to an end. When the appeal ended, the brothers also concluded their intercession. Upon opening their eyes, they rejoiced to see their brother up in front along with others who also made their decisions.

Several years later, Freddy and his brother were talking. Freddy then asked his brother, "Do you remember what you told me when I attended that meeting that I had no desire to be in?" "No," said his brother. "Well, I was determined not to respond to the invitation given by the preacher. I felt that I had to hold on to my seat in order not to respond. Then you showed up and said, 'Why don't you respond?' I retorted, 'I am not serving anybody.' To which you said, 'If you are not serving God, you are in essence serving the enemy.' That statement shocked me into reality. I then determined that I was not going to serve the devil. And if not the devil, then I was going to serve God."

APPEAL:

Friend, Elijah posed this question to the Israelites on Mt. Carmel: "How long halt ye between two opinions? If Baal be God then serve him: But if the Lord be God, then serve Him" (1 Kings 18:21). What about you? "No man can serve two masters: for either he will hate the one, and love the other; or else he will hold to the one, and despise the other. Ye cannot serve God and mammon" (Matthew 6:24), Jesus said. Maybe, like Freddy, you had determined not to serve anyone, but now you see that there is a choice to be made. Will you choose God now? Will you decide to surrender to Him? Will you do it just now?

MONEY TO THE CROCODILES

Two poor children of five and six years old were visiting the zoo for the first time. They were excited to see the huge and different animals. They were greatly intrigued as they saw the monkeys scamper from limb to limb and from trampoline to rope. The lion's roar was deafening, and the screech of the peacocks was a new unusual sound.

Then they arrived at the crocodile pit. They were large ones. But were they dead? They just lay motionless. They did not even appear to breath. As the children gazed at the great reptiles and chatted about the seemingly lifeless creatures, a man stood next to them overhearing their inquiries.

He took a dollar out of his pocket and threw it into the pit. Then recognizing the impoverished lot of the children encouraged them to climb over the fence and go fetch the much-needed money. The children not knowing the danger thought it a good idea to get this easy money. After all, they were convinced that no harm would come from the apparently harmless creatures.

Fortunately for them, their stepfather had just caught up with the children and happened to overhear the cruel man's suggestion. He immediately grabbed his children. With anger, he blasted the hateful man and threatened to throw him into the pit to retrieve his dollar. The man made a hasty retreat never to be seen again.

APPEAL:

Isn't that just like the devil? He tempted Eve to partake of the outwardly harmless fruit. But think of what that apparently harmless act has done. Think of the sickness, pain, death, hatred, violence, murders, broken-up homes, and misery that innocentfall has brought. Think how that act has placed the human race in the cruel grip of the devil.

Perhaps you have been led into a seemingly harmless act of sin, only to find yourself in the grip of the powerful claws of transgression. That small digression from the right—what harm would it do? But the consequences are painful. Oh, if you had only listened? If only you had not... - but listen! "If the wicked turn from his wicked way, then he shall live." Many have been led down the same-blinded path, only to awake to the reality of the dreadful condition that sin brings.

Oh, friend, you might have innocently been involved in something you now regret. But remember, "if we confess our sins, He is faithful and just to forgive us our sins, and cleanse us from all unrighteousness." Flee from lustful desires. They will appear harmless.

But remember! "There is pleasure in sin for a season." As the Scriptures say, "He goeth after her straightway, as an ox goeth to the slaughter, or as a fool to the correction of the stocks" (Proverbs 7:22). Oh why not flee from temptation? Turn ye, oh turn ye, for why will ye die? Will you turn and heed your father now? Will you arise and come to the safety of your heavenly father?

TURNED UPSIDE-DOWN IN THE TRUCK

He had grown up in a Christian home but was wearied from the bondage he felt from all the rules. He made up his mind to abandon all notions of religion as soon as he was old enough to throw off the restraints. And so he did. Gerry got together with the wrong crowd. Oh, how free he was now! He could do anything he wished, and no one was around to tell him what he could do and could not do.

To keep his drinking and drug habit going, he got a job as a truck driver. How he enjoyed sailing down the highway and feeling the breeze of freedom! One day he was driving on Interstate 80, a main highway, through the state of Wyoming. In his altered state of mind, he did not notice the signs warning about the gust of winds that blew through the open canyons. Though the windsock was horizontal, indicating a strong wind, Gerry never noticed until it was too late.

Almost instantly, the truck was on its side on the ledge of the precipice. Just as immediate was Gerry's wake up call. He was trapped inside a truck that was rocking to and fro on the edge. No longer high, he looked out his side window. All he could see was hundreds of feet down.

Sensing his danger and dire need, it was then that Gerry decided to cry out to God. "God," he said, "if you save me, I will serve you." Some very tense moments of reflection about his abandoned life followed his cry. Fortunately for him, the answer to his agonizing plea came. Not long after his vow of commitment, the police arrived and were able to get him out of his predicament.

APPEAL:

"God, if you save me!" was his cry. Maybe you do not find yourself in the same predicament as Gerry. Perhaps your need may not be as immediately dire as his was. But like him, you recognize that God has been more merciful to you than you deserve. Just as your soul cries out, "God save me," you desire to return to the true freedom.

Remember, the thief on the cross sensed that he did not have much time. His only hope was to turn to the Savior. In that final hour, he cried out, "Lord, remember me" (Luke 23:42). The answer came immediately, you shall "be with me in paradise" (Luke 23:43). Oh, friend, it matters not in what condition you may find yourself. All you have to do is call on the name of the Lord. Will you call on His name now? Who here will rise calling on the name of the Lord?

Chapter 30

BACKSLIDERS

BRYAN

Bryan had been away from the church for twenty years. Deep inside he knew he should have continued with the commitment he had made to God. Circumstances with his wife became very trying. She did not want him to be a Christian, let alone, an Adventist Christian. Bryan was pushed to have to make a decision—either her or the church. Fearing that his home was about to collapse, he chose his wife.

Through the years he wondered how long God would extend mercy to him. At times when trouble loomed over his head, he wished he could find himself under the shelter of God's wings. Time passed on into retirement, but Bryan's heart was not at peace. Would God take him back after knowingly turning his back on Him?

One day Bryan went to fetch his mail. In the bundle there was a flyer advertising a series of meetings on prophecy. He determined to not miss out this time. Night by night he attended. As Bryan listened to the Word of God, old memories would come to him of his first love for God. Tears would well up as conviction once more took hold of him. Then came the night when the invitation was made for anyone who had once known the Lord but had drifted away from Him to respond to the appeal. Bryan rose to his feet, and with tears flowing, he bowed at the altar. "I am coming home," he thought. "I am coming home."

APPEAL:

Have you wandered away from the Lord? Have you found yourself drinking from empty cisterns? You know where you should be, but you have not had the courage or strength to come back to the Lord. But just now, your heart is stirred. Like Bryan, you do not want to miss this opportunity. Will you then rise to your feet and come back home? God invites you. Come home! Just as the father waited for the returning prodigal son, so God waits for you. Will you come? I know how difficult it is to respond in public. But friend, if that woman in the Bible who was sick for years had not stretched forth her hand and touched the hem of Jesus, she would never have been healed.

THERE IS NOTHING OUT THERE

Physically sick, and worn with the dog-eat-dog life on Broadway in New York City, Rick and his model girlfriend were walking down a Manhattan street. Though deep in conversation about the disappointments and frustration of show business, Rick's eye noticed a colorful flyer on the edge of the sidewalk. Picking it up, he was impressed with the topics. It was a Bible prophecy seminar. Not having anything in particular to do that evening, they decided to "check it out."

Rick was gripped by the passionate presentations made by a former gang member—now turned preacher. As Rick listened, thoughts came back of a forgotten time when, as a child, he sang in church. Memories of a childlike faith in God revived. Rick could not remember the last time he prayed. Things from the Scriptures he had been taught began to resurface. Heartsick for the years he wasted, and sensing the beckoning of a voice he had long ago stifled, Rick desired to return to the God of his father.

When the invitation was made to forsake all and follow the Lord, Rick said to himself, "There is nothing out there." Rising to his feet, he began his journey back home. By his side walked the tear-stained model. Together they both decided to turn their lives over to Christ and live for Him.

APPEAL:

Yes, friend, "There is nothing out there." Once you have tasted of the Word of God and the presence of the Spirit, you will never find another substitute. Yes, Satan will promise you fun, excitement with heartaches, and finally a dark, dreadful end. Christ promises you a life filled with trials but peace in your heart and a wonderful hereafter.

As you contemplate your own condition, can you identify with

Rick? Do you sense God calling you back home? Hear the word of the Lord: "And I will give them an heart to know me, that I am the LORD: and they shall be my people, and I will be their God: for they shall return unto me with their whole heart" (Jeremiah 24:7). Will you respond to your heart's promptings? As you hear the voice of the Lord speaking to your heart, will you not harden it? Will you arise and come back home? Will you do it just now?

THE PRODIGAL SON

Head strong, and desirous to get himself from underneath his father's control, the prodigal made his request. "Father, give me the portion of goods that falleth to me." Though in reality he had nothing that was his, the father nonetheless "divided unto him his living." "Not many days after, the younger son gathered all together, and took his journey to a far country, and there wasted his substance with riotous living" (Luke 15:13).

Perhaps the "life of the party," the young man was living it up. Things went well until he became penniless. Yes, when you have money, you have lots of friends, but when the bank runs dry, then the stark reality hits—gone are the friends.

Forsaken to feed pigs, the young man came to himself. The Bible says, "and when he came to himself" (Luke 15:17), there he was—eating the husks of the swine and down in morality, decency, and broken in spirit. Finally, the thought of his home life swept before him.

Things were much better than supposed. "I will arise and go to my father, and will say unto him, Father, I have sinned against heaven, and before thee, and am no more worthy to be called thy son: make me as one of thy hired servants. And he arose, and came to his father. But when he was yet a great way off, his father saw him, and had compassion, and ran, and fell on his neck, and kissed him" (Luke 15:18-20).

APPEAL:

Notice that the young man "came to himself." The backslider has known better things spiritually. For him the way of selfish gratifications quickly brought satiation and an inner dissatisfaction.

A backslidden person knows the way home. The only problem is that he has not come to himself. Perhaps just now you are hearing the voice of the Lord speaking to you, saying, "Return oh, backslidden children, and I will receive you."

As you hear the invitation, have you come to yourself? And like the lost son, will you arise and say, I will go to father. Notice these words, "I have blotted out, as a thick cloud, thy transgressions, and, as a cloud, thy sins: return unto me; for I have redeemed thee" (Isaiah 44:22). Oh, friend, He is waiting for you come return home. But, you must arise. Will you arise just now? Will you humble yourself and say; I have sinned against heaven, and against you. Will you come?

LARRY

Larry had gone into the world to gain the most from it. By the time he was fifty, he had built quite a financially comfortable life. There were times when his conscience would trouble him. But he justified himself that he was living a good life. He now owned several motels. Everything that life could offer, he had. But the words of the Lord became more and more real. "What shall it profit a man if he gain the whole world and loose his own soul. Or what shall a man give in exchange for his soul" (Mark 8:36, 37).

Nothing seemed to give him inner peace. Larry sensed he needed something that materialism could not supply. Then one day a prophecy seminar came to his town. Upon hearing about it, Larry decided to attend.

From night to night, he listened as if spellbound. Old feelings for God seemed to revive. A welling-up in his throat like a knot came to him one night. He could fight it no more. Larry realized what he was missing; why it was that nothing seemed to satisfy him.

When the appeal was made, Larry headed for the altar. Broken in spirit, and remorseful, he at last decided to return to his God. It was so good to go home, he thought. Larry immediately began to turn away from all that had turned him away from God. At last, Larry had regained that which he had lost for so long—his peace of mind and heart.

APPEAL:

Perhaps like Larry, you have gained all that life can offer. You have gained everything except peace of heart. As you contemplate the life of Larry, you can identify with him. Yes, you have it all, but there is still a nagging void—a sense that there is still something missing. There might have been a long absence from all that you knew as a child, but as you have heard this message, you long to return.

You might be thinking, I have been away too long. God will not have me back. Listen, "O Israel, thou shalt not be forgotten of me. I have blotted out, as a thick cloud, thy transgressions, and, as a cloud, thy sins: return unto me; for I have redeemed thee" (Isaiah 44:21, 22). If your heart is throbbing, if while you hear this appeal you have an awaking desire to come back to God, then come. God has broken through the barriers and hardheartedness. He is calling you. Will you return to God? Will you open your heart to Him again? Why not arise and come? Will you do it just now? Yes, come, and God will receive you. Come just as you are.

Listen to God's invitation. "Seek ye the Lord while he may be found, call ye upon Him while he is near: Let the wicked forsake his way, and the unrighteous man his thoughts: and let him return unto the Lord, and he will have mercy upon him; and to our God, for He will abundantly pardon" (Isaiah 55:6, 7).

I AM NOT GOOD ENOUGH

An attorney was invited by a friend to a youth convention. They had not seen each other since childhood though they had kept in touch with one another through the years. The friend, who was from New York, thought it a good opportunity to see each other in as much as the convention was near where the attorney lived. At the convention many different seminars were being offered by various speakers.

The inviting friend suggested they attend a seminar on "Gaining Decisions for Christ." As they sat in the audience, the speaker made mention that he needed a volunteer, and pointing to the attorney, he asked if she would be willing. Shyly, she walked to the platform. The speaker asked her to sit down and then began with the illustration he wanted to demonstrate to the attendees.

Step by step, the presenter carefully led her through the process of leading a person to accept Christ. Upon turning to the book of Revelation, he asked her to read chapter three and verse twenty. After asking several questions, he looked at her and asked, "Is there anything that would keep you from inviting the Lord Jesus into your heart?"

Though it was supposed to be only a demonstration, there came over both the presenter and the audience an awestricken sense that to her this was real. She had not been confronted with that question till that moment, and it caused her to consider it. There was a long pause, and then with a reverential tone she said, "I am not good enough."

Realizing that the live demo turned into a real-life experience, the presenter asked, "Have you tried to become good enough?" Pensively, she said, "Yes." Have you succeeded?" the speaker asked. "No," she responded.

"Then if you cannot become good enough in your own strength, whom do you need to make you 'good enough'?" he asked. Looking at the pastor, and now with teary eyes she said, "Jesus!" "Then," the pastor asked, "is there anything that will keep you from inviting the Lord into your life so He can make you 'good enough'?"

APPEAL:

There are many just like this attorney. Her smitten conscience dictated that she was not good enough. Though a professional and living a good moral live, she did not think her life acceptable enough to God. Perhaps as you have been listening your heart bears witness that you are not good enough. And while that may be true, you will never in your own strength or intellect become good enough. The Scriptures say, "There is none righteous, no, not one" (Romans 3:10). All of our righteousness is as filthy rags.

Only Jesus can make you all that you can become. In Him shall be your righteousness and goodness. Only He can make you whole. Do you desire to be clean? Do you long to come to the Lord but think that first you must become good, and then He will accept you? Do not wait any longer.

Maybe you do not have the strength to come. Then why not pray, "Turn thou us unto thee, O LORD, and we shall be turned; renew our days as of old" (Lamentations 5:21). Additionally, the Scriptures say, "I will heal their backsliding, I will love them freely: for mine anger is turned away from him" (Hosea 14:4). God looks at backsliding as a disease. Only the divine Physician can cure the maladies of the soul. God will help you if you will only cast yourself on him. Will you do that just now?

The idea that we need to be "good enough" comes from no one but the great deceiver. He knows that you can never become whole without Jesus. That is why he suggests the thought, hoping that you never turn to the One that is altogether merciful. Arise then! Come to the Savior. He has promised, "Though your sins be as scarlet, they shall be as white as snow; though they be red like crimson, they shall be as wool" (Isaiah 1:18). Oh, sinner, come as you are. Will you lift your hand toward heaven and say, "I want you to make me clean." Will you respond while the Lord is calling?

ERNEST HEMINGWAY

In 1899, Ernest Hemingway was born into a religious home. His parents were both avid, God-fearing Christians. They raised him with church and God being part of his early life. However, as Ernest grew into manhood, he departed from the path his parents had laid out for him. He began his writing career in a newspaper office in Kansas City.

After returning from his involvement in World War I, he wrote his first novel entitled, *The Sun Also Rises* (1926). This, in part, had some reflection from Hemingway's reading of the book of Ecclesiastes. After a while, he went headlong into an abandoned life. Ernst's life of debauchery led down the path of immorality, with both men and women. He went into deep depression. Oftentimes he could be found asleep in a drunken stupor in the gutters of the streets.

He lived in Key West, Florida and then in Cuba. It was while in Cuba that he wrote his famous work, *The Old Man and the Sea* (1952) and received the Nobel Prize.

In this short novel, he wrote of a fisherman that had become old. The younger fishermen had taunted the old man that he had become a has-been. His days of usefulness were past. Determined to put the words to silence, he went out fishing. To his fortune, he hooked the largest swordfish he had ever seen.

Excited for the turn of events, he wrestled with the fish for hours. The hours turned into a few days. The fish fought for his life; the fisherman fought for his hopefully restored dignity. The battle concluded with the man's hands worn; his skin was sunburned, and he was almost at the peek of exhaustion; yet, he was satisfied in his winning.

Since the fish was as big as the boat, he could not bring it aboard. So he tied it to the side of the boat and began to paddle back home. While on his way, sharks appeared and began to tear away at the swordfish. Anxious over the awful turn of events, he took a knife and began knifing at the sharks. Thankfully, he was able to repulse the sharks for a time, but they returned. So he took a wooden stick and began beating the sharks. Once more he succeeded in repelling the attackers breaking, but he broke his stick.

He continued his journey home when once again, the sharks returned. In desperation, he took his oars and began to beat the intruders, but to no avail. As he neared the shore, he was greatly dismayed at the sight. All he had was a skeleton. Who would believe him? In his exhaustion, he collapsed onto the sand and slumped into deep depression over the victory that had ended in defeat.

This was Hemingway's tragic life. He never returned to the faith of his parents. He was a backslider to the end. Though knowledgeable of the counsels in the Bible, he chose not to follow them. His portrayals in his books of his fictitious characters were a reflection of the reality in his life. Vanity, vanity, all is vanity. In 1961, he took a rifle and shot himself, committing suicide.

APPEAL:

The Scripture says, "There is a way which seemeth right unto a man, but the end thereof are the ways of death" (Proverbs 14:12). How sad the ending of such a life. It could have ended so differently. Friend, there are those who have not been satisfied with living the Christian life. In their dissatisfaction they go on their pursuit of happiness. Sooner or later, they come to the place that King Solomon had reached—all is vanity and vexation of the soul.

Perhaps like this man, you have tried to find meaning in life by the things offered by worldly fare. But in your quest, like Hemingway you find your soul vexed. You can take his way out, or you can take God's way out. Like the prodigal, the Lord invites you to return to Him. Don't let the enemy of the soul goad you with feelings of distress and despair.

Perhaps like the prodigal you have found the attractions of the world turn into the husks given to the swine. It does not satisfy you anymore—it has lost its flavor. You desire to return to God, but you may be apprehensive that he will not receive you. Don't allow those feelings to haunt you. Remember, the Father waits for you. Jesus said, "Him that cometh to me I will in no wise cast out" (John 6:37). Will you come? Will you by faith accept the invitation and return to God? Will you do it just now?

SELL MY HOUSE

Lamont was a very talented child. At an early age, he had learned to become very proficient on mouth organs (harmonica) of different sorts and sizes. His talent was so great that the famous *Little Rascals* television series begged his mother to let him become part of it. Fearing the baleful worldly effects of that type of life, his mother refused. His mother, being a God-fearing mother, had other hopes for all those talents—God's service.

Lamont's musical talents continued to increase. From the piano, he mastered the organ as well. His singing abilities also were commensurate with his instrumental aptitude. Sadly, the attraction of show business beckoned, and Lamont acquiesced to its call. His praying mother became gravely concerned for her boy, but there was no turning him from his pursuits.

The night came when Lamont was to have his debut at the Grand Old Opry—on Friday night. Though quite conscience that this was the beginning of the Sabbath, Lamont was defiant.

The moment came, and the symphony began its introduction. The conductor gave him his queue. When he opened his mouth to sing, nothing came out. "You missed your queue, Francisco," the conductor exclaimed. "I did not miss my queue." responded Lamont. "Do it again." Once more, the symphonic music began to fill the hall. The audience anxiously awaited the lovely tenor voice to blend with the melodic strains. As Lamont opened his mouth, not a sound was heard. The same thing occured. Chagrined, and sensing that the finger of God was upon him, Lamont left the stage.

Still defiant, he determined to stay in show business contrary to his praying mother's concern. Fashion shows became his avenue to satisfy his cravings for big money and the bright lights of Hollywood. His skills furnished Lamont with two white El Dorado cars and a mansion in the south. But this was not the answer to the agonizing prayers of his mother. She had committed him to the service of the Lord. But Lamont had too much to gain in show business and little to gain in ministry.

Though engrossed in his quest, in the back of his mind he knew he should have been using his talents for God. Conscience stricken at times, he felt guilty about what he was doing, justifying it by his giving large offerings as an excuse for continuing his course. But his conviction strengthened. He could see that his talents were being used to encourage the complete opposite of what he had been taught and believed. Finally, not able to handle the conviction any longer, he said, "Alright God, if you want me to use my talents for you, then, sell my house."

Later that day, a woman drove up his driveway and knocked on his door. When he opened the door, the lady said, "I was driving back, and I spotted your house. Would you be interested in selling it?" Upset that the answer seemed to have come so quickly, he determined to drive the woman away by asking a high price. "Two hundred and fifty thousand dollars," he said (a lot of money in those days).

"Alright," said the woman, "I'll buy it." Amazed at the way that God removed the objections, Lamont finally decided to stop fighting and surrendered his life to the service of ministry.

APPEAL:

My friend, have you felt God calling you? Have you been running from Him, chasing your own pleasures and pursuits? Though deep inside you know where and what God wants you to be doing, there has been a determination to follow your own aims and goals. But no matter what you do, you still sense you are not where God wants you to be. Will you stop running? Will you decide just now to give your heart to the Lord? No matter what you have accomplished, no matter what your achievements, your heart tells you that you will never find happiness until you are serving the Lord. Will you dedicate your talents and your all to God? Will you respond just now? Raise your hand toward heaven, and by so doing indicate your desire to accept the invitation.

Chapter 31

OTHER EXAMPLES
OF APPEALS

The call to repentance was sounded with unmistakable clearness and all were invited to return. "Seek ye the Lord while He may be found," the prophet pleaded, "call ye upon Him while He is near: let the wicked forsake his way, and the unrighteous man his thoughts: and let him return unto the Lord, and He will have mercy upon him; and to our God, for He will abundantly pardon" Isaiah 55:6, 7.

"Have you chosen your own way? Have you wandered far from God? Have you sought to feast upon the fruits of transgression, only to find them turn to ashes upon your lips? And now, your life plans thwarted and your hopes dead, do you sit alone and desolate? That voice which has long been speaking to your heart, but to which you would not listen, comes to you distinct and clear, 'Arise ye, and depart; for this is not your rest: because it is polluted, it shall destroy you, even with a sore destruction.' Micah 2:10. Return to your Father's house. He invites you, saying, 'Return unto Me; for I have redeemed thee.' 'Come unto Me: hear, and your soul shall live; and I will make an everlasting covenant with you, even the sure mercies of David.' Isaiah 44:22; 55:3.

"Do not listen to the enemy's suggestion to stay away from Christ until you have made yourself better, until you are good enough to come to God. If you wait until then you will never come. When Satan points to your filthy garments, repeat the promise of the Savior, 'Him that cometh to Me I will in no wise cast out.' John 6:37. Tell the enemy that the blood of Jesus Christ cleanses from all sin. Make the prayer of David your own, 'Purge me with hyssop, and I shall be clean: wash me, and I shall be whiter than snow.' Psalm 51:7."[50]

---

50. E. G. White, *Prophets and Kings*, 319-320..

"The work dearest to the heart of Christ is that of drawing souls to Him. . . . Look at Jesus, the Majesty of heaven. What do you behold in His life history? His divinity clothed with humanity, a whole life of continual humility, the doing of one act of condescension after another, a line of continual descent from the heavenly courts to a world all seared and marred with the curse, and in a world unworthy of His presence, descending lower and still lower, taking the form of a servant, to be despised and rejected of men, obliged to flee from place to place to save His life, and at last betrayed, rejected, crucified. Then, as sinners for whom Jesus suffered more than the power of mortal can portray, shall we refuse to humble our proud will?

"Study day and night the character of Christ. It was His tender compassion, His inexpressible, unparalleled love for your soul, that led Him to endure all the shame, the revilings, the abuse, the misapprehensions of earth. Approach nearer Him, behold His hands and His feet, bruised and wounded for our transgressions. 'The chastisement of our peace was upon him; and with his stripes we are healed.'

"Lose no time, let not another day pass into eternity, but just as you are, whatever your weakness, your unworthiness, your neglect, delay not to come now. . . . The call of Jesus to come to Him, the presentation of a crown of glory that fadeth not away, the life, the eternal life that measures with the life of God, has not been of sufficient inducement to lead you to serve Him with your undivided affections. . . .

"Be no longer on Satan's side of the question. Make decided, radical changes through the grace given you of God. No longer insult His grace. He is saying with tears, 'Ye will not come to me, that ye might have life.' John 5:40. Now Jesus is inviting you, knocking at the door of your heart for entrance. Will you let Him come in?"[51]

"Were you following Christ, the Word of God would be to you as a pillar of cloud by day and a pillar of fire by night. But you have not made the honor of God the first object of your lifework. You have the Bible. Study it for yourself. The teachings of the divine directory are not to be ignored or perverted. The divine mind will guide those who desire to be led. Truth is truth, and it will enlighten all who seek

---

51. E. G. White, *That I Might Know Him,* 56.

for it with humble hearts. Error is error, and no amount of worldly philosophizing can make it truth.

"'Ye are bought with a price: therefore glorify God in your body, and in your spirit, which are God's.' 1 Cor. 6:20. What does the Lord require of His blood-bought heritage? The sanctification of the whole being—purity like the purity of Christ, perfect conformity to the will of the Lord. What is it that constitutes the beauty of the soul? The presence of the grace of Him who gave His life to redeem men and women from eternal death. . . .

"No entreaties are so tender, no lessons so plain, no commands so powerful and so protecting, no promises so full, as those which point the sinner to the fountain that has been opened to wash away the guilt of the human soul." [52]

"'I must repent first,' some say. 'I must go so far on my own without Christ, and then Christ meets me and accepts me.'

"You cannot have a thought without Christ. You cannot have an inclination to come to Him unless He sets in motion influences and impresses His Spirit upon the human mind. And if there is a man on the face of the earth who has any inclination toward God, it is because of the many influences that are set to work to bear upon his mind and heart. Those influences call for the allegiance to God and an appreciation of the great work that God has done for him.

"Then don't let us ever say that we can repent of ourselves, and then Christ will pardon. No, indeed. It is the favor of God that pardons. It is the favor of God that leads us by His power to repentance. Therefore, it is all of Jesus Christ, everything of Him, and you want to just give back glory to God. Why don't you respond more when you meet together in your meetings? Why don't you have the quickening influence of the Spirit of God when the love of Jesus and His salvation are presented to you? It is because you do not see that Christ is first and last and best, and the Alpha and the Omega, the beginning and the end, the very Author and Finisher of our faith. You don't realize this, and therefore you remain in your sins. Why is this? It is because Satan is here wrestling and battling for the souls of men. He casts his hellish shadow right athwart our pathway, and all that you can see is the enemy and his power.

---

52. E. G. White, *This Day with God,* 188.

"Look away from his power to the One that is mighty to save to the utmost. Why doesn't your faith plow through the shadow to where Christ is? He has led captivity captive and given gifts unto men. He will teach you that Satan claims every soul that does not join with Him as his property."[53]

"Meetings were held all through the day. My husband spoke in forenoon; Brother Andrew in the afternoon. I followed with remarks quite at length, entreating those who had been interested through the meetings to commence from that day to serve God. We called forward those who wished to start in the service of the Lord. Quite a number came forward. I spoke several times, beseeching souls to break the bands of Satan and start then. One mother went to her son and wept and entreated him. He seemed hard, stubborn, and unyielding. I then arose and addressed Brother D, begged him to not stand in the way of his children. He started, then arose, spoke, said he would commence from that day. This was heard with glad hearts by all. Brother D is a precious man.

"Sister E's husband then arose, testified that he would be a Christian. He is an influential man—a lawyer. His daughter was upon the anxious seat. Brother D then added his entreaties to ours. Sister D's also to their children. We entreated and at last prevailed. All came forward. The fathers and all the sons and other fathers followed their example. It was a day of gladness. Sister E said it was the happiest day of her life.

"I spoke in the afternoon from 2 Peter. I had freedom in talking. After I had spoken one hour I invited those who wished to be Christians to come forward. Between thirty and forty came forward quietly without excitement and occupied the front seats. I spoke with them in regard to making an entire surrender to God. We had a praying season for those who came forward. We had a very precious season of prayer. Those who wished baptism were requested to signify it by rising. Quite a number arose.

"I spoke in the afternoon {at Stanley, Va.} from John 17:3. The Lord gave me much of His Holy Spirit. The house was full. I called those forward who wished to seek the Lord more earnestly and for those who wished to give themselves to the Lord a whole sacrifice. For a time not one made a move, but after a while many

---

53. E. G. White, *Faith and Works,* 72-73.

came forward and bore testimonies of confession. We had a precious season of prayer and all felt broken down, weeping and confessing their sins. O that each may understand!"[54]

More copies of *Great Stories for Gaining Decisions* are available at **www.louistorres.org.**

54. E. G. White, *Selected Messages,* Vol. 1. 144-146.